TORCHY

TORCHY

THE HUMBLE LIFE OF
A COACHING LEGEND

FOREWORD BY ROCKY BLEIER

BO CLARK

Torchy: The Humble Life of a Coaching Legend

For information about this title or to order other books
and/or electronic media, contact the publisher:

Bo Clark Publications
2800 N 6th St, Unit 1
PMB # 222
St. Augustine, FL 32084
boclark37@gmail.com

Library of Congress Control Number: 2019904418

ISBNs
Hardcover: 978-1-7329746-0-9
Softcover: 978-1-7329746-1-6
eBook: 978-1-7329746-2-3

Printed in the United States of America

Cover and Interior design: 1106 Design

Dedicated to Mom and Dad

Contents

CONTENTS

Foreword

By
Rocky Bleier

L egends are not born, they are made; and what may seem easy, is an illusion forged from hard work, sweat and tears. The beginning of a belief system, as fragile as it is, is cradled and held and rocked until its roots take hold and become a part of who you are. Success comes only after that foundation is set. This book is about a man who created his own destiny and made a difference in the lives he touched.

Growing up in Appleton, Wisconsin, in the mid-'50s, my life was contained in about an eight-block radius. I only knew two kinds of kids—public kids and Catholic kids. Within that radius there happened to be two Catholic grade schools, separated by three blocks: St. Joseph's Catholic School, the German parish where our family went; and St. Mary's Catholic School, the Irish parish where those other people went. One of those other people was a dynamic young coach by the name of Gene "Torchy" Clark.

He was a whisper amongst us German kids, and we didn't like him, or his school, or those Irish kids because they always beat us, primarily in basketball. We finally got the best of them when I was in eighth grade and we won the grade school title. I would like to think we won that title because we were better, but I believe the real reason was that they lost their leader. Coach Clark had left the program that year to become the athletic director, head football and basketball coach, and teacher at the brand-new Catholic High School—Xavier.

The baby boomers were taking over the world back then. New schools had to be added, and a new athletic conference was born. Suddenly, this Irishman became our coach, my coach, and we weren't St. Joe's, or St. Mary's, or Sacred Heart, or St. Therese anymore, we were Xavier. Our destiny and future unknown. What happens will unfold in this book, but it wouldn't have happened if it weren't for Torchy.

The man simply wanted to win, and he would drive his players to want the same thing. He demanded your best and he would get it, otherwise you wouldn't play. He wasn't looking for perfection, he was looking for heart. He wanted you to believe, as much as he believed, that second place wasn't good enough!

In simple terms he would let you know if you weren't doing well—a word here and there, a glare, a look, his voice would raise, veins would stick out, the bleacher would be kicked, and you just knew you had to play harder.

He set a standard. He became a legend. He was our coach. We are who we are today because Gene "Torchy" Clark entered our lives and made a difference.

CHAPTER 1

I'm from Oshkosh

The long and lasting impression a teacher and coach can make on one's life is remarkable and timeless. This is the story of a coach who leaves an incredible, yet humble, legacy that lives in the hearts of those he touched—his family, former players, students, managers, coaches, and friends. In 1929, his fascinating life begins in Oshkosh, Wisconsin, an hour and a half north of Milwaukee.

What a nice thing to be able to say, "I'm from Oshkosh!"

This beautiful city of approximately 67,000 people is located off Wisconsin's largest lake, Lake Winnebago. Often referred to as "Oshkosh B'Gosh," the city was named for Menominee Chief Oshkosh. Every summer close to a million people descend on the community for the EAA AirVenture Oshkosh, the world's largest air show.

The people are friendly, outgoing, and proud of their deep Wisconsin roots. The fiercely devoted sports fans love to laugh, play card games such as Sheepshead and Cribbage, drink beer, eat pizza, and cheer for their beloved Packers every Sunday.

Eugene Allan Clark was born on New Year's Day, 1929, on the brink of America's Great Depression, to Florence (Mueller) and Donald Clark. Donald, a native of North Fond du Lac, Wisconsin, and Florence, from Oshkosh, met on a blind date for dinner in nearby Menasha. In 1924, Donald and his lovely bride Florence were married and raised three boys: Dutch, Eugene, and Jim. Florence was the heart of the family as Donald worked as a plant manager at American Axle. Eugene's parents were a perfect match, yet had completely different personalities. They lived in a modest upstairs apartment on High Street, one block away from the historic museum. In retrospect on his family, the young Eugene said, "They say the middle class is a good place to be. We didn't have a lot of money, but nonetheless, still had a great life." The future coach would jokingly tell his grandchildren, family, and friends, "My parents named me Eugene because they didn't like me."

Oshkosh was a kid's paradise with great parks, fabulous schools, plenty of water and a college with elite sports facilities. The skinny redhead played many sports, including baseball, basketball, and football, with his neighborhood buddies who would become life-time friends.

On a cool summer day in 1937, eight-year-old Eugene was playing sandlot baseball at local Bauman Park. With runners on second and third and his team losing 4–3, Eugene stepped to the plate. He passed on two pitches as he waited for the perfect one to hit. A chubby 11-year-old playing in the outfield quickly yelled at Eugene, "Swing the bat . . . Come on, swing the bat 'torch head,' swing the bat 'torch head,' we want to play and not stand here all day." The feisty Eugene snarled at the chubby outfielder as he waited on the third pitch, which he promptly singled up the middle, scoring the two runners. Eugene was harassed the remainder of the game with the "torch head" taunts. As time went on, the nickname "torch head" became "Torchy," and the *Torchy* legacy was born!

Reflecting back on his High Street childhood Torchy remembered, "At six or seven years old, I was in trouble most of the time. I'm not sure why, but I was in general . . . a pain." The Clark family, like many American families across the United States, was living with the effects of the Depression. Entertainment and eating out were few and far between opportunities for the Clarks. Most of the time, they enjoyed their privacy with relatives, just visiting and talking sports.

"I was always politely advised to get lost and go outside and do something," said Torchy. On the command from his parents, he quickly grabbed a baseball-sized rubber ball and his glove. The energetic Torchy began throwing the ball against the apartment wall, playing catch by himself for hours and hours. He recalled years later, "To this day, I am convinced this is how my athletic career started. In one minute, you can throw and catch the ball 40 times. In two hours, it becomes a high-grade motor skill workout. Doing this activity five or six days a week in the summer gave me excellent fielding skills, quick hands, and improved footwork."

Torchy added a trick to his hobby: "Later that summer, I discovered the roof and would make high tosses and wait and run like an outfielder to catch the ball as it rolled down. You had to move forward, backward, and laterally. I enjoyed it so much that I started to play imaginary games between the Chicago Cubs and the St. Louis Cardinals. I began to broadcast the play-by-play action of this make-believe game. It seemed like my favorite team always rallied to win! And I realized this house ball game did improve my motor skills."

Tommy Heinrich, the World Series hero of the New York Yankees (1937–42 and 1946–50) nicknamed "The Clutch" and "Old Reliable," once stated that the average Little Leaguer bats seven times a week in two games and gets two hits. Henrich recalled as a youth playing in a sandlot baseball game, "I once got 52 hits in 57 at bats."

Torchy emphasized this theory of the importance of constant repetitions, the cornerstone of his Hall of Fame coaching career, by saying, "To me, like Tommy Henrich, the more you do it, the better you'll get. Proper practice and repetition are the keys. Every young boy should run, throw, field, and broadcast his games. If you practice a specific sports skill 10,000 times in any sport, it will be yours for life."

In 1937, Oshkosh State Teachers College, now the University of Wisconsin Oshkosh (UWO), had an enrollment of 450 students. Back in those early days of Titans' glory, Coach Bob Kolf Sr. was practically the entire athletic department. He was the head coach of all sports at the small college, including football, basketball, tennis, and track. The well-respected Kolf had an excellent reputation, not only in the state of Wisconsin, but across the country.

Today, UWO's spacious and first-class sports arena is fittingly named and dedicated in his honor. The Kolf Sports Center was considered a state-of-the-art facility when it was built in 1971. The facility contains an all-weather indoor track on the second floor. The Kolf Center hosted the 1994, 1997, and 2001 NCAA Division III Indoor National Championship Track Meets.

Torchy attended St. Peter's Catholic Grade School in Oshkosh. The Clarks, a devout Catholic family, made the financial sacrifice for their three boys to receive a Catholic education. Coach Kolf's son Bobby Jr. and Torchy were third-grade classmates at St. Peter's. Fellow third-grader Ben Meixl was another chum of this group. The three boys bonded immediately as a result of their passion for sports and similar upbringings.

"After school each day, Bobby, Ben, and I would walk to the college to watch his dad's teams practice, whatever sport season it was. During football, we threw passes to each other and played a game called 'interception.' Basketball practices gave us opportunities to shoot baskets on the side goals.

"We also went into the training room and tossed the heavy medicine ball back and forth. Many days, we ventured into the equipment room to try on the football and basketball uniforms which were ten

4

sizes too big. We had a blast!! We were in heaven, and Coach Kolf treated us like family. He gave us opportunities for simple and old-fashioned fun," said the spunky Torchy.

All three buddies would play college sports: Torchy played basketball at Marquette University; Bob Kolf Jr. played basketball at the University of Southern California alongside NBA Hall of Famer and Boston Celtic great Bill Sharman; and Ben Meixl played college football at UW-Lacrosse. Coach Kolf (Sr.) was a positive role model through his kindness and encouragement to three lucky eight-year-olds. Appropriately, Clark, Kolf, and Meixl all became college coaches in their future careers.

Torchy emphasized how important those formative early years were: "We had a fourth friend named Bill Hesser. At an early age, Bill had great skills and would sometimes play with us at the college. But, his dad ran a used car lot, and he was usually working around cars with him. Did he become a college coach too? No, but you guessed it. For many years, Bill ran a successful Oldsmobile dealership in town."

Another boyhood reflection close to his heart was the Oshkosh All-Stars. In 1937, the "Sawdust City" had a professional basketball team called the Oshkosh All-Stars who played in the National Basketball League (NBL). A local business, the Hunkel Seed Company, sponsored the team which was a collection of some of the best college players in the nation. One of these college phenoms was All-Star Leroy Edwards, nicknamed "Lefty," who had an outstanding career at the University of Kentucky.

Edwards, a six-foot-five NCAA All-American center who left Kentucky after his sophomore year, was one of the first true "stars" of professional basketball in the United States. A huge gate attraction in the NBL, Edwards led the league in scoring his first three seasons. He was also named NBL Most Valuable Player all three years he played as an All-Star.

When reporters asked the legendary George Mikan who was the toughest player he ever played against, Mikan responded, "Lefty Edwards."

Torchy remembered the thrill of watching the All-Stars as a young boy. "I could name the whole team. They were really good, and the games were played at South Park and Merrill Junior High Schools." Opponents in the NBL included the nearby Sheboygan Redskins, Toledo Jim White Chevrolets, New York Renaissance, Fort Wayne Zollner Pistons, Akron Firestone Non-Skids, Chicago American Gears, Akron Goodyear Wingfoots, and the Harlem Globetrotters before they went into show business. The All-Stars was one of the most successful pro franchises of their era, winning six NBL Western Division Championships. In the 1940s, Oshkosh was well known as a "basketball city."

Admission to the NBL games was $1.20 to sit downstairs, $.88 for upstairs, and $.50 for a seat on the stage. "Naturally, I always sat on the stage. You had to get there early to get a side seat. There weren't any glass backboards to see through in those days, so you tried to get the angle seat in which you could see the whole court and part of the net. The rest of the action you could see perfectly," Torchy recollected with a gush of excitement.

Some of the great players in the NBL at this time were Bobby McDermott of the Fort Wayne Zollner Pistons, Soup Cable and Johnny Moir of the Akron Firestone Non-Skids, Ed Dancker of the Sheboygan Redskins, Bob Davies of the Rochester Royals, and Chuck Chuckovits of the Toledo Jim White Chevrolets. The great George Mikan of the Chicago American Gears played a few years later.

Torchy recalled watching the amazing center at South Park. "I saw Mikan play one of his first pro games. He had just signed an enormous contract with the Gears for five years at $12,000 per year for a grand total of $60,000 ($25,000 signing bonus)." Mikan, a future

Hall of Famer and the NBA's first outstanding big man, played college basketball at DePaul for legendary coach Ray Meyer. As a rookie, Mikan led the Gears to the 1947 NBL Championship.

"To me, the whole environment was fabulous and became a part of me and my future in coaching. Today, when I tell my college students about it, they sort of smile and snicker. Then I tell them this was the beginning of the present-day National Basketball Association (NBA) and that Fort Wayne Zollner team I mentioned earlier became the Detroit Pistons," explained Torchy.

Besides the All-Stars, the Wisconsin Flyers of the Continental Basketball Association also played in Oshkosh from 1982–87. In 2017, professional basketball returned for the third time in the city's history with the Wisconsin Herd of the Gatorade League, or G-League, of the NBA. The Herd competes in the action-packed, highly entertaining minor league as an affiliate of the NBA's Milwaukee Bucks. The franchise plays their home games in Oshkosh's plush and fan-friendly Menominee Nation Arena.

Celebrating the great success and gloried history of the two-time NBL World Champion Oshkosh All-Stars (1941 and 1942), the Wisconsin Herd wore throwback uniforms for a G-League home game in 2018. The All-Stars' throwback jerseys were then auctioned off, with the proceeds donated to a local charity.

The Clarks survived one of the toughest financial periods in our country with immense love and support. Florence, an excellent cook and housewife, was frugal in her spending during the rough times.

Torchy shared a story from a Christmas in 1940. "On a frigid December day my mother (Florence) and I took the bus downtown to buy a tree. I was a sixth-grader and we did not own a car. We got off the bus and walked a block to a large open tent selling trees. After 10 minutes, the freezing salesman told us the beautiful tree she was looking at was $1.25. My mother said, 'We never pay that much;

Christmas trees are so high!' 'O.K, lady. I'll charge you one dollar,' said the salesman. 'A dollar, oh no, that's too much,' said Florence. Before his lips froze completely shut, the salesman finally said, 'O.K, $.75.' Florence responded firmly, 'That's still pretty high. They sure have gone up in price.' The annoyed, worn-out salesman said, 'All right, lady, $.50.' My mother without batting an eye said, *Do you deliver?*'"

The All-Stars and the NBL provided the spirited Torchy with a treasure chest full of memories. "I had a seat for $.50 to witness the highest level of basketball in the world. What a fun experience to watch these outstanding players and excellent teams up close, in person. And virtually right in my backyard! But sometimes in life things are like vapors: here and then gone. But the memories remain."

CHAPTER 2

Let 'em Play

Growing up in Oshkosh in the 1940s, the three Clark boys, Dutch, Torchy, and Jimmy, enjoyed watching and playing sports. According to their father Donald, sports served as a solid foundation to teach good morals, build character, and become better people. Dutch, Torchy's older brother, was an outstanding basketball player at St. Mary's Menasha High School. Following graduation, Dutch then attended Marquette University in Milwaukee.

At the end of his freshman year, Dutch withdrew from school and joined the U.S. Navy (post-World War II) for a two-year enlistment. After serving his country admirably, the eldest son of Donald and Florence was excited to come home and begin a new career. He eagerly desired to enter the coaching profession or become a businessman. However, during his return to Oshkosh, Dutch was tragically killed in a train accident in California at the age of 21. This was a devastating blow to the close-knit Clark family. Their strong faith and the support of family and friends pulled them through this difficult period.

Jim, Torchy's younger brother, was the most outgoing of the three boys. His personality, charm, and charisma could light up a room.

Jim was a star basketball player at Oshkosh High School. He then attended local UW Oshkosh, majoring in education, with the dream of teaching and coaching basketball at the high school level.

A short time later, Jim's dream would become a reality. At the age of 26, he moved his young wife, Diane Naparalla of Ripon, Wisconsin, and their four children to Orlando, Florida, to become the new basketball coach at Bishop Moore Catholic High School. The first-year coach led the Hornets to the 1966 State Final Four of the Class A Florida High School State Basketball Championship, losing in the semifinal to Hollywood Chaminade, 44-37.

The Hornets, in Jim's second year (1967), fell short of a repeat Final Four appearance, falling in the Class A Regional Semifinal to Winter Garden Lakeview, 55–54. During his four years at Bishop Moore, Jim, like his older brother Torchy, was an intense motivator and a tremendous role model. As an American History teacher, he was a beloved member of the school's faculty.

Before the 1969 school year, Jim decided to enter the business world, becoming a Gillette Razor district representative based in nearby Altamonte Springs. After two years, he was transferred by Gillette to the Philadelphia region, and then to Denver, Colorado.

Sadly, Jim died of a brain tumor on August 4, 1975, in Denver at the age of 36. His wife was three months pregnant with their sixth child when Jim died. Diane remembers her husband as a "kind and caring father to our children, Debbie, Lisa, Kelly, Jackie, and Tara. Michael was not born yet."

Revered at Bishop Moore, Jim was inducted into the school's Athletic Hall of Fame posthumously in 1995. Each Christmas since 1987, Bishop Moore Catholic's Athletic Director Mike Malatesta has honored his legacy by hosting the "Jim Clark Classic."

Losing both brothers so young was emotionally and physically draining for Torchy. He was extremely close with his brothers, sharing common values of faith, family, and sports. Torchy had a strong relationship with the Lord and relied heavily on his faith during these turbulent times. He would miss Dutch's smile and Jim's laugh, but looked forward to their glorious reunion in heaven.

Torchy was in the Denver hospital with Diane the night Jim died. His faith helped him understand death as he often quoted St. Thomas Aquinas who said, "After death, the day of man is ended; And the day of Christ begins." The tremendous adversities lit an internal flame in his teaching and coaching career. Torchy was proud of his brothers and loved them dearly.

Donald, who died in 1960 at the age of 61, strongly influenced his three boys. He was hard working, quiet, but very opinionated on topics of the day. His primary talking points centered around sports: Notre Dame, the Green Bay Packers, and revolutionary ideas or concepts he envisioned in sports. "My father belonged in the big time. He didn't miss much. My mother said 'He would have been president of the company if he ever would have shut his mouth.' My father was sharp, perceptive, and progressive," said the proud redhead.

As a youngster growing up, Torchy observed his father's classy and kind gestures. "My father always tipped his hat passing a Catholic church. He always stood perfectly erect for the flag. Somehow, he always had a $10 bill to drop in an envelope at the funeral home for the family of the deceased.

"Many mornings, my father woke us by calling, 'Daylight in the swamp.' He never left the house without saying, 'Good-bye' and 'God bless you.'" Notre Dame football games were always on the radio at the Clarks' apartment, as Torchy recalled, "We sat and listened closely to Fighting Irish announcers Bill Stern and John Harrington. My father loved Notre Dame. Those were special times for our family."

While today's modern technology of cable television, social media, and smartphones keep families up-to-date, the Clark family depended on the radio and family conversations in the living room. "My father would tell us that Knute Rockne discovered George Gipp on a playground," said Torchy. "Gipp punted the ball so far, it took two guys to kick it back to him using a relay system."

Donald understood the heartbeat of sports and loved baseball. Torchy recalled his father saying, "'When the opposing pitcher has a no-hitter and your team is losing by five runs in the ninth inning with two outs . . . you strike out and give him his no-hitter.' He taught us the 'Infield Fly Rule' before we could catch. My father's favorite baseball players were Red Rolfe and Charlie Gehringer. He also loved Dizzy Dean for backing up his round-the-clock bragging."

In the 1940s, both college football and professional football scores were low, because offenses and defenses were bunched up and tight in their formations. Donald said, "Spread your offense out and use the whole field. This will open the game up." Years later, football teams started using spread formations, flankers, slot receivers, and wide-outs.

He, too, was opinionated on the placekicker's role in football. "'Coaches should put their dropkicker or placekicker in an area by himself. Let him work out privately and become an expert or specialist. Bring him in just to kick at games.' My father's forecast became true. In 1949, Tad Weed of the Ohio State Buckeyes practiced at a side field away from the team. He was inserted into the lineup for Saturday games and used solely as a kicking specialist."

Naturally, Donald had progressive ideas on basketball. "My father said, 'Shoot it! Shoot the ball! Cut out the unnecessary passing. You'll throw the ball away or travel before you even take a shot.' He was right again . . . years later most teams began to shoot more. The shot became the big weapon and shot charts exploded in numbers."

A wise and avid sports fan, Donald believed that a basketball team "is only as good as its guards." How true that is today at all levels. While attending one of Torchy's high school basketball games, he observed his son's excellent passing skills but lack of scoring, bluntly saying, "Who wants a five-foot-ten guard who can't score?"

Like many parents, whether it be 1947 or any year, Donald had personal critiques of basketball officiating. "There's too much whistle blowing by the refs—too many fouls are called—*let 'em play*. They should keep their whistles on the opposite end of the floor. When an official sees a foul, he should run down the court and get his whistle, and then run back, and if the foul is still going on, blow the whistle. Otherwise, let it go," he said sarcastically. In the middle 1940s, many college and professional games began to use cameras to film game action. "Cameras never lie. Any time they put a camera on the officials, it's worth a lot of money to officiate," added Donald.

Torchy often told the story of an Ivy League football game and how effective the use of the camera was in this particular situation. "An Ivy League football championship in the 1940s was won by a team scoring the winning touchdown on the fifth-down as a result of an official's error. The camera replay of the extra down was shown to the winning school's president, who immediately conceded the championship to the losing team."

The Clarks' two-bedroom apartment was located near the many paper mills of the Fox Valley. "Get a job in the mill and you'll be set for life. The world will always need paper," emphasized the elder Clark. Both Torchy and Jim skipped the mill option and became coaches.

Donald was the breadwinner of the family. He worked long and hard hours at American Axle. Torchy remembered the lasting influence of the Clark patriarch. "My father was a neat guy who believed in the truth. You better bet your lunch, he was my *hero*. But sometimes in life things are like vapors: here and then gone. But the memories remain."

CHAPTER 3

Sister Joseph Mary

In 1939, as a fifth-grader at St. Peter's Grade School, Torchy was blessed to have a Dominican Sister as his teacher. Many of his favorite childhood memories revolve around the *kindness* of Sister Joseph Mary. "My mother had recently given birth to my little brother Jimmy. He was the best-looking baby I'd ever seen," said Torchy. The devout Sister asked the fifth-grader if his mother could bring the baby to the convent for her to see the newest of God's creations. "My mother, who lives in Chicago, is visiting Oshkosh this weekend," said Sister. "She, too, would like to see the baby."

The Clarks brought Jimmy to the convent. "We had a wonderful visit and it meant so much to them," reminisced Torchy. Sister Joseph Mary's mother was a successful attorney in the Windy City.

Three months later, on another trip to Oshkosh, her mother invited the Clarks back for another chat. This time, they gave Torchy a new leather basketball from DePaul University, a tremendous gift in 1940.

"The following spring, her family invited me to Chicago, which was 175 miles from Oshkosh. I took the train by myself as we pulled into the Northwestern Terminal. I was in seventh heaven being in the grand city of Chicago. What an opportunity for a kid from a small town to be in the big time," said the excited Torchy. "We went to see the Cubs play the White Sox in an exhibition game at Comiskey Park. Beforehand, I was introduced to Grace Comiskey, who was the owner of the White Sox." Grace was the daughter-in-law of Charles Comiskey and inherited control of the team (1939–56) upon the death of her husband, the late J. Louis Comiskey. Sister Joseph Mary's family and the Comiskeys were close friends. "We always had great seats behind home plate for the games," he recalled from when he was a 10-year-old.

"Later that year, I saw the White Sox play the Detroit Tigers in Chicago. After the game, I got to meet Tigers Hall of Famer Charlie Gehringer who went three-for-five at the plate that day. I remember how quiet and humble he was. Years later, I read that Gehringer's nickname was 'The Mechanical Man,'" Torchy added.

Gehringer was a second baseman who played 19 seasons with the same franchise. He was named to the American League All-Star team six times, and his No. 2 jersey was retired by the Tigers.

In 1941, Sister's gracious family gave Torchy a baseball autographed by Cleveland Indians Hall of Famer Bob Feller. "It was not just any ball, but one of the actual baseballs used in his no-hitter against the White Sox in 1940," said Torchy. "The ball said, 'No-Hit Feller, 1940.' To this day, it was one of the top fifty games of all time." Hall of Famer Stan Musial believed Feller was "probably the greatest pitcher of our era." Torchy looked back at his misfortune with the baseball: "The ball was worth $10,000 plus; however, it went down a city sewer playing catch, two weeks after I got it. Wow! But what do you know in fifth grade?

"The next fall, I went back to Chicago and her family took me to South Bend to see a Notre Dame football game," he added on the thrill of seeing the gorgeous campus and the Golden Dome. "Notre Dame beat Indiana, 19–7. Steve Juswik was a standout for the Irish and Billy Hillenbrand starred for the Hoosiers. That weekend, we also went to the Brookfield Zoo and Chicago's Board of Trade."

Sister Joseph Mary's brother Joe had played fullback at athletic power Mount Carmel High School. "One visit, he took me to see DePaul and Kansas play at Chicago Stadium in a college basketball game," said Torchy. "I had the opportunity to watch the legendary Phog Allen, the University of Kansas coach."

Allen played college basketball at Kansas for Dr. James Naismith, the inventor of basketball. But it was Allen's brilliance as an innovative tactician which earned him the title "The Father of Coaching Basketball." Torchy recalled as a youngster the thrill of Chicago Stadium: "We sat courtside and watched two of the nation's best teams. What a great fifth-grade teacher I had! My mom and dad could not believe the generosity of her family. I lost track of Sister Joseph Mary for almost a decade.

"In September of 1949, when I was dating my future wife Claire, we went to watch Marquette play Wisconsin in football at Camp Randall Stadium in Madison." Marquette lost to Wisconsin that day, 41–0, before a crowd of 42,000 fans. He recalled the chilly Saturday afternoon: "Our football team was really overmatched against the Badgers. The school dropped the sport in 1960."

Torchy had heard through friends that Sister Joseph Mary was still serving our Lord and had been assigned to Blessed Sacrament School in Madison. "After the game, Claire and I went to the convent to see her," said Torchy. "I asked the Mother Superior who answered the door if Sister Joseph Mary was there. Claire and I were ushered into the parlor of the small convent, as we waited anxiously."

Torchy remembered as a 21-year-old, "And lo and behold there was Sister Joseph Mary—much smaller than I had expected. I had not seen her since fifth grade, and I was naturally taller. We had a nice visit as I told her about my life: St. Peter's, St. Mary's in Menasha, Marquette, and my beautiful Claire."

After the brief reunion in Madison, the holy Sister wrote her former pupil a meaningful letter that he received in the mail after returning to Milwaukee. "In her letter, she mentioned the 'Beatific Vision After Death' that I'll never forget," said Torchy. "It's too bad more people don't read some of the writings of the 'Beatific Vision.' It always stayed with me."

Torchy fondly added, "I wish I had kept the letter from Sister Joseph Mary. I wish I still had the Bob Feller no-hit baseball. But, sometimes in life things are like vapors: here and then gone. But the memories remain."

CHAPTER 4

Road to Marquette

Torchy had an outstanding grade school basketball career at St. Peter's. The many hours of practicing on the side goals at Oshkosh State alongside Bobby Kolf and Ben Meixl had paid off. The redhead recalled the awe-inspiring memories of St. Peter's: "In the eighth grade we had a really good team. The three (Torchy, Bobby, and Ben) of us had played together since third grade. We entered the 16-team Diocesan tournament in Menasha. There were teams from Green Bay, Manitowoc, Appleton, Oshkosh, Neenah, Menasha, Kimberly, and Stevens Point. The tournament was the state's best and had over 200 participants. And I remember the games like it was yesterday!"

The narratives of the unforgettable 1943 tournament are etched in Torchy's heart and mind forever. "Our St. Peter's team won our first game over a tough Holy Name Kimberly. Then we edged St. John's of Green Bay by one point. In the semifinals, we defeated St. Steven's of Stevens Point and then won the tournament, beating St. Pat's of Menasha by 10 points in the championship game. I was picked the Most Valuable Player in the tournament, one of my most remarkable accomplishments to this day. I felt like I had won the Heisman Trophy.

"Winning the championship for St. Peter's was like winning the National Invitational Tournament (NIT) back in 1943. I was hoping there would be a victory parade for us downtown. The parade never happened, but our pictures were on the front page of the *Oshkosh Northwestern* sports section. The Diocesan tournament is one of my greatest sports memories."

Torchy's family encouraged him to attend St. Mary's Menasha High School, the alma mater of his brother Dutch. The school was a 20-minute drive from the Clarks' High Street apartment. Donald arranged for his 14-year-old son to live with the Broeren family, who were friends of the Clarks in Menasha. During the week, Torchy stayed with the Broerens, allowing him to attend school at St. Mary's, and then returned to Oshkosh for the weekends.

In August 1937, the Broeren family invented the napkin dispenser in the paper-producing region and patented the new convenience. Torchy was comfortable living with the Broerens and enjoyed his Menasha experience as a St. Mary's Zephyr.

The Zephyr name originated from the Pioneer Zephyr, the first diesel-powered streamline passenger train from the Burlington Railroad. On May 26, 1934, the Pioneer Zephyr traveled non-stop with record speed from Denver, Colorado, to Chicago for the World's Fair.

In high school, Torchy competed in three sports: football, basketball, and boxing. Yes, that's right . . . boxing. As a wide receiver for the Zephyr football team, he played for St. Mary's Hall of Fame coach Doug Trish. While playing against Appleton High School, Torchy caught five passes as a receiver with incredible hands. Later in life he would kiddingly say, "Throw me anything and I'll catch it. I never dropped a pass."

Torchy excelled in basketball, averaging 16 points per game for the St. Mary's varsity cagers. Under Trish, who coached football and basketball, the Zephyrs played a demanding schedule, many times playing larger public schools.

The ball handling, quickness, and basketball savvy of Torchy Clark led the Zephyrs to one of their greatest seasons in 1946, finishing with a 19–3 record. Trish's Zephyrs lost all three games that season to powerful Edgewood Catholic High School in Madison. The confident Torchy scored his career high of 30 points against Edgewood in a highlight reel of driving layups and jump shots. In both his junior and senior years, Torchy led the Fox Valley Catholic Conference in scoring (basketball). He, proudly, is a member of the St. Mary's Menasha Sports Hall of Fame. The Oshkosh native has fond memories of his Zephyr days: "Father Becker was our principal. He was one of the finest religious-athletic administrators I ever met (tie with Brother Peter at Xavier). Father Becker emphasized often, 'We have an obligation to meditate on the crucifixion.' I'll never forget that. He was a genius. He could remember the name of every student at St. Mary's."

Donald's support at his son's high school games was extraordinary. Torchy recalled, "My father attended all my high school home and road games. Our family, unfortunately, did not own a car. Many times our home games did not end until 9:30 p.m. Remember, we lived in Oshkosh, 15 miles from St. Mary's."

Without a car, Torchy explained, Donald had to be creative with his transportation to football and basketball games: "My father would leave our gym at 9:20 p.m. to catch the 9:40 train back to Oshkosh. But if he took the 9:40, he'd miss the last five minutes of our game. During an exciting or close game, he would stay for its entirety, miss the 9:40, and then take the next train to Oshkosh, which did not depart until 1:33 a.m. Once the train arrived in Oshkosh, he walked two miles to our High Street apartment. Every once in a while, he took a cab from the train station. There were some games he didn't get home until 3:00 a.m."

Torchy remembered another example of his father's dedication: "Once we played a road game against a team from a Catholic seminary which was in the deep country of central Wisconsin. Very few could describe how to get there or where the seminary was located. Our team arrived at the gym an hour before tip-off. I saw a person sitting in the stands. It was my father! I said, 'Pa, how did you get here?'

"He responded, 'None of your business.' He got home the same way. My father never asked for anything for himself. He always went beyond to support, instruct, and motivate like no other. No one was more loyal than him."

As a junior and senior Torchy competed on the St. Mary's boxing team. "I boxed in high school to release fears. We got our hands taped and then waited and waited for our fight," said Torchy. "You'd say to yourself, I'm so nervous . . . I can't lift my arms. How will I be able to fight? Naturally, this fear leaves you in the ring," noted the three-sport star.

Torchy detailed the athlete's general nervous arousal in all sports: "Wrestlers, football players, and all athletes have the fear 'in the waiting.' Any golfer trying to win a tournament may honestly say he couldn't feel the club in his hand putting the last stroke." He used the same analogy in football: "A kickoff returner waiting to catch the ball says, 'Here it comes—why me Lord?'" He reiterated his thoughts on fear: "Some of this fear is good for everybody to know and feel."

One winter for Christmas, Torchy recalled buying boxing gloves for his four sons, Mike, Tom, Bo, and Bob. "I once bought boxing gloves, just so my kids could go at it a few minutes," said the father of five. "I wanted them to get this feeling and necessary understanding.

Bob was the toughest of the four. I wish he could have boxed in high school. Bob had happy feet," he added. An avid boxing fan, Torchy tells the story of Ezzard Charles, the once-heavyweight champion of the world in 1949 and 1950, and the *overpowering* anxiety he experienced riding the taxi in New York City on his way to fight the undefeated Rocky Marciano.

Initially, Torchy had a chance to play basketball at St. John's University in Minnesota. St. John's is an all-male college located in Collegeville six hours from Oshkosh. He planned on attending the Catholic college with seven other seniors from St. Mary's. Torchy remembered the tough decision he faced: "At the last minute in August, I decided not to attend St. John's. A month earlier, I had talked to Bill Chandler, the basketball coach at Marquette University. Chandler emphasized to me, 'You are pretty small but if you make the team, we will help you with a scholarship.'"

The St. Mary's flash took "a leap of faith" and tried to attend Marquette. Torchy recalled the 1947 scenario: "My father and I traveled by train to Milwaukee to inquire about getting accepted into the school. When we got there, Marquette's incoming class was completely full. The Admissions Department had closed the enrollment for new students for the fall semester several weeks prior. My father said, 'Let's go see the president of Marquette.' I said, 'Pa, you gotta be kidding!'" Reluctantly, Torchy obeyed as the two went to talk to the president, Father Brooks, at his housing quarters. Upon knocking on the front door, Father Brooks, a Jesuit priest, greeted them. Torchy remembered, "My loving pa said, 'I'm Donald Clark and this is my son, Gene. I attended Marquette in 1924, but ran out of money and couldn't pay my tuition. My son really wants to be here. He is a basketball player and has talked with Coach Chandler.' The president quickly remarked with great pride, 'I went to Marquette in *1924* too!!' And miraculously, the president approved my acceptance into Marquette for the fall. I was admitted into the university because of my father's love and persistence. And thank God for 1924," said the grateful Torchy.

After a year on the freshman squad, Torchy earned a scholarship for his next three years. Bill Chandler, an excellent athlete at the University of Wisconsin-Madison, was Marquette's coach from 1930-51. His teams played a difficult schedule against the giants of college basketball: Ohio State, UCLA, Indiana, Notre Dame, and Wisconsin. Torchy, who wore jersey No. 37, was used as a scoring weapon off the bench backing up three excellent guards, Gene Berce, Sammy Sauceda, and Jack Meyers.

Berce, after graduating, played professional basketball in the NBL with the Oshkosh All-Stars. Sammy Sauceda was the first Hispanic to receive a scholarship at Marquette, playing both football and basketball. He later became the athletic director at the university (1970–73). Jack Meyers was an excellent ball handler with an outstanding basketball IQ. And a lifelong friend that introduced Torchy to a person who would change his life forever.

Torchy recalled another act of kindness from his father his sophomore year: "I was standing in line for breakfast at the Marquette Union when a student told me the university was dismissing all Education Majors [his major] under a 2.5 grade point average (GPA). I had a 2.2 GPA. I thought to myself, *I'll be gone.* I called my father at work in Oshkosh 85 miles away. He said, 'I'll come to Milwaukee and meet you in front of the Gesu Church at 2:00 p.m.' The Gesu Church is located on downtown's Wisconsin Avenue and sits across from Marquette's campus."

Donald took the train from Oshkosh and then the bus to the church. Torchy remembered the cold 1950 day: "My father immediately said, 'Let's go see the head of the Education Department.' And I replied, 'I'm not going in there, Pa.' Donald was fit to be tied and mumbled, 'OK, you always think you know everything.' Off marched my father by himself to the department head's office trying to bail me out as I headed to practice. I returned later that afternoon to my Aunt Katie's house where I lived in Milwaukee for three years. My Uncle Ed opened the door and said, 'Torchy, you're set with the Education Department and they approved you remaining in your major. Your Pa got the issue settled.' Donald was not at Katie's and was already on the train back to Oshkosh. I was lucky to have a father that cared. My mother was an unbelievable person but usually stayed out of any trouble or conflict."

The Marquette Hilltoppers played their home games in the on-campus gymnasium; but in his senior year, the team moved to the new, state-of-the-art Milwaukee Arena. The downtown venue opened in 1950 with a capacity of 8,500. Torchy recalled, "Marquette University is a great institution and was a wonderful experience for me. But sometimes in life things are like vapors: here and then gone. But the memories remain."

CHAPTER 5

Claire

Marquette University was a perfect fit for Torchy, both academically and athletically. His greatest treasure, however, was his introduction to Claire Theis, a beautiful Marquette sophomore from Southgate, Kentucky. She was a devout Catholic and the daughter of Bill and Dorothy Theis. Her father, a brilliant man, owned and operated a drugstore in nearby Newport. Claire worked at the drugstore during the summer months.

Torchy remembered his first encounter with Claire: "My teammate Jack Meyers and I had just finished basketball practice. We were driving home in a new Ford his dad had given him to use for the week. Jack was 24, an excellent player, ex-veteran, and I was only 20."

Jack said, "Torchy, let's call Mary Jane Lacey." Torchy replied, "Naw, let's go home." Hesitantly, the former Zephyr caved in. He recalled his teammate's conversation: "Jack was older, wiser, and sharper than I. He called Mary Jane at the girls' dormitory. They talked for a while on the phone, then Jack said, 'I've got a friend . . . anybody around for him? We'll all go out for a beer.' Mary Jane responded, 'Claire Theis is here.' The cool-handed Jack swiftly said, 'Torchy knows her really well.'" Laughing at the irony of the life-changing scenario, Torchy remarked, "I had never seen or met Claire before, but that is how I met the future Mrs. Clark."

The Oshkosh native looked back at his Marquette days with a smile. About Claire he reflected, "Was she popular? She was well-bred in everything and morally so good. She was rushed by every sorority." On her outgoing and charismatic personality, Torchy recalled, "I don't know anyone who didn't like Claire. They say in life there are givers and takers. Claire is truly a *giver*, and everybody that knows Claire . . . knows she is a giver."

Torchy continued his adulation: "She was Division I in every department and didn't know what selfishness was. A big fraternity guy told me, 'Oh, she'll date you, but she won't go steady with you.' Five children, seventeen grandchildren, and fifty-seven years later, he was wrong!" The proud husband humbly added, "Claire is a perfect mother, a perfect grandmother, and a perfect coach's wife. The Bible referred to the good wife 'as a jewel.' I definitely married up! Claire looks like Sophia Loren."

In 1950, Torchy and Claire were married at St. Peter's Catholic Church in Oshkosh. Both were still undergraduates at Marquette: Torchy was a junior and Claire was a sophomore. After getting married, the couple made the decision for the Hilltopper basketball player on scholarship to continue his education and basketball career and Claire dropped her classes. To help the couple's budget, he worked part-time at a brewery in Milwaukee.

One of his Marquette teammates amusingly quipped, "Why on earth did she marry you, Clark?" Torchy shot back, "Claire wore contact lenses when they first came out and didn't see too well." A year later, the Clarks would welcome their first of five children, Michael James Clark, born on July 13, 1951, in Milwaukee. A new chapter in the newlyweds' life was on the horizon.

In May of 1951, Torchy graduated from Marquette. He promptly began to search for a teaching and coaching job. Job hunting was difficult and highly competitive, with many veterans returning from World War II looking for employment. Torchy recalled, "Jobs were almost impossible, so I went to the jobs in the toughest, most rural parts of Wisconsin. I was 22 years old, but looked 17. I had two possible opportunities: one at Fish Creek High School and one at Gilman High School, located in the rugged Wisconsin farmland. I chose the latter first and was interviewed by Gilman's principal. He took me to two separate farms to meet the farmers who served on the job search committee." The interview process continued. "We next met the local grocer. The principal detailed my possible teaching responsibilities which included two classes of American History, two classes of World History, and one class of English. My coaching duties included serving as the head football and head basketball coach." After a minute of silence, gazing afar at the tall corn stalks in the nearby field, the principal made a firm job offer: "And the salary is $2900." Torchy replied with no hesitation, "I'll take it."

"My mother-in-law Dorothy Theis warned me sternly, 'You have a newborn son, wife, and no job yet!' Dorothy was one of the greatest human beings God put on this earth and lived to be 102. We had a great relationship and she was right!" added Torchy. Claire stayed in Milwaukee to get her six-week checkup after the baby. He traveled alone to Gilman to begin his coaching career; Claire and Mike would follow later.

Torchy's first recollection of the school: "Gilman High School looked exactly like the high school in the movie *Hoosiers*. The school's original colors were purple and gold, but the administrators working on a tight budget received a huge discount on some green and white football uniforms. They quickly changed the school's colors to green and white, but for basketball, it was too late. We wore purple and gold uniforms for the first season," reminisced the young coach. Torchy remembered his time in Gilman: "I went to a movie after arriving there, and the theater was 15 miles away in Cornell. The movie was *Valentino*, which starred Eleanor Parker and Anthony Decker."

A strong wave of anxiety hit Torchy as he awaited his first "official" practice as a coach: "I was really nervous: anxiety, acute anxiety . . . you name it. My wife and son were four hours away—I was alone. Tomorrow, I was starting my first job at 9:00 a.m., and worse than that, it was football! I was a basketball coach, and at the age of 22, I wasn't even sure of that! Anyway, it was a great movie."

Torchy returned to his tiny apartment and went to bed, as the next morning, a new chapter in his life would begin. He distinctly remembered his first day: "How was I? To my surprise, I was a complete dictator. I had never seen or noticed this before in my personality, but I could decidedly give orders and be in charge."

The village of Gilman had 410 residents and was located in north-central Wisconsin. The high school's mascot was either a purple and white Pirate or a green and white Pirate, depending on which sports team was playing. The first-year coach remembered arriving at school one morning and seeing a crowd of students crying near the hallway bulletin board. He asked a student, "What happened?" The student replied, 'Hank Williams just died.' Now I knew Frank Sinatra, Gene Autry, and Louie Prima, but I had never heard of Hank Williams."

Another special memory from Gilman involved baseball. "I had to stop listening to the radio broadcast of the National League Pennant race (1951) between the Dodgers and the Giants to coach my football practice," said Torchy. "Fifteen minutes later, three Gilman teachers sprinted out to the field telling us the Giants won the Pennant on Bobby Thompson's walk-off home run. This was the historic home run called by Giants announcer Russ Hodges, a sports call that lives forever: 'The Giants win the Pennant' four times in a row . . . and then said it one more time. This was the 'Shot Heard Around the World.'"

A few weeks later, Claire and Mike arrived in Gilman, thus making life easier for the Pirates' new coach. Torchy recalled a story about a local restaurant: "The only steakhouse or nice dining establishment was two miles out of town . . . it was called Kool Mo's Supper Club." Many of the Gilman faculty often frequented Kool Mo's.

One weekend, Torchy and Claire decided to go out to dinner. "On Saturday, we got a babysitter and went out for a steak at Kool Mo's. We had a delicious meal, socialized with the Gilman faculty and had a wonderful time," he said with a glow of satisfaction. "Claire is a beautiful woman and has a vivacious personality. I always said if Claire had my records in coaching, she'd be the head coach at UCLA, Notre Dame, or Purdue." As the two were leaving the restaurant, the owner approached them and asked, "How was everything?" Claire replied, "The meal was elegant and your place is gorgeous, but why on earth did you give it a crazy name like Kool Mo's?" The owner replied, "I'M WENDALL KOOLMO."

The small village had a weekly newspaper called *The Gilman Herald*. The paper had no national news and just covered local events. The young couple made extra money writing the sports for the *Herald*. "We received 10 cents for every inch. We never made much. Our biggest article (80 cents) was when I resigned as coach," he noted with a touch of humor.

Gilman was Torchy and Claire's beginning as a family. "I'll always have lasting memories of the town and school. And the great opportunity the Gilman administration gave me right out of Marquette. But sometimes in life things are like vapors: here and then gone. But the memories remain."

CHAPTER 6

Appleton

In 1953, the Clarks' next part of their journey took them to Appleton, Wisconsin, three hours southeast of Gilman. The city is the hometown of the famous magician and illusionist Ehrich Weiss, also known as Houdini; former United States Republican Senator Joseph McCarthy; and Pulitzer Prize winner Edna Ferber. The mighty Fox River runs through the heart of the city. Back in 1953, the population was 50,000 (now 75,000).

Appleton was settled in 1847 and incorporated as a village in 1853. With the financial backing of Amos A. Lawrence, the Lawrence Institute was chartered during that same period (the late 1840s). Samuel Appleton, Lawrence's father-in-law from New England, donated $10,000 to the school's new library. Appleton's name was given to the community for his kind generosity.

The Lawrence Institute became Lawrence University. Today, the school's athletic programs are proud and highly successful members of the NCAA Division III. The Wisconsin Timber Rattlers are a Class-A affiliate of the Milwaukee Brewers who compete in the Midwest League. The team is located in Appleton and plays its home games at picturesque Neuroscience Group Field at Fox Cities Stadium.

St. Mary's Catholic Church is the oldest Roman Catholic Church in Appleton. In 1953, St. Mary's Grade School began a search to find a young, vibrant coach to lead its school's basketball and football teams. The new hire would serve as athletic director and also teach physical education and two classes of English.

Torchy interviewed for the teaching and coaching position that summer. Monsignor Adam Grill, pastor at St. Mary's, was deeply moved by his humility and sincerity. The school was ecstatic to hire a former college athlete and role model for St. Mary's students and players. Howard Crabb and Tom Miller, both church parishioners, highly recommended the devout Catholic. Miller, too, played a key role in his future hire at Xavier. Roy Lindgren (Oshkosh) and Roger Rindt (Appleton) also guided the up-and-comer immensely in his life and career.

The appointment of Torchy Clark fired up St. Mary's eighth-grader Bill McGinnis. He remembered meeting his new coach for the first time as a 13-year-old: "We were all thrilled to have a former Marquette player as our coach. My first impression of Torchy in 1953 . . . Boy, is he young-looking with the baby face. He looked like a 17-year-old."

The school was in the process of constructing a multipurpose gym, which was invigorating for the entire community. McGinnis observed each day the building of the St. Mary's Gym . . . the laying of bricks, the mounting of the jumbo scoreboard, and the installation of the permanent wooden bleachers on each side of the court. The excitement grew bigger and bigger each day as McGinnis anticipated taking his first shot in the new facility with the maple-wood floor.

St. Mary's fielded a football team of 14 players, including Bill McGinnis, Chuck Kunitz, Joe Eich, and Jimmy Holzer. Football practices were held at several sites, but Pierce Park was the most common. The boys hopped on their bikes after school and pedaled to the park in their football gear. Donald, Torchy's father, attended practice occasionally in Appleton to watch his son coach. "We had a lot of fun. We played our home games at Goodland Field. St. Joe's was the class of the league and our big rival," said McGinnis of his cherished memories.

Torchy's St. Mary's basketball teams in the 1950s were ultra-successful. The 24-year-old guided his first team in 1953 to a surprising 21–9 record. It was in Appleton where he developed "coaching confidence" with a system of play ahead of his time. This system employed a high-powered fast break and an aggressive, trapping full-court press. McGinnis, who played in the eighth and ninth grade, warmly reminisced, "That first year, Torchy bought us brand-new uniforms . . . shiny gold tops and blue shorts. Our basketball team was very good, and he did a great job teaching us how to press."

Torchy was strongly influenced by his *own* St. Peter's champion-ship experience in the 1943 Diocesan Basketball Tournament as an eighth grader. Now ten years later, he was the director of a similar, 16-team Christmas Tournament hosted by St. Mary's in Appleton. McGinnis remembered, "Torchy did a brilliant job organizing Catholic grade schools from all over to play in the tournament. It lasted three to four days, and it was an awesome experience to play teams from different areas."

For other games, the Colts traveled to Oshkosh to play St. Peter's and St. Vincent's. "Every time we played in Oshkosh, Torchy treated us to ice cream cones after the game at Sunlight Dairy. It is a golden memory of St. Mary's I'll always remember," said McGinnis.

Torchy recalled the story of his first basketball clinic at St. Mary's in the late 1950s: "It was winter of 1958 and I was chaperoning a dance in our gym. I was standing next to a high school athlete and said, 'You know, it's a shame the gym doesn't get used in the summer.' The athlete said, 'That would be fun if we had some type of summer basketball in the gym.'" The groundbreaking coach continued, "The following summer I started a basketball clinic at St. Mary's. One week of basketball with fundamentals, demonstrations, lectures, and scrimmaging. I charged $2.00 for the week!!

"The following year I added football and charged $8.00 a week. Coaches in the area heard about it and started calling me to pick my brain. Instead of coaches peddling ice or working in parks and recreation as a summer job, they could make $800.00 running sports clinics. I knew I was onto something," reflected Torchy. "Medalist Sporting Goods followed my idea and entered the camp industry around 1957. It took off in the 1960s. I wish now I would have patented the idea! But it all started at St. Mary's with my clinic for $2.00!" he added.

The teacher-coach was an influential mentor to his students and players. McGinnis remembered Torchy's random act of *kindness* in his freshman English class taught by his coach: "Our class was reading out loud the story *Tale of Two Cities*. Each student would read a page to the entire class . . . followed by the next person reading a page and the next, etc., . . . going down the row of desks." As a ninth grader, McGinnis was terrified of reading out loud. Torchy knew of his anxiety and genuine fear. McGinnis recalled, "When it was my turn to read, Torchy skipped over me, calling on the next person. He did that several times and bailed me out. We never talked about it, until years later when we coached together at Xavier."

At St. Mary's High School in Menasha, McGinnis lettered in three sports. His passion was baseball, and he played collegiately at UW-Stout in Menomonie. As the starting catcher for the Stout Blue Devil baseball team, McGinnis had a standout career; however, several times he wanted to quit school. "Torchy motivated me to stay in college, and I am grateful for the guidance and encouragement he gave me during that time," said McGinnis.

The two would forge a friendship for life. It was Torchy's recommendation of McGinnis as a history teacher in 1963 that helped him join the renowned Xavier faculty. McGinnis became a trusted asset and confidant to the Hawks' legend in his phenomenal success.

The protege recalled the story of a basketball scouting trip he took with the veteran coach. "Torchy and I drove to scout Messmer in Milwaukee, a two-hour drive. Messmer Catholic High School had incredible talent and were well-coached. We were scheduled to play them in a week. As the game started, Torchy watched the action closely, scribbling on a notepad a few of Messmer's tendencies and identifying their best shooters. At the end of the first quarter, he said, 'Bill, I'm ready to go. I've seen enough.'"

After leaving Appleton in 1969 to coach at the University of Central Florida (UCF), Torchy and McGinnis remained close, talking frequently on the phone, having conversations centered around family and sports. Bill McGinnis and his wife Peg still live in Appleton and have six children and 20 grandchildren. Their oldest son, Brian, was a pitcher for Appleton West High School. Brian wanted to play college baseball in Florida's warm weather. He received a baseball scholarship to Seminole Community College in Sanford, Florida, near Orlando.

A week before the fall term began, Brian had a scheduled flight to Orlando from Appleton. His 6:00 p.m. flight was to arrive in Orlando at 9:00 p.m. The prearrangement was made for Torchy to pick Brian up at the airport. However, the plane had maintenance issues and the departure was delayed until 12:15 a.m. McGinnis remembered calling his mentor that night, "'Torchy, don't worry about picking up Brian. His flight isn't arriving until 3:00 a.m. It's too late . . . One of his teammates can go to the airport.' But, Torchy insisted on picking him up in the middle of the night, and he did!"

McGinnis fondly looked back with deep respect and appreciation. "Torchy has been one of the most important and influential people in my life . . . as a father, grandfather, teacher, referee, and coach. I think of him often." And by the way, Bill McGinnis' FIRST shot (1953) as a 13-year-old in the newly constructed state-of-the-art St. Mary's Gym with the gleaming wood floor was a 16-foot right elbow jumper. The shot was nothing but net!

On his reflections of 1953–59, Torchy recalled, "St. Mary's Appleton was a very special place for the Clark family. We enjoyed the quality teachers and the warm-hearted, kind families of the parish. I have indelible memories of my six years. But sometimes in life things are like vapors: here and then gone. But the memories remain."

CHAPTER 7

Soul of Xavier

In 1959, a new Catholic high school opened its doors in Appleton. The school was led by the Institute of the Brothers of the Christian Schools (Christian Brothers) and the Franciscan Sisters of Christian Charity (Manitowoc Franciscans). After six successful years at St. Mary's Grade School, Torchy Clark was hired by the school's board headed by Brother Peter of the Christian Brothers. The multiple duties of the position included teaching History, athletic director, and serving as head coach of the football, basketball, and tennis teams.

The 30-year-old Torchy recalled that historic period: "The Christian Brothers and I together liked the name 'Xavier.' The Diocese of Green Bay's patron saint was St. Francis Xavier, which was a major influence in the school's name." Torchy reminisced proudly, "The name 'Xavier' was appealing to me and close to my heart. Jim Bunning, the Hall of Fame pitcher (1996) who played for the Detroit Tigers, Philadelphia Phillies, Pittsburgh Pirates, and the Los Angeles Dodgers, was my brother-in-law. Jim and I married sisters." Torchy married Claire Theis in 1950, and Bunning married Mary Theis in 1952.

Jim Bunning was an excellent baseball and basketball player at Xavier University in Cincinnati, Ohio. "I always liked the name 'Xavier' because of Jim's loyalty and pride for his alma mater," Torchy emphasized.

After 16 years (1955–71) in the major leagues, Jim Bunning, the master of the strikeout, would later enter the political arena as a staunch, conservative Republican spending a combined 24 years representing Kentucky in the House and Senate. He is the sole Major League Baseball player to have been elected to both the United States Senate and the Baseball Hall of Fame. Bunning, one of baseball's all-time greatest pitchers, threw a no-hitter for the Tigers (1959) and a perfect game for the Phillies (1964).

Torchy reflected on that special time in his career: "It was the perfect name, and it was exciting to be on the ground floor of the school's integral and humble beginning. Xavier's great tradition and expectation of excellence would soon be second-to-none."

The beautiful campus located on Prospect Avenue began with a freshman and sophomore class in the fall of 1959. The following year, the school added a junior class; and then the following year, added a senior class. In 1961, Xavier began interscholastic competition and postseason competition with other schools in Wisconsin, becoming a member of the Fox Valley Catholic Conference (FVCC).

As the school searched for an identity in its early history, Claire called her uncle, Father Stan Tillman, a Jesuit priest and teacher at Xavier University, for some advice. "I called Stan to get a copy of the sheet music of the school fight song," said Claire. Xavier High School adopted Xavier University's fight song with permission, changing the words to make it fit accordingly for the Appleton school.

Claire spent many hours on the Clark's piano diligently practicing the song. An excellent pianist with a sweet, harmonious voice, Claire's

Xavier fight song echoed in the halls of their Prospect Avenue home on many days.

Torchy remembered the historic decisions that he as the athletic director, together with the Christian Brothers, made in 1959: "We used Xavier University's colors of navy and white. The Christian Brothers wanted to add a touch of Columbia blue to the school colors. They thought a Columbia blue 'X' would look classy on the navy letter jackets and sweaters. The committee was sold on the nickname of the 'Hawks.' I had the wonderful opportunity to be a part of the *soul* of Xavier High School that included assisting the Christian Brothers and Franciscan Sisters with:

- The school's name
- The school's expectation of excellence
- The school's colors
- The school's nickname
- The school's fight song
- The buying of the first athletic uniforms
- The organization of the athletic program
- The trophy case"

The upstart Hawks coach witnessed firsthand the construction of the new Xavier gym in 1959: "I watched it all . . . the wood floor, the gym equipment arriving, and the eight baskets being installed. One day, I walked out of the gym and into the lobby. I saw two huge trophy cases that were being assembled. They were the largest trophy cases I've ever seen. Naturally, the cases were empty and I said to myself, *How on earth will we ever win a conference championship with the tough league (FVCC) we would be joining in a few years?* I personally played in that league. The conference was loaded with unbelievable talent, gifted coaches, and great traditions."

In Xavier High School's inaugural academic year, the boys were taught by the Christian Brothers on one wing of the campus. On the opposite wing, the girls were taught by the Franciscan Sisters. During a school day, the only time the boys and girls saw each other was at lunch in the Xavier Commons. The other faculty members were made up of lay teachers.

The Hawks were not eligible for any high school state championship playoffs until 1961, when all four classes were fully operational. The school's sports teams competed against junior varsity and freshman squads the first two years. Xavier's feeder schools included St. Mary, St. Joseph, Sacred Heart, and St. Therese. All provided Torchy with an excellent pool of athletes who wanted to attend the elite school for its strong academic reputation; and to play football or basketball for this trailblazing, energetic coach, as *rumors* of potential championships swirled around the Fox Valley. Occasionally, students from Menasha, Neenah, Kimberly, or Freedom commuted each day to attend Xavier— many would play crucial roles in Torchy's legacy.

Looking back to 1959, "Xavier's original strategic plan was to: (1) Accent on excellence in Academics and doing the little things extraordinarily well; (2) Xavier wanted strong Music; and lastly (3) Athletics was an integral part of student development/growth, improving school spirit and school morale," emphasized Torchy with great pride.

The integrity of the administration and the Christian leadership in Xavier's infancy impressed the 1951 Marquette graduate: "Academically, we had outstanding principals leading our school. The principal of the boys' wing was Brother Peter, one of the sharpest and most dedicated religious men I've ever known. Coincidentally, the principal of Xavier's girls' wing was Sister Peter. I didn't know Sister Peter as well, but she was deeply committed and a humble guiding light.

"The excellent academic culture was created immediately at Xavier in 1959. By reputation, the Christian Brothers were distinguished teachers. The group we had in my mind were the best-of-the-best. The priests were exceptional—Father Al Lison and Monsignor Adam Grill were two of my all-time favorites."

The proud father liked to tell the story of son Tom, who attended Xavier his freshman year before the family moved to Florida. "Tom, who worked for Delta Airlines for 30 years, said that Bob Strick (Xavier faculty) was the best Math teacher he ever had, including college."

Torchy affectionately remembered the great *honor* and *privilege* it was to be a part of Xavier's early foundation: "The faculty was brilliant. When you looked at the faculty picture in the school's yearbook, it was one fabulous teacher after another. Xavier will forever hold a special place in my heart. But sometimes in life things are like vapors: here and then gone. But the memories remain."

CHAPTER 8

Perfection—1962–63

On November 22, 1963, the assassination of President John F. Kennedy in Dallas, Texas, by Lee Harvey Oswald shocked the entire United States. The first-ever Catholic president was a strong advocate and voice for civil rights in our nation. Many baby boomers can remember the exact time and place they were in 1963 when Kennedy was assassinated.

That same year, an English rock band called the "Beatles" caught the attention of the entire world. The enormous popularity of the Beatles became "Beatlemania" as the group toured the country. Beatlemania lasted 10 years (1960–70), but their songs live forever.

The Xavier Hawks' inaugural campaign (1961–62) as a full-fledged member of the FVCC was astonishingly successful, winning conference championships in both football and basketball. In 1961, Torchy's football Hawks finished with an unblemished 9–0 record. However, they finished second in the final regular season Wisconsin State Football Poll (no state playoffs in Wisconsin until 1968). The basketball Hawks also had a spectacular first season with a 22–3 record, winning the conference championship before losing to Eau Claire Regis in the first round of the Wisconsin Catholic Interscholastic Athletic Association (WCIAA) State Basketball Tournament at the Milwaukee Arena.

The city of Appleton was blown away by the stunning success of Xavier's teams. The new Catholic high school not only established their strong academia, but also made a surprising impact on the Wisconsin prep sports scene.

In only Xavier's second year as a four-year school (1962–63), the Hawks began their steep climb to the summit. The football Hawks were led by junior phenom Rocky Bleier, a five-foot-ten, 180-pound All-State halfback, and finished with another incredible undefeated season at 9–0.

Xavier not only won the FVCC Championship, but more importantly finished as the No. 1 team in the final Wisconsin State Football Poll. The Xavier Hawks were 1962 WISCONSIN STATE FOOTBALL CHAMPIONS!!

Bleier's strength and beauty as a runner were uncanny. His athleticism, explosiveness, and toughness fueled the Hawks' offense. Quarterback Dick Weisner, whose brother Tom played football in the Big 10 for the Wisconsin Badgers, completed 50 percent of his passes. Besides Bleier, the Hawks' backfield was made up of halfback Kip Whitlinger and fullback Tom Peeters. Whitlinger was a shifty runner, while the 215-pound Peeters was Torchy's power running back. Seniors Dick Boots and Bobby Rammer led the wide receiving corps. Boots scored seven touchdowns and did the kicking.

The intensity and fire of Torchy drove the football Hawks to great success. His teams played with an unrelenting passion and the fear of letting him down. That obligation and a basic *Lombardian* playbook ignited Xavier to State Championship glory. Torchy and brilliant assistant Harry Nelson taught fundamentals consistently as execution, work ethic, and a team-first attitude were mandatory.

On July 30, 1960, on the floor of the maternity ward at St. Elizabeth's Hospital in Appleton, Torchy met Harry Nelson for the first time. On that day, Claire gave birth to daughter Patty, and Harry's wife Jan gave birth to daughter Heidi. Nelson had played college football at UW Oshkosh as a lineman and developed an instant connection with Torchy. Both Clark and Nelson would create a powerful, dynamic coaching alliance for the football Hawks in the early 1960s.

Nelson coached both the offensive and defensive linemen. Xavier's defense was one of the nation's finest, shutting out five foes and never allowing more than 12 points in a single game. The stingy Hawks held their opponents to a mere 35 total points for the entire season. Meanwhile, the Hawks' offense piled up 334. In addition to offense, Rocky Bleier played defense and became an All-FVCC defensive back and an All-FVCC linebacker. Whitlinger and Rammer also doubled on both sides of the ball as defensive backs.

The key linemen in the trenches for the State Champion Hawks were: tackle Jim Captain, center Tom Schueppert, and guard Kelly Kornely. "Harry did a fabulous job with the line. Our guys were physical, disciplined, and opened huge holes," added Torchy. Hawks' athletes Kornely, Rammer, Paul Putzer, and Tim Garvey also played basketball and football for Torchy at St. Mary's Grade School. In 2004, Kornely was instrumental in the renaming of the Xavier Gym to the Gene "Torchy" Clark Gymnasium in a tremendous tribute to his former coach. Today, the Xavier students call it "The Torchy."

In 1964, Harry Nelson moved to Florida to run his own football program at Bishop Moore Catholic High School in Orlando. "Harry the Hornet" led his Hornets to a 1970 Florida Class A State Championship. The leadership and poise of Mike Malatesta, the Hornets' quarterback, was decisive in the 21-12 victory against Quincy Shanks in the title game. Nelson had a legendary career at Bishop Moore, and the school's on-campus football field was proudly renamed "Harry Nelson Field at Memorial Stadium" in 2008.

The 1962–63 basketball Hawks were led by senior sharpshooter Kip Whitlinger, the son of ex-Ohio State basketball player Warren Whitlinger. The five-foot-ten, multi-talented guard who averaged 26 points per game, was a resident of Neenah, Wisconsin, and commuted 20 minutes each day to attend Xavier.

Whitlinger, like his father, would play basketball at Ohio State after his storybook career. His shooting, athleticism (great driver), and ability to score in bunches were huge strengths for the 1962–63 Hawks. "Kip was one of the best ever. He was the purest of pure shooters," said Torchy. "By far, Kip was the best shooter I ever coached." Whitlinger will be remembered as one of Wisconsin's finest prep players.

Dick Weisner, a five-foot-ten point guard/quarterback, was another Neenah commuter. His toughness and intelligence helped the Xavier teams to crowning success. "Weisner was so good at making decisions and was like a coach on the field . . . and on the court. He was excellent with the ball in his hands. I trusted him," reflected Torchy. The basketball Hawks raced through the regular season with an undefeated 22–0 slate. Xavier easily dispatched their opponents in the FVCC behind Whitlinger's prolific scoring, Bleier's defense, Weisner's leadership, and the scrappy rebounding of blue-collar bigs, Bob DeBruin and John Heinritz, both undersized at six-foot-two.

Torchy's intensity teaching the full-court press was like a hurricane ready to hit the coast. Time after time at practice, he blew his whistle, stopped the action when a defender got beat denying the inbounds pass, or when a trap was split. In only his unique and passionate way, Torchy ripped the player. Over and over, the hurricane-force winds kept blowing until the Hawks got it right. Little by little, the Hawks improved each day as Torchy's intensity and emotion bled into his players. "The face-guard press is difficult to teach, but can turn around a game quickly. It's a momentum-changer! Boy, did it win some games for us!" said the high-energy coach.

His system of transition basketball, running the floor with great spacing, unselfish teamwork, and the full-court press was unstoppable in 1962–63. Game after game the Blue and White sold out the hot and noisy Xavier Gym: The tradition, the spirit, and Appleton's love of the Hawks grew each game and each season.

In March of 1963, the Hawks were off to Milwaukee for a second consecutive trip to the (WCIAA) State Basketball Tournament. Xavier won their quarterfinal game against Wausau Newman, 79–51. They then pounded conference foe Green Bay Premontre in the semifinal, 74–53, advancing to the State Championship. The opponent for the title game was Milwaukee Marquette High School, an all-male Jesuit school who came into the championship after defeating 1962 State Champion Madison Edgewood 60–51 in the other semifinal.

The Hilltoppers were playing in their backyard—the school was only three miles from the arena. Marquette High was coached by John Glaser who, like Torchy, was a former Marquette University player (1955–58). Glaser is one of the Golden Eagles' (MU) all-time leading rebounders. Marquette High had a highly respected basketball reputation in the state. The school was the alma mater of coaching great Rick Majerus and Al McGuire's son, Allie. The younger McGuire would go on to have an outstanding career as a point guard/floor general for his legendary father at Marquette University.

The 1962–63 Hilltoppers had an excellent team with a record of 19–3. They were led by sophomore sensation Chuck Nagle, a six-foot-three forward; Pete Brewer, a six-foot-three senior center; and Dan O'Neil, a six-foot-three senior scoring forward. Chuck Nagle, the son of Jack Nagle, former Marquette University basketball coach (1953–58), was the Hilltoppers' best all-around player. A four-sport letterman at Marquette High, he would later play college basketball for the Badgers at UW-Madison, scoring 1,064 points.

Marquette came into the title game riding a nine-game winning streak; Xavier had won 26 straight. "They had tough kids, and Glaser was an excellent coach. We knew Nagle was very good. And our guys knew we'd have to play well to win," said Torchy of his team's daunting task. The chatter among fans, coaches, and the media in Milwaukee was Xavier's relentless, smothering press. The championship was a game for the ages as 7,095 fans attended the Sunday night classic. At the time, the massive crowd was the largest attendance ever for a Wisconsin prep basketball game. Marquette's fans echoed proudly in warm-ups, chanting, "WE ARE . . . MARQUETTE! WE ARE . . . MARQUETTE!" The 2,000 Xavier fans who trekked down Highway 41 for the two-hour trip south began cheering, "LET'S GO HAWKS! LET'S GO HAWKS!"

Marquette jumped out to an early lead the first five minutes behind the play of Nagle and O'Neil. Both Hilltoppers had been playing confident basketball in Marquette's drive to the title. In the second quarter, Xavier stormed back like a freight train, using the full-court press on one of the game's key Hawk scoring spurts. The charge was led by the phenomenal shooting of Kip Whitlinger and the defensive tenacity of Rocky Bleier as Xavier took a commanding 38–29 lead at the intermission. Bleier's two lightning steals from the press before halftime resulted in four quick points.

Behind the play of Tim Garvey, Bobby Rammer, and Tom Rankin, Xavier's bench was instrumental and gave the Hawks valuable minutes. As he did often in his career, Torchy used only eight players in the championship game. Both teams made key halftime adjustments. Marquette wanted to throw the long pass against the press and switched to a 1–2–2 half-court zone defense, trying to shade the scoring-ace Whitlinger. Torchy's adjustments included trapping and swarming Marquette's best ball handlers, Tom Collentine and Tim Larkin, forcing deflections and turnovers. In addition, he wanted the Hawks to run with greater pace against the slower Hilltoppers in the hunt for easy baskets.

The undersized Hawks were manhandled on the boards by a whopping 48–28. Pete Brewer of Marquette collected 18 rebounds in the game. But the Hawks were much quicker and in better basketball condition. The hours and hours of working on the full-court press had paid huge dividends for Xavier's "toughness of steel."

In the second half, Marquette gritted its teeth and fought through Torchy's press to tie the game 49-all with a minute left in the third stanza. The Xavier faithful nervously awaited to see if the Hawks could handle the pressure of an outstanding Marquette team. The game's fourth quarter would be the Hawks' biggest test of their almost perfect season.

Xavier, a team with the striking power of a team of commandos (Bledsoe, 1963), responded quickly in the decisive fourth with a basket off a steal. At the 6:36 mark, Marquette's Brewer scored on a reverse layup as the Hilltoppers retook the lead 55-54. Xavier's Whitlinger then hit a huge 20-footer to put the Hawks up, 56–55. Marquette turned the ball over on the next possession. The confident Whitlinger, who was absolutely brilliant in the second half, rose to the occasion again with a short pull-up jumper slicing through Marquette's 1–2–2 zone. The Hawks now led 58–55.

Marquette's Brewer followed with another layup, this time against the Hawks' press to cut Xavier's lead to one, 58–57. Torchy was livid . . . as his team gave up an easy bunny. The supreme shooter, Whitlinger, again swished a 25-footer as the Hawks now led, 60–57, with 4:50 left in the game. This was a nail-biter in Milwaukee.

Claire sat in the 15th row above the Xavier bench. She anxiously wrote the scoring tallies of each Hawk on the back of an envelope. This was a Claire tradition at every one of his stops in his coaching career. "I always rode to the games with Torchy," said the loyal Claire. "I felt by keeping the scoring, I'd be able to talk to him about the game on the way home. Plus, the games were so nerve-wracking . . . it gave me something to do."

The exhilaration of the title game lived up to its media hype in the *Milwaukee Journal* and the *Milwaukee Sentinel*, with the game's outcome not being decided until the closing minutes. With 4:01 left and Xavier up 60–59, the Hawks would go on another key scoring spurt. The run was sparked by John Heinritz, a pivotal role player who missed a six-foot jumper, got his own rebound, and followed up with a basket to put the Hawks up, 62–59. Heinritz and Bob DeBruin were true unsung heroes, not only in the Marquette title game, but throughout the magical season.

With 3:20 to play in the game, Xavier's flurry continued as Whitlinger hit another 25-foot jumper. The Hawks now led 64–59. Marquette made a critical turnover, and with 2:50 left in the game, Bleier nailed a decisive 12-foot baseline jumper to put the Hawks up, 66–59. "The legion of Appleton fans on hand almost deroofed the Arena with a mighty roar." (Paustian, 1963)

Torchy took off his full-court press to play his tight zone as Marquette scrambled for quick scores. The Hawks ran their disciplined "triangles-delay" game to perfection with precise passing and state-champion confidence. The Hilltoppers could not get any closer than five points. The Hawks knocked down several crucial free throws in the waning seconds. Xavier defeated Marquette, 71–66!!

When the final horn blared at the arena, Bob Lloyd of Appleton's WHBY radio station, who was broadcasting the game back to the hometown, went wild with hysteria, calling the historic victory for Xavier. Lloyd, a veteran announcer, knew his sports and truly loved the Hawks.

On the air, Lloyd enthusiastically proclaimed, "The Hawks have just won the STATE CHAMPIONSHIP . . . The Hawks have won the STATE CHAMPIONSHIP, beating Marquette, 71–66, here in Milwaukee. What a game.!! And remember, folks . . . they were *No. 1* in football too. The players have Torchy on their shoulders, and oh what a sight . . . Bedlam Reigns Supreme!"

After the game, the State Championship Trophy was presented to Torchy and his two seniors, Kip Whitlinger and Dick Weisner, at center court. The joyous, euphoric Xavier players and fans cheered wildly in celebration of the school's second state championship in a little over four months. An *amazing* feat!! An Associated Press (AP) picture of the three clutching the trophy in jubilation was carried by many Wisconsin newspapers. The victorious coach was tossed into the showers by his ecstatic players in the post-game hoopla.

John Paustian, an *Appleton Post-Crescent* sportswriter who Torchy deeply respected and appreciated, summarized the remarkable triumph: "Appleton Xavier's all-conquering basketball team won the 1963 state Catholic championship Sunday night in a flaming climax to the school's meteoric rise to athletic greatness. Guard Rocky Bleier boomed in 16 points—all but four of which came on 6-for-12 field goal shooting—led the team in assists with five, and was a bulwark on defense with fiery perpetual-motion coverage. Senior Dick Weisner was outstanding as the floor general and added 12 points to the attack. Junior Bob DeBruin punched in eight points and combined with John Heinritz, a senior, to pace the Hawks' board-clearing. DeBruin retrieved nine rebounds and Heinritz eight. Whitlinger closed one of the most fabulous scoring careers in Fox Cities' prep cage history by pacing all point-makers with 26 points."

The 1963 Wisconsin Catholic State Tournament broke attendance records for the three-day event. The official attendance of 24,409 smashed the previous high of 9,000 in 1961. Three of the players from the State Championship game played college basketball or football at major universities: Kip Whitlinger (basketball) at Ohio State, Chuck Nagle (basketball) at Wisconsin, and Rocky Bleier (football) at Notre Dame.

The Hawks were greeted by hundreds of cheering fans as they arrived back in Appleton after midnight. The festivities for the Hawks' players, managers, and coaches continued as they rode fire trucks provided by the city of Appleton Fire Department. Many enthusiastic fans lined up on College Avenue in rainy downtown to greet the State Champions. The welcome home championship events were coordinated by Jim Choudoir.

Xavier's school director and principal of the boys' wing, Brother Peter, reflected on the Hawks' 71–66 championship win: "It is a very pleasant feeling to know that your school has won a championship. Everyone worked hard to achieve the goal. We have a wonderful group of players and a top-notch coach *who is as good in the classroom as on the playing floor.*"

Sister Peter, director of the girls' wing, added her fond memories: "We're all thrilled about winning the championship; it should have a tremendous effect in a good sense. It was a frightening thing when our lead got cut to one point, but we knew our boys would come through."

Early the next morning after the state title game a reporter called the Clark's house at 8:30 a.m., trying to get some quotes from the Hawks' coach. The Clark's youngest son Bobby, a four-year-old, answered the phone and told the reporter, "I think my daddy is still sleeping. You know my daddy's team won the championship last night." The reporter laughed at the innocence of the moment and asked to talk to his mom.

The proud, delightful Claire, working on three hours of sleep, recounted the joy of Xavier's state championship victory: "No matter what happened last night, we were proud of our boys (Hawks)." Claire choked up with deep emotion, pride, and at a loss for words managed to exclaim, "It's just so wonderful . . . ohhh . . . it's just wonderful." A lot of others thought so too!!

The sheer excellence of Torchy's 1962–63 Xavier football and basketball teams can never be overlooked. A flawless masterpiece!! It was *perfection* at its highest point. The Hawks reached the *summit*. The humble championship coach fondly remembered, "Both teams had exceptional chemistry and everyone bought into their roles. *There were no egos.* The leadership we got from Weisner, Whitlinger, Kornely, and Bleier was the best I've seen. But sometimes in life, things are like vapors: here and then gone. But the memories remain."

CHAPTER 9

Rocky

A 1964 graduate of Xavier High School, Rocky Bleier went on to play football at Notre Dame (captain) and was a 16th-round draft choice of the Pittsburgh Steelers in 1968. Following his rookie season, Bleier was drafted into the Army. He had a tour in the Vietnam War, where he suffered severe foot and leg injuries. Bleier received the Purple Heart and the Bronze Star for his courage and bravery in the war. Following his return to the U.S., Bleier spent the 1970 NFL season on the Steelers taxi squad. He made the active roster in 1972 and went on to be a starter during all four of the Steelers Super Bowl Championships from 1975 to 1980. Bleier's heroic return to football was chronicled in the book and made-for-television movie called *Fighting Back*. His No. 23 football jersey was retired by Xavier, the only football player to be so honored in the school's 58-year history.

—Mike Woods, *Appleton Post-Crescent*, 2007

Bob "Rocky" Bleier Jr. was born to Bob Sr. and Ellen Bleier in Appleton, Wisconsin. His parents were gentle, hardworking, and humble people who owned a bar/restaurant off the main drag of downtown Appleton. The bar was named "Bob Bleier's Bar," and it was one of the city's finest.

The bar not only served alcohol, but more importantly had delicious food, especially on Fridays when lake perch (Bleier's was the best perch in Wisconsin) was on the menu. The bar also served great steaks, ribs, and chicken on other nights of the week. Many Friday nights there was an hour wait at Bob Bleier's Bar. It was "the place to eat" in Appleton. The family of six lived in the back section and second floor of their Walnut Street bar.

The name "Rocky" was tagged on him as an infant by his father, Bob Sr., who was opposed to the idea of his son being called "Junior" the rest of his life. Instead, he occasionally brought bar customers back to the bedroom to peek at his newborn "just lying there in the baby's cradle looking like a little *rock*." The name "little rock" stuck, and an accidental but perfect football nickname of "Rocky" sprung up in the Bleier family.

It's hard to believe this sensational running back who ran for 21 touchdowns in Xavier's 1962 Wisconsin State Football Championship season came pretty close to not playing football at all. When Rocky was in sixth grade at St. Joe's, his family doctor, Dr. Arthur Taylor, advised his parents he should stay off his feet and refrain from playing sports for three years. He was so active as a child, Rocky began to develop a knee condition called Osgood-Schlatter disease—a bone disorder that causes pain and swelling below the knee joint during the early years in growing adolescents.

According to his dad, Rocky nearly tore his heart out having to watch from the sidelines. All sports activities halted with the hope and goal of getting his knees stronger as he continued to grow. After a year of idleness, he began to secretly play basketball without telling his parents.

Rocky remembered the sneaky dilemma he was in as an 11-year-old: "I was getting away with it quite craftily until one afternoon when a teammate's father walked into my dad's bar and said, 'Hey Bob, you going to watch Rock play tonight?' My dad just laughed. 'Well, are you going, Bob?' My dad said, 'Rocky can't play basketball. He's got Osgood-Schlatter disease.' 'Well if he does,' the man said, 'then all those kids should have it.'"

In 1959, X-rays revealed his knees to be normal. The stage now was set for the legendary story of Rocky Bleier to play out. His path to glory, despite a one-year stoppage on sports participation, began as his knees were healthy and strong . . . built for greatness. As a freshman at Xavier, Torchy was immediately *awed* by Rocky's exceptional talent, his ability to change speeds, his relentless effort, and his humble "teachable spirit."

Torchy remembered his first encounter as coach with Rocky at St. Mary's: "I first met Rocky when he was a sixth-grader at St. Joe's. He was a good-looking kid wearing a white T-shirt and blue jeans. Rocky had a great smile and a perfect attitude. His hairline was extremely high—the sign of a pro in sixth grade.

"The next time I saw Rocky he was playing in an eighth-grade basketball tournament. His team was losing by eight points in the first half, and I've never seen anyone work or press harder. Then his team was up ten points with 15 seconds left in the game. It was over! And with two seconds to play, Rocky was playing defense like a mad man."

In 1961, Xavier's third year as a school, Rocky competed in football, basketball, and track (the Hawks were not eligible for conference or postseason play his freshman year). The Torchy-Rocky football and basketball teams of 1961–64 combined for a spectacular 96–4 record. That is correct, 96–4.

Rocky was also an excellent trumpet player and first chair in Xavier's nationally acclaimed band, and a member of the National Honor Society. Torchy remembered, "He was the perfect person: a good student, served Mass and tried to please everybody." Torchy always said, "Rocky was so nice that Mother Teresa wore a Rocky Bleier medal."

In his book *Fighting Back*, Rocky recalled playing for Torchy: "I say without reservation, Xavier was probably one of the best high schools in the country. Nothing at Xavier was as good as the athletic department for two reasons. First, we had a marvelous pool of talent. Second, we had Gene 'Torchy' Clark. His records at Xavier were phenomenal, 178–14 in basketball and 63–8–1 in football. He won 15 out of a possible 16 Fox Valley Catholic Conference championships.

"More important for me, Torchy brought out and developed the competitiveness I would need later in college and the pros. Torchy used to say I always had that intensity. But I remember watching Torchy coach St. Mary's basketball into a frenzy, trapping and pressing all over the court. They were the first grade-school team I ever saw that pressed—zone press, man-to-man press—non-stop pressure the whole game. After the shock of playing St. Mary's, I thought to myself, *Gee I'd like to play for Torchy someday.* Freshman year, I got my chance when I started on Xavier's varsity."

Rocky reflected on the special 1963 Xavier basketball season: "It was a team of discipline led by one of the all-time great coaches in Torchy. We had great floor leadership from Dick Weisner, our quarterback, uncanny scoring from Kip Whitlinger, and the rest of us played our roles. Our offense was our defense. We pressed and pressed just like Torchy's team pressed at St. Mary's. The full-court press and Kip's shooting were keys for us winning the State Championship."

As a basketball player, Rocky was a defensive stopper and the catalyst for Xavier's full-court press: The basketball Hawks in the Torchy-Rocky era finished an astounding 69–4. "He was a great presser, and one of the best I coached. I really believe Rocky was underestimated as a basketball player because of his unprecedented success in football. In the Marquette 1963 title game, Rocky hit two big free throws and scored 16 points, hitting a clutch jump shot in the closing minutes," said Torchy.

In three football seasons, the star halfback never lost a game as the Hawks went 27–0. For football opponents, Rocky was unstoppable: "Once in a Xavier football game at Goodland Field, he carried the ball six times and had four touchdowns," noted Torchy. "If I had let him go, Rocky would have scored a dozen or more touchdowns in that game." As a halfback/linebacker, Bleier played both sides of the field for the invincible Hawks. Torchy was a big believer in his best athletes being on the field as much as possible, maximizing their athleticism.

A gifted athlete, he developed a statewide reputation as football fans throughout Wisconsin got to know Rocky Bleier. For his sophomore, junior, and senior years, Rocky was named as a Wisconsin All-State selection. He ran for 2,985 yards averaging a surreal 9.4 yards per carry and scored 55 career touchdowns for the Hawks.

The great respect opponents had for Rocky was unequaled. Torchy shared one of the lasting memories: "In a preseason scrimmage against an excellent team, we took the ball first to start the action. The opponent's defense was waiting for Rocky to run, but on the first play, we didn't run him. On the second play, we pitched to Rocky on a sweep around the end. You could see the bulging eyes of the defense and see the fear. I heard a couple of their players simultaneously yell, 'HERE HE COMES—IT'S BLEIER!'"

Describing another story of Bleier's gallantry, Torchy continued, "At another game, we had a big lead, and I had our subs in the game. We stopped our opponents on our two-yard line. Our second team offense had the ball, and on first down we struggled out to the three-yard line. On second down, we stumbled for another yard to the four.

It was third-and-eight deep in our opponent's territory. I yelled for Rocky and said, 'Go in, Rocky, and run it out of there.' On the next play, third down, he took the hand-off and ran 45 yards to midfield. Then I took him out and let the subs finish the game."

One of his many feats as a Hawk football player was the famous Green Bay Premontre run in 1961. Torchy reminisced of the magnificent play, "In a barn burner against Premontre at the old Packer Stadium with the score tied 9–9 late in the game, Rocky took a quick pitch from quarterback Dick Weisner and got shoved out of bounds. His left foot was inside the out-of-bounds line, while his right foot hung off balance. But, Rocky regained his footing for a crucial 23-yard touchdown. It was an unbelievable run of athleticism and skill."

The touchdown was the difference in the game as the Hawks beat the Cadets, 23–16. A framed picture of Rocky's spectacular Premontre run and a bronzed replica of his left shoe rests in the Xavier trophy case today commemorating the historic run.

Rocky detailed the game in Green Bay as a sophomore: "Premontre was the dominant school in the conference and had all the great athletes. It was a hard-hitting back-and-forth game. It was late and we needed a touchdown." Football teammate Kip Whitlinger recalled the Premontre game: "Rocky threw about five or six guys off of him. It was an incredible play. From that time on word got out that Bleier was something special."

In 2007, Mike Woods of the *Appleton Post-Crescent* remembered Rocky's last football trip to Marinette for a game against Catholic Central in 1963, emphasizing it was a typical Rocky Bleier day.

He found the end zone as a running back, and as a punt returner. He also played defense and picked off a couple passes. As the Hawks gathered in their locker room following the

39–13 win, there was a hard knock on the door. "They wanted to see Rocky," said Torchy. Who exactly was they? "The whole Marinette Catholic Central team was out there," added Torchy. "They wanted to meet Rocky. So he goes outside and he still had his helmet on and takes it off and says, 'Jeez, you guys are really a good ball club.' He really praised them. They thought he'd be real cocky. But he was never a cocky kid, just a bucket of humility. They were very impressed with him."

Rocky's elusive running electrified the crowd every time he touched the ball. Co-captain Kelly Kornely remembered Torchy's three "secret" plays: "Bleier to the right . . . Bleier to the left . . . and Bleier up the middle."

The all-around "good guy" had a close relationship with his Hawks' coach, stopping by the Clark home every other Sunday to watch football and visit the family. On many school days, Rocky walked from his home, Bleier's Bar, to the Clark's house three blocks away to hitch a ride with Torchy to school.

Mike Clark, Torchy's oldest son, a Xavier graduate and three-sport letterman for the Hawks, relived a Rocky memory of his own: "In 1969, several months after he was wounded in Vietnam, he came to visit us in Orlando. Rocky stayed with our family for a week on leave from the Army, wanting to enjoy some warm Florida weather; but more importantly, he needed a shot of confidence and reassurance from his trusted mentor, his trusted confidant. I remember Rocky being on crutches and showing us his severely injured foot. We were all worried about his recovery."

At Notre Dame, the Fighting Irish and Rocky won a national championship in 1966 with a 9–0–1 record under Coach Ara Parseghian. The Pittsburgh Steelers and the city of Pittsburgh have embraced Rocky Bleier as a crown jewel and a beloved citizen. He remains one of the most popular players in the history of Pittsburgh sports. If the mere fact of winning four Super Bowl rings wasn't enough, Rocky's passion, courage, and comeback won the hearts of millions of sports fans.

For many Appleton youngsters in the 1960s, Rocky was a positive role model and hero to emulate. The grade schoolers playing sandlot football at Pierce Park or Jones Park in the cool Indian summer or the December snow took turns pretending to be Xavier's No. 23 Rocky Bleier running for another Hawk touchdown!

One of those impressionable grade schoolers was Torchy's son Bo, who attended St. Mary's before moving to Florida at the age of 12 when Torchy began at UCF. Bo went on to have successful high school and college basketball careers at Orlando Bishop Moore Catholic High School and UCF, respectively. With all humility, Bo's jersey No. 23 is retired at both Bishop Moore and UCF. "I wore No. 23 (Rocky's Xavier football number) because Rocky was my hero, my idol. I started wearing it in sixth grade at St. Mary's in Appleton and wore it my entire career," said Bo.

In 2007, Xavier renamed their football field "Rocky Bleier Field on the Knights of Columbus Sports Complex." Kip Whitlinger and Kelly Kornely, both former Rocky football teammates, were on the planning committee. "It was a labor of love," Whitlinger said. Rocky addressed the next generation of Xavier Hawks while on campus for the special weekend. Kornely recalled, "There aren't too many people in this world who have four Super Bowl rings, and he's earned them all. You could hear a pin drop in that assembly. Rocky had those students, and they just loved him," added Kornely.

Rocky says he was humbled, yet proud of the field dedication. "It was a great honor. It was a wonderful tribute to see my name attached to the field. My fondest memory was helping establish the future of Xavier High School, its great tradition and expectation of excellence."

Torchy's lasting memories on coaching Rocky: "Probably no one who has ever played two major sports has had a more outstanding career than Rocky Bleier. Teams become championship teams when your hardest worker is your best player, and that's what I had in Rocky. But sometimes in life things are like vapors: here and then gone. But the memories remain."

CHAPTER 10

Knee and the Ankle

The local hero, Rocky Bleier was honored in 2007 by the city of Appleton when they named a street after him. "Rocky Bleier Run" is located near his former grade school and two blocks from the site of his childhood home.

Kip Whitlinger was Xavier's all-time leading scorer until February 16, 2018, when Hawks' point guard Hunter Plamann shattered Whitlinger's 1,656 career points record. His scoring mark lasted an unbelievable 55 years (1963). The night Plamann broke his record at a home game in Xavier's Torchy Clark Gym, Whitlinger was in the house. A three-time All-State Basketball selection in Wisconsin, Whitlinger's No. 22 is the only Hawks' basketball jersey retired (2013). Today, the jersey is proudly displayed in "The Torchy."

Whitlinger still owns the Xavier record for points in a single game with 46 against St. John's Little Chute in 1963. In two other games, he scored 42 and 39 points, all before the advent of the three-point shot. During his state championship senior year, Whitlinger was named as a Catholic All-American selection, highlighting a sensational career.

Torchy chuckled at the memory of a football practice in 1962 and the unusual dilemma he stumbled upon. Both Bleier and Whitlinger, like many Hawk athletes, played football and basketball. "One day at practice, we ran a crossbuck. This means that the players X or cross as the receivers look for the pass," recalled the Hawks' mentor. "Once in a while, a player thinks he goes first, when actually he should go second.

"This causes a horrific collision like two trains crashing into each other. You always worry about Yankees' Mickey Mantle running into Roger Maris in the outfield fielding a fly ball. You could lose 100 home runs if it caused injury to both on the play," added the coaching veteran.

Torchy detailed the drama unfolding: "Whitlinger and Bleier collided on a pass route. Both were hurt: Bleier's knee and Whitlinger's ankle. They were lying on the field 100 feet apart. This was the time and era when high schools didn't employ a certified trainer or team doctor at practice. The head coach was the trainer.

"Now the question . . . who would I go to first? Actually, this all flashed through my mind instantaneously. I hesitated, and then went to Bleier's knee injury." The sensitive coach quickly thought of the conjecture and discernment his 38 football players would make from his immediate response of attending to Bleier first.

Torchy reminisced on the pickle he was in: "What was Kip Whitlinger's reaction? Kip was a thoroughbred and looked at me— 'Coach, I know . . . you picked Rocky,' but he was still with me. In coaching, you call this *transparent realism*. Kip saw my vulnerability in the touchy, delicate situation."

Later that spring, at the Hawks' 1963 postseason basketball banquet in the Xavier Commons, Torchy credited his team's defense and "focused" mental toughness as keys to success. More than *300* people attended the banquet to honor the State Basketball Champions.

Torchy continued his adulation of his Hawks players: "Rocky moved defense ahead ten years with his dedication to that phase of the game. But he also developed a scoring eye and offensive confidence to turn into an All-Conference and All-Tournament selection. Rocky proved to everyone what a tough and talented basketball player he was."

At the sold-out event, the Xavier coach resumed his praise of the Hawks: "Dick Weisner was the team's floor general and a tremendous leader . . . you can't replace him. He rose to the occasion in so many big games."

John Heinritz, his post player, was a true inspiration with his resilience and physical toughness. Torchy added on Heinritz's importance, "He came back with great determination after getting cut from the freshman team. John triumphed over adversity by starting at center as a senior and winning a State Championship at the Milwaukee Arena. What a powerful example of perseverance and courage John Heinritz was for every grade school basketball player at St. Mary, St. Joe, Sacred Heart, and St. Therese."

Junior Bob DeBruin, a versatile player on the championship team, shook off the effects of a severe ankle sprain, coming on strong after Christmas. Torchy declared at the podium, "Bob was all about the team and turned Xavier into a championship team." Tom Rankin was also praised for his "yeoman's work" off the bench. "Tom will be one of the best in the Fox Valley next year," said Torchy of Rankin's bright future. Guard Bobby Rammer was commended for his "clutch play as sixth-man and as a major wheel in the Hawks' championship."

Torchy also complimented junior guard Tim Garvey: "He was an excellent teammate who I trusted to make the right play." The baby-faced coach also praised the toughness of Bill Timmers, who was huge for the Hawks off the bench. Bill Fischer, Bruce Greisbach, Jim

Rather, Bob Zwicker, and Paul Putzer were thanked for their valiant team efforts and contributions. The Xavier coach also lauded his two team managers, as he always did throughout his career. Everyone was important in Torchy's eyes, as Tim Hardy and Paul Stumpf were recognized for their hard work, dedication, and loyalty.

Xavier's basketball success was fueled by the full-court press, an essential component of Torchy's system he calls "organized confusion." With Xavier's press and fast break, the Hawks discovered there's more method than madness in their approach to the game. Torchy joined other coaches such as St. Mary's Menasha's Ralph McClone ("Cyclone McClone") and Menasha High's Eric Kitzman, who have pressed their way to gloried success. McClone's 1960 State Champion Zephyrs (St. Mary's) featured the press, as did Kitzman's 1953 State Public Champion Bluejays (Menasha High). The brilliant Zephyrs' coach Ralph McClone was a huge *early* influence on Torchy's style of play and system. Both coaches were dear friends and had a mutual admiration for each other. A proud St. Mary's Menasha graduate (1947), Torchy used his "organized confusion" his entire Hall of Fame career.

John Paustian of the *Appleton Post-Crescent* remembered, "When Torchy was racking up astronomical winning percentages at St. Mary's Grade School in the 1950s, the cynics said, 'Wait until he gets into high school varsity sports.' Well, the returns for the first four years (1959–63) are in, and Clark's Xavier record is just as astounding as was the grade school record. That record reflects outstanding knowledge-ability in both major sports, exceptional dedication to his job, and a unique ability to inspire players." Paustian continued the Torchy accolades: "Quickness, one of the Hawks' greatest basketball assets, is a natural gift—it can't be taught. However, a good coach helps channel such an attribute to the maximum advantage of the team. Other Xavier 'plusses' are hard work, teamwork, and a *conspicuous absence of jealousies among squad members.*"

When it was time to recognize Kip Whitlinger, every attendee knew that Torchy could talk for two hours about his bright star from the East. Whitlinger was spectacular all the time but was "money" in the second half of the Hawks' 71–66 state championship victory. The fleet-footed guard was a *perfect* fit for Torchy's up-tempo transition and full-court press game. The 34-year-old coach took full advantage of the accomplished scoring of his Neenah commuter. He emphasized clearly to the Hawks' faithful in The Commons how truly *special* Kip was. And the humble *privilege* he had in coaching him . . . this once-in-a-lifetime player.

Warren (Baba) Whitlinger, Kip's dad, was born in Barnesville, Ohio, on April 4, 1914. He attended Zanesville High School in Ohio where he was a three-sport athlete and senior class president. He went on to Ohio State University, graduating in 1936. He played collegiate baseball and basketball. As a Buckeye basketball player, he led the Big Ten in scoring and was All-Big Ten and team captain his senior year. He returned to Ohio State in 1939, getting his MBA in 1940.

After receiving his degree, he accepted a job with Kimberly-Clark Corporation, moved to Neenah, Wisconsin, and worked 35 years for the company. He retired as director of quality assurance in 1975.

Warren then got involved in junior tennis. Although not a player himself, he developed and coached three national champions in his own family—son John and granddaughters Tami and Teri. He also coached and helped many other junior players.

In 1991, he served as corporate coach for Mercury Marine in Fond du Lac, Wisconsin, where he worked with the president/CEO, his direct reports, and other key players in self-management and leadership skills, team building, and mental toughness.

Warren was married to his greatest love Naomi for 66 years. When his wife was diagnosed with Alzheimer's, Warren became totally committed to her care. He showed his unconditional love, his loyalty, his faithfulness, and his passion to help her. As hard as it was to lose her in 2007, he understood that her death was her ultimate healing (*Timeless Tips, 2009*).

Warren (Baba) Whitlinger wrote, "When someone becomes a memory, the memory becomes a treasure." Torchy warmly reminisced, "Kip and Rocky were very special. Both had wonderful parents who were outstanding role models and good people. They *trusted* me and let me coach their sons. But sometimes in life things are like vapors: here and then gone. But the memories remain."

CHAPTER 11

Ouch! Who's Al McGuire?

Jim Bunning retired 27 New York Mets in a row on Father's Day, June 21, 1964, pitching a perfect game at Shea Stadium. His wife Mary and oldest daughter Barbara were in the Big Apple for the historic day. The Phillies won 6–0, and few people knew that Bunning hit a double in the game, driving in two Phillie runs.

Ten months prior to Bunning's perfect day, Torchy's Xavier Hawks in August 1963 sought their second straight year of perfection both on the football field and the basketball court. The football Hawks in 1963 steamrolled through the Fox Valley, winning the conference championship with another undefeated 9-0 campaign. However, like 1961, the Hawks finished second in the Wisconsin State Football Poll. Rocky Bleier was not only the talk of the state but garnered national attention, being named as a *Parade* All-American.

The supremacy of the basketball Hawks in 1963–64 continued, winning the FVCC championship with a dazzling 20-0 regular season. Xavier High School now was within grasp of a second consecutive year of flawlessness. The Hawks won the regional championship, winning two games at the Brown County Arena in Green

Bay, qualifying for their third consecutive trip to the WCIAA State Basketball Tournament.

Coming into Milwaukee, the Hawks had missed the high scoring of graduated top gun, Kip Whitlinger. But a defensive-minded and cohesive group led by Rocky Bleier, Paul Springer, Paul Rechner, Tim Garvey and forwards Tom Rankin, Bob DeBruin, and Bill Timmers united together in Torchy's system, riding a 47-game winning streak.

Xavier's conference foe, Marinette Catholic Central, also qualified for the 1964 State Tournament, winning their regional championship by edging Don LaViolette's Squires of De Pere Abbot Pennings in double overtime. At State, Marinette drew the easier tournament bracket with Madison Edgewood, Stevens Point Pacelli, and Superior Cathedral. The Hawks were seeded in the "Milwaukee Bracket," as Torchy called it, which included Racine St. Catherine's, Milwaukee Marquette, and Milwaukee Pius. The "Milwaukee Bracket" was the more difficult road to the finals, but the Hawks' coach emphasized "everybody is tough at State."

Xavier won their opening quarterfinal game, beating St. Catherine's 47–44 behind the steady play of DeBruin and Bleier. The Hawks in the semifinals beat Marquette High 46–38 with an aggressive 2/3 zone that suffocated the Hilltoppers. Marinette defeated Edgewood in double overtime 50–46 in their quarterfinal; and then shockingly in the semifinal edged Pacelli 51–39 in a *three* overtime slugfest. The Cavaliers of Marinette played in an almost unimaginable *seven* overtimes their last three games, all heroic wins for well-respected coach Marty Crowe.

Yes, the Hawks would face Marinette Central a third time . . . this time for the 1964 State Basketball Championship. Torchy recalled after watching the Cavaliers' narrowing Pacelli triple overtime win, "There was no other team I wanted to play least than Marinette. We'll play anybody but them." Some of the Milwaukee reporters thought Torchy was joking, but he was dead serious. All-Conference Hawks' guard Rocky Bleier also witnessed the upstart (19–5) Cavaliers squeeze out another nail biter and remarked, "Marinette is playing good ball now. They are playing with a lot more confidence."

During the regular season, Xavier defeated Marinette twice. The first game on the road, the Hawks trailed the Cavaliers at intermission, 22–11. Torchy waited and waited before entering the Hawks' locker room at halftime, wanting his players to *stew* over their poor play. FINALLY, with two minutes left on the clock, he angrily stormed into the tiny locker room and demonstratively laced into his team. Torchy's short but intense rip was highly effective, as the Hawks played inspired ball the second half, winning 56–41.

The second game at Xavier was no country picnic for the Hawks. It was a chess match amid the brilliant coaching minds of Torchy and Crowe. Bob Goemans, a referee and Fox Valley insurance agent who officiated the game in Appleton, recalled the battle of wits: "I never saw two coaches with so much thinking going on." The baby-faced Clark remembered the close, hard-fought 45–41 win: "We're lucky to get out of here with a 'W.' It was one of the few games in my career that I needed to shower right after the game. I was drenched with sweat. It was hard work."

Torchy and Crowe had a high regard and appreciation for each other. Both not only coached basketball at their school, but were also head football coaches battling each other three or four times a year. There were no coaching skeletons hidden in either closet, and both knew each other's deep secrets. Torchy affirmed the worrisome challenge ahead: "This time at the 1964 State Tournament we were the favorite on paper, which meant nothing. Crowe was such an excellent coach; he was my father's *favorite* coach. Marty Crowe was the best high school coach I ever coached against. And he did wonders with his team. We beat them twice that year, but both games were 'white knucklers.'"

For Sunday night's title game, the Marinette coach wore his customary game attire: black pants, black turtleneck and a black blazer. Torchy wore a traditional navy blue suit.

Crowe knew if his Cavaliers had any chance to win, his team would have to control the game's tempo for its entirety. His strategy of limiting Xavier's possessions, a disciplined shot selection and a rugged defense were keys. Crowe was adamant and confident about keeping the score in the 40s for the Cavaliers to have any chance of winning gold. The pressure was solely on the Hawks . . . 49 in a row, defending State Champions and the title game would be Bleier's finale. Xavier's winning streak was the longest in Wisconsin Scholastic Sports at the time.

Claire sat in the 15th row behind the Xavier bench with envelope and black Flair pen in her hands. She was nervous about this one, feeling Torchy's external pressure. Like many Hawks players, the winning streak was on everybody's mind. Xavier sophomore Paul Rechner in Adrian Martin's *Marty: The Man Who Refused to Punt. The Life and Times of Legendary Coach Marty Crowe* remembered, "The pressure of the win streak was out there, and when the streak got in the 40s, we survived some close games down the stretch."

Yes, Xavier and Torchy felt the pressure. To exacerbate the stress or maybe totally coincidental, the arena public address announcer Duane Miller did the Cavaliers a monumental favor. At the 9:45 mark on the pregame clock, seconds before the two teams were about to leave the court and retreat to their locker rooms for last-minute reminders/prayer, Miller made a complimentary, but *untimely* announcement to the 5,564 fans. With the microphone ON he said:

Xavier has a 49-game winning streak and are the defending State Champions. Four of the Hawks' players: Tim Garvey,

Bob DeBruin, Jim Rather, and Bill Busch have won 82 games in a row during their high school career. They've never played in a losing game.

Torchy was furious and enraged at Miller! This was the last thing his 17–18-year-olds needed to hear before a State Championship game. The streak pressure already existed, but Miller's proclamation pounded the stake deeper into the ground for the unscathed Hawks.

Adrian Martin tells the story of a fan's reaction to the rather peculiar pregame announcement. "Sportswriter Dennis Hernet was sitting right behind the scorer's table with his cousin Norb Wishowski, a young high school basketball coach at the time who decades later would be inducted into the Wisconsin Basketball Coaches Association Hall of Fame. After the announcement, Wishowski turned to his cousin and said, 'I'm taking my entire bank savings and betting it on Marinette Catholic Central, because that was just the kiss of death.'"

As the title clash began, both Fox Valley teams were tight as they jockeyed for position. Torchy was 99.9 percent sure what Crowe would do—a patient, grind-it-out, deliberate style of play. The Cavaliers decided to go right to the jugular: Rocky Bleier. The 1964 Hawks did not have a prolific scorer, a player who could get 25–30 points. The closest was Bleier, and Marinette would target him by doubling the Hawks' legend with scrambling, aggressive traps.

Sam Komp, a five-foot-eleven senior guard and pure shooter who was Marinette's second leading scorer, detailed the Cavaliers' defensive strategy: "Rocky was the heart and soul of the Xavier team. He was the flagship of what Xavier sports had been for three years. When it came to crunch time, we knew we had to stop Rocky." Besides Komp, the Cavaliers were led by Jan Roland, a six-foot-three mobile center, who was an excellent post player and rebounder. Roland, a junior, was Marinette's leading scorer.

Bob DeBruin's basket at the end of the quarter put the Hawks up 9–7 in the snail's pace of the game. The first quarter score closely resembled St. Joe's of Appleton playing St. Pat's of Menasha in the Diocesan Grade School Tournament. But that was precisely Crowe's "plan for glory" for his underdog Cavaliers. In the second quarter, the Hawks jumped out to a 15–9 lead before Marinette quickly rattled off six points before intermission to tie the game at 15. Claire was worried, as well as the other 1,800 Xavier faithful in the arena.

Marinette's sharpshooter Sam Komp hit three jump shots and a layup in the third quarter as Crowe's troops took a commanding 31–23 lead. Torchy and his Hawks put themselves in an *uncomfortable* position. Marinette Central's radio color man Bob Haase, who called the 1964 classic, said, "Xavier had to come after us. If they hadn't, we would have frozen the ball."

And Xavier did. With 6:52 left in the game, Torchy turned to his full-court press; however, this time Crowe's Cavaliers were fully loaded and ready. Marinette had practiced their press attack relentlessly over and over in anticipation of playing Xavier. Crowe not only wanted to break the press, he wanted to aggressively score against it. The constant repetitions at practice were the *miracle cure* for the Cavaliers as they dominated Xavier's press. Adrian Martin who was at the 1964 game remembered, "Four straight times Marinette got the ball down court in less than five seconds. Boom—boom—boom—the ball never touched the floor. The Cavaliers scored each time and didn't turn the ball over once."

Xavier lost 43–37 and were denied a second consecutive State title and a second straight year of perfection. The winning streak was over! According to many at the tournament, the little team (Marinette) from the northwoods with an abundance of heart, but little talent, had pulled off the biggest upset in the storied 35-year history of the

Wisconsin State Catholic Basketball Tournament (Martin, 2010). The Hawks players and fans were stunned after not losing a game in over two years. On congratulating Crowe after the horn, Torchy said, "This was no fluke, Marty. You deserved it! Your boys played great ball." Xavier's Bob DeBruin, a hard-nosed rebounder in Adrian Martin's book, *Marty: The Man Who Refused to Punt. The Life and Times of Legendary Coach Marty Crowe* emphasized, "They came to play and we didn't. If we played them 20 times they would only beat us once. But tonight, was their night."

Martin fondly recalled the Xavier contingency: "When Marinette came forward to receive the 1964 State Championship Gold Ball, the entire Xavier cheering section stood and applauded the Cavaliers." Tim Garvey, who lost for the first time in his high school career, remembers seeing the Xavier fans and a tear welled in his eye and thought to himself, "Now that's class!"

In hindsight, on the loss, Torchy explained, "Sure it hurt. Losing always hurts! John Lawther said in his book *Psychology of Coaching*, 'You are supposed to remain a gentleman in losing. But if one does hate to lose, and loves to win, he deserves no credit for his behavior. He is controlling no emotion. He has no emotion. He is only half man.'"

Torchy's deep intellectual thoughts on the loss mirrored the life lessons of sports: "I love Lawther's definition. We naturally lost like champions. Losing is right around the corner. By preparing to lose, you usually don't lose. You never want it to sneak up on you or come like a thief in the night."

The *Milwaukee Journal* ran an editorial the next day on the class and dignity displayed by the Xavier team in the loss. With one minute left in the game and his team down 11, Torchy called a timeout to convey his powerful message: "I told our players and managers, we are going down with our boots on and remember, 'WE ARE XAVIER and WE ARE CLASS!"

Torchy and Claire headed home by car after the heartbreaking loss . . . the players would later board the team bus for the two-hour drive back to Appleton. The humble Xavier mentor who had not tasted defeat the prior two seasons until that night described the couple's trip home: "We took the wrong road. At 1:00 a.m., we ended up in Sheboygan. Claire said to me with a speck of frustration, 'Torchy, we're in *Sheboygan!*' I half-heartedly responded, 'We aren't going any place, anyway.' Yes, I was disappointed but knew my guys gave me everything they had."

A month after the championship loss, the Marquette University basketball job came open. "I applied for the position. I was a Marquette graduate and played there," said Torchy. "My dad and brother Dutch both attended the school. Plus, I had just won 49 of my last 50 basketball games. The *Milwaukee Journal* ran a story and picture about my strong interest in becoming Marquette's new coach," he added.

In Spring of 1964, Torchy and Claire attended a dinner party in Appleton when a close friend mentioned he had heard a coach from a small college called Belmont Abbey got the Marquette job earlier that day.

"What's his name?" Torchy asked.

The friend said, "Al McGuire."

Torchy said, "Now, I'd heard of the great Frank McGuire and the pro Dick McGuire, but who's Al McGuire?" Now we know.

Every adversity, every failure, every heartache carries with it the seed of an equal or greater benefit (*Timeless Tips*). Life doesn't allow for us to go back and fix what we have done wrong in the past, but it does allow for us to *live each day better than our last* (unknown author). To finish his reflections of 1964, Torchy concluded, "The Marinette loss was one of the toughest I ever experienced. We handled it like true champions. When you win like we did at Xavier, there is a tendency to evaluate the losses painstakingly, instead of enjoying the remarkable feats of accomplishment. I was so proud of my football and basketball teams; the character of my Xavier players was impeccable! But sometimes in life things are like vapors: here and then gone. But the memories remain."

CHAPTER 12

Frankie McGinnis and Torchy's Tales

Frankie McGinnis, a 1965 Xavier graduate, played football for the Hawks in 1963 and 1964. After his days as a player, Frankie and Torchy remained close. As a third-string halfback for the 1964 squad, Frankie seldom played, but had a positive attitude and was dutifully loyal. The Frankie McGinnis story and the other tales in this chapter illustrate Torchy's engaging, yet corny sense of humor. Yes, he was serious; but more importantly, he valued the *lifelong relationships* he developed with his former players, students, and coaches over the precious years.

Torchy loved to tell the story of Frankie and his dad, Vern McGinnis, at a Xavier preseason football practice in August 1964 on a hot and humid Appleton day. "We were almost done with our second practice of two-a-days," said the focused coach. "Our team had a great morning workout. The intensity was exceptional during our second practice despite the heat. We were in our last segment. Xavier's football field was located on the north side of campus off busy Prospect Avenue," explained Torchy. "The school didn't have a fence or any type of privacy around the field. Any passing cars could watch practice . . . many times I worried that opponents were scouting us from the road," he said with a little anxiety.

The Hawks' football coach was a dear friend of the McGinnis family. Frankie's brother Bill played football and basketball for Torchy at St. Mary's in the 1950s. Bill McGinnis would later work for his mentor as an assistant football/basketball coach at Xavier.

On that "dream come true" day in August, Torchy yearned to give Frankie and Vern 30 seconds of fame. Toward the end of practice, Vern pulled up near Prospect Avenue on a side street to catch a short glimpse of the workout. At Xavier and UCF, Torchy had no problem with parents watching practice, though few ever did. The elder McGinnis did not want to interfere, but parked close enough to see the action. Vern lit up a cigarette and leaned against his car.

Torchy remembered the sequence of events: "I saw Vern pull up and recognized him right away. We were finishing up our 11-on-11s live offense/defense.

"With Vern in sight 100 yards away, I had a plan," said the football coach. "I first huddled up with our defense, telling them that on the next live play, the offense was going to run 22-dive, a halfback-dive play off right tackle for Frankie. Speaking softly in the huddle, I told the defense to let Frankie run. Do not tackle him . . . make it look real and live, but no one tackle Frankie. Just let him go."

Torchy continued his plan of action: "I quickly huddled up with the offense. I told McGinnis to replace Paul Springer at halfback for the next play." Frankie anxiously snapped his chinstrap on his plain white Xavier helmet with the navy blue stripe down the middle. "I then told the offense in the huddle, we were going to run 22-dive on 2. I said to Frankie, 'Show me what you got,'" added Torchy. Frankie replied, "Thank you, Coach—I'll do my best." Frankie was not aware of what was to happen. Vern, too, was also unaware as he watched from a distance.

The Hawks' defense was cued and ready. As the ball was snapped, Xavier's quarterback Paul Rechner reverse pivoted, and handed the ball to Frankie on 22-dive. Frankie hit the hole, bounced off two defensive line would-be tacklers, made a terrific inside cut avoiding the middle linebacker, darted around two defensive backs, and ran 50 yards to *daylight*.

Torchy warmly reminisced, "Vern was ecstatic . . . smiling and clapping like a proud papa! His son had just burst through the Hawks' defense for a 50-yard run. On that August 1964 day, Vern witnessed Frankie run like Packer Paul Hornung. Frankie and Vern got their 30 seconds of glory and a memory for the ages. I wish the whole world was like the McGinnis family."

■　■　■

Another tale is called "Just Before the Kickoff." In Torchy's words, "No one could make this story up . . . it's true. During pregame, football officials will bring the captains out to midfield and introduce them to each other before the coin toss. The referees will say, 'Captain Pollock and Captain Meyer, meet Captain Becker and Captain Johnson.'

"While coaching football at Xavier, I had a player named Jimmy Captain and another player (no relation) named Louie Captain. My goal was to send those two out to meet the officials and have them say, 'Captain Pollock and Captain Meyer, meet Captain Captain and Captain Captain.'

"I'm probably the only coach in the history of football to have had that once-in-a-blue-moon opportunity. No, I didn't do it. I never changed my captains unless we lost, and we were in that special 31-game football winning streak (three and a half years without a loss)."

■　■　■

This tale is called "Humility," which Torchy shares: "Rocky Bleier was the best player I've ever coached. We won 96 games and lost four and were extremely close, having an incredible player-coach bond.

When Rocky was in Appleton on summer break from Notre Dame, I saw him while he was working out at Xavier.

"On this July afternoon, Rocky said to me, 'Coach, do you know who or what has influenced me the most in my life?'" Torchy pondered the question, "Naturally, I knew it was me—in all humility, it had to be me: all the pressures, thrills, adversities, and championships we had been through together. So I humbly said to Rocky, 'Who or what?'"

"Rocky replied, 'This morning I went into Schiedermayer's Hardware Store [downtown Appleton] and saw a grade school buddy of mine from St. Joe's. My friend said, "Rocky, I just flunked out of the University of Wisconsin-Madison." Rocky continued, 'Coach, that was the most powerful lesson I've learned. It really made me realize everything I've got at Notre Dame.'"

Torchy reflected if the story bothered him: "No, it didn't, but we all think we're so darn important."

■　■　■

Kelly Kornely, one of Torchy's loyal soldiers at Xavier from 1959–63, remembered a cherished high school memory: "Torchy had just moved his family into an Appleton home he recently purchased. He asked six or seven of his Xavier football players to help him paint the trim of the 100-year-old house in preparation for new maroon siding which would be delivered the next day.

"At this time in 1961, the popularity of the hit movie (musical) *West Side Story* starring Natalie Wood had swept the country. Every high school guy at that time had a crush on the gorgeous Wood. We loved the movie and were familiar with the characters, storylines, and music. Kip (Whitlinger) and I were working up high on a scaffold at the old two-story house painting white trim. Towards the end of the day when we finished painting, Kip and I had a brilliant idea. To show our devotion to *West Side Story,* and to have some fun, we painted JETS vs. SHARKS (white paint) in giant letters on the old dark gray siding of Torchy's house. Cleverly, we knew that the new siding would be delivered and installed tomorrow. We painted it on the front, most visible side of the house facing Appleton's busy Prospect Avenue. The next morning, we saw Torchy at football practice and he told us the new siding delivery was on back order and would not be delivered for three weeks. Torchy laughed it off with us, and the Clark family lived with *West Side Story's*, JETS vs. SHARKS emblazoned on their house for three weeks. We all loved Natalie Wood."

■   ■   ■

The last tale of this chapter is known as "Where Did the Flu Go?" Torchy remembered in 1963, "We had just won the State Basketball Championship. The following day my three best players were sick and missed school. They were not skipping; they were sick. Naturally, if the tournament had lasted another week, their infirmities would have been delayed.

"It got me thinking how we usually don't get the flu on the day of the big event. While coaching at UCF, I was visiting with our two veteran war horse coaches, legends Bill Peterson, athletic director, and Lou Saban, UCF's football coach. Including me, the three of us had a combined total of 90-plus years of coaching experience.

"I knew the answers before I asked the questions. I said to Coach Peterson, 'In your 25 years of coaching, did you ever miss a game because of the flu?' Pete replied, 'Never.' Then I asked Coach Saban, 'In your years of coaching, did you ever get the flu on game day?'

'Absolutely not,' he said. I'm sure if four or five more coaches were added at random to our group, the answers would have been the same. Perhaps, the answer is the adrenals do a great job of pumping temporary health and help. You have to admit it's interesting: over 90 years of coaching, over 1,200 games, and no flu. But sometimes in life things are like vapors: here and then gone. But the memories remain."

CHAPTER 13

Obligation—Preparation

Torchy loved to make people smile or laugh. He had an engaging personality and a sincere, genuine concern for the dark horse. However, once the practice or game began, his inner drive, obligation, and "insecure" competitiveness were unleashed, helping him prepare his football and basketball teams.

Kelly Kornely reflected on the wisdom of his coach: "Torchy always had us prepared to win. I'm not sure where he got his information, whether it was a scouting report or another coach, but every game we were ready to play. At practice, he would tell us, if so-and-so lines up here, this is what's going to happen . . . it's going to be this play. Sure enough, come game time, it was exactly like Torchy had said. We were prepared not to play the game, but to win the game."

Torchy's intense preparation and knowing that defeat is right "smack" around the corner was the foundation of his teaching. In preparation for the always tough and physical St. John's Little Chute (next game), Kornely remembered a football practice he will never forget: "Our senior year in 1962, we knew we were pretty good. We were No. 1 in the state, and we had Rocky Bleier.

"Torchy loved to get in the offensive huddle, kneeling down and chewing on a blade of grass in his mouth, ready to call a play. In this particular huddle, he began to emphasize over and over how good St. John's was. He repeatedly warned the offensive huddle all the ways they were going to beat us. He went on a tirade about the toughness and fight of the Dutchmen. There was a moment of silence within the huddle. And then Dick Weisner, our starting quarterback, point guard on our state championship basketball team, and the school's valedictorian who was on the far side of the huddle, innocently asked, 'Coach . . . Coach, do you really think they can beat us?' I'm thinking to myself, 'O God, Weisner, you shouldn't have said that. We are going to run wind sprint after wind sprint, gasser after gasser up and down the field after that. You don't second-guess Torchy.' He immediately ripped into his offense and sent the entire team home for the day. Practice was over! The defensive eleven on the other side of the field were completely oblivious to why practice had abruptly ended."

At Xavier, Dick Weisner was a fearless clutch and top-notch athlete. He led the Hawks to two 1962–63 Wisconsin state championships (football and basketball) in the same academic school year as the starting quarterback and the starting point guard. Yes, the football Hawks soundly defeated St. John's that Friday night in early October of 1962. Torchy's fiery, yet successful motivation put the fear of the Dutchmen in each player. This essential component was a huge part of his game preparation. He never wanted to overlook an opponent, as defeat was always lurking in his eyes.

Kornely recounted another Torchy football story and his meticulous attention to detail: "We were preparing to play Wausau Newman who had a tall, strong Jim Thorpe-type fullback. This guy was huge, powerful and hard to tackle. To get us ready to play against the 'giant,' Torchy had one of our defensive backs jump on the shoulders of a Xavier lineman, riding piggyback style. He then told us this is what you will see Friday night. He specifically said not to tackle the 'giant' above the waist because the guy will drag you another ten yards as you try to bring him down. Torchy instructed us to tackle him low around the knees or ankles, and that's what we did Friday night in our Newman win. We had the exact imagery of who we were going up against through his teaching and the precise technique of how to tackle the 'giant.'"

Torchy defined the word 'obligation' as a duty, a commitment, a serious responsibility, a vital concern for the players, the team, and what affects them both. He preferred the word 'obligation' over 'accountability.' His deep thoughts and philosophy on 'obligation' are further explained *in his own words:* "Don't let your teammates down, a player reminds himself. Don't let your coaches down, a player also reminds himself. And lastly, don't let your players down, coaches remind themselves." *Torchy believed that* all *players and coaches* have serious "obligations" to each other, a togetherness. Players to players, players to coaches, and coaches to players.

"Here are my feelings and my own personal obligations. I deeply feel a responsibility that our overall team record for the season should be as successful as humanly possible; not sitting back on a 25-game basketball schedule and saying we were 15 wins and 10 losses, when we should have been 22–3. This is very rooted in me, whether it be insecurity, or what.

"I feel the responsibility to give everything I have to my team, from the first practice to the last minute of the season. I realize there are many variables involved such as humor, compassion, understanding and change of pace, but I do not stray far from the word 'obligation.' I would like my teams when the season is over to say, we were our best in our efforts, overtime losses, one-point losses and all phases of winning.

"We have to know what our best is and then give it. The expression that he or she gave 110 percent is bull. You can only give 100 percent, and most people run at 60 or 70 percent. But, you have to know what your best is.

"Each season I set up these specific football or basketball *team* goals:

1. To have the best record we can have (this is my number one goal above all others).
2. To win the conference championship.
3. To qualify for the State Championship.
4. To play well at the State Championship."

John Paustian (1963) of the *Appleton Post-Crescent* wrote, "Xavier's perfect football and basketball records in the same school year have made history. To the best of my knowledge, this feat has never been accomplished in the Fox Cities area—and only rarely in the entire state. The fact that the same coach—Torchy Clark—directed both unbeaten teams makes the achievement even more momentous. The vast majority of head coaches have a *specialty*—at least in the major sports—but the amazing redhead has proved he's equally adept in both sports."

Torchy's top-notch assistant at UCF for six years (1974–80) was Ray Ridenour. A native of Dayton, Ohio, Ridenour was a member of Dayton's Belmont High School 1964 Class AA Ohio State Championship team under coach John Ross. Ray Ridenour was the captain of the historic team that finished 26–1. The former Georgia Tech player and graduate worked as an assistant to Ross at Wright State University before joining Torchy in 1974. Torchy recalled, "Ray always said, 'Coach, you always give your teams a chance to win at the end . . . whether it be stalling, conditioning, the press, the intensity, the little things, the work, work, and more work.' It is called your obligation to your team."

A major component of this obligation was to clearly define roles within the team. Kip Whitlinger remembered the Xavier basketball teams of the 1960s: "Torchy was really good at having his players understand and embrace their roles. Each player knew what his specific job was and how valuable their part was to the whole. His attention to detail made us championship teams."

Torchy focused on winning. He wasn't interested in the politics of the team or the politics of the parents, or if a player didn't get enough touches, shots, or minutes. The team was his car, a 1965 Ford Country Squire, and he was driving it the entire trip! Yes, there would be bumps in the road, and possibly a detour along the way. But his obligation was to give his team the best opportunity to win, the best chance to beat Marquette High School or Furman University.

Whitlinger fondly recalled a heartfelt post-game discussion with teammate John Heinritz, an impactful player on Xavier's 1963 State Basketball Championship team. "We were in the locker room changing after a regular season game. Heinritz, our strong-willed center, asked me, 'Kip, how many points did you score tonight?' I responded, 'I'm not sure, but close to 25.' I then humbly asked, 'John, how many points did you score?' Heinritz said, 'I didn't score tonight. I didn't take any shots.' Heinritz that night had 10 rebounds for us. Not scoring or not taking any shots did not bother him a bit. Torchy was great at getting guys to buy-in. That's why we were so good."

The Xavier football and basketball practices were always intense, as Torchy *demanded* his teams to be mentally and physically prepared for every game and every situation. He stressed to coaches the importance and "championship significance" of role players to your team. Torchy then added, "Heinritz and DeBruin in my eyes were just as important to the success of the team as Whitlinger and Weisner. That was my obligation, my duty . . . to prepare my teams. But sometimes in life things are like vapors: here and then gone. But the memories remain."

CHAPTER 14

The Big Play

Xavier's football teams in the Torchy era were 63–8–1. The Hall of Fame coach always believed he was a better football coach than a basketball coach. Two of his greatest football memories are from games against Green Bay Premontre. The first memory is described in Chapter Nine ("Rocky")—the 1961 Rocky Bleier 23-yard historic, tightrope-sideline run of sheer athleticism and incredible balance in a 20–16 Hawks' victory. The second flashback is the 1967 Hawks-Cadets game in Green Bay he shared numerous times with his teams and classes. It is aptly named *The Big Play*.

Now at this time, Premontre was a larger school than Xavier with an all-male enrollment. The school literally sits in the backyard of storied Lambeau Field (four minutes away). "They had a great football tradition; plus, they were a talented basketball school. By some mystique, we had their number in both sports," said Torchy. He remembered the 1967 season and his anxiety going into the Premontre game: "We were in an off year, and Premontre was a powerhouse. I scouted them before our game and they won 54–6. They were really good! We had nice kids, but no outstanding athletes. I thought we had one chance to hit them on the first play of the game with a big play, but I guess all underdogs feel like that."

On the Monday before the Saturday game, the Hawks' football coach added *The Big Play*. "You remember the famous long pass play in 1935 from Notre Dame's Bill Shakespeare to Wayne Millner in the Fighting Irish 18–13 come-from-behind victory in the closing minute to upset Ohio State in Columbus with 65,000 fans at the game. The pass was executed perfectly, and the game was a classic," fondly reminisced Torchy. "I taught a similar version of the Shakespeare play privately to the team. I decided to run it once each day for the five practices before Saturday's game. Why only once? Our practice field was fairly unprotected and highly visible. I didn't want the play to be scouted from the road," added Xavier's master play caller who had a trick up his sleeve.

Torchy explained the intricacies and precise timing of *The Big Play*: "My quarterback was Greg Steinhorst: a good kid, a gifted Appleton Little League pitcher and an average high school quarterback. I liked him—he was a tough kid. Greg was one of the most loyal players I had in my tenure, and I loved coaching him. Steinhorst was simply to roll out right behind the Xavier blockers. One quick, dive-fake and just roll out and run for your life. My wide receiver was Jeff Bartosic—another great kid. Neither one of these two were going to play college football, although both were gamers I *trusted* on the big stage."

The footwork of the Hawks' wide receiver was the key to the execution of *The Big Play*. The great motivator continued: "Now I turn this story over to Bartosic and myself. I told him to split out at the right-end position 10 yards from our right tackle. The plan was simple; or was it? I told Bartosic to run straight at their defensive back Tony Canadeo Jr., an excellent athlete whose father was the great Tony Canadeo—former Packer hero from Gonzaga." Torchy accentuated the finite details to his young receiver: "I want you to run deadpan with no eye expression directly at Canadeo, then cut to the right. Now Jeff, here's exactly what I want . . . take step one toward the sideline, then take step two toward the sideline. You will want to turn and go upfield. Don't do it, or Canadeo will be right with you!"

Torchy emphatically said to his receiver, "NOW, YOU GOT IT?" (The intense coach was one-inch from his receiver's nose . . . their eyeballs were touching.)

"Okay, Jeff?" barked the demanding Torchy.

"I got it, Coach," said the confident Jeff.

Torchy continued the footwork fundamentals: "Remember, Jeff, don't go upfield on your third or fourth step. Canadeo's *mind* is what we are interested in. You've got to make him think you are going to the sideline. Then go upfield on the fifth step."

Bartosic said, "I got it, Coach . . . I got it!"

Torchy concluded, "Now that's either communication or motivation. Maybe both? I like Jeff, but you'd never know it.

"I was hoping Saturday we'd win the coin toss for possession and get the opening kickoff," said Torchy. "Coaching is all repetition, but we just practiced this once each day for fear of somebody scouting *The Big Play*," he added on the secrecy of the quick hitter.

Torchy continued: "On the first Monday practice, we ran the play; it didn't work. On Tuesday, we ran the play; it didn't work. On Wednesday, we ran the play; it didn't work. On Thursday, we ran the play; and it WORKED!! We tried it again on Friday, our last practice; and it didn't work."

Saturday morning, Claire and Torchy enjoyed a hearty Wisconsin breakfast at home. The time was 8:00 a.m. Kickoff was at 2:00 p.m. "Claire knows we are going to lose to the powerful Cadets (Premontre) today," said Torchy. "To give her some hope, I told her, I added a big play, but it only works on Thursdays. She asked me if I wanted another English muffin."

The time was 1:55 p.m. at the old Packer City Stadium. The referees and captains met at midfield for the coin toss. Xavier's captain, quarterback Greg Steinhorst, then sprinted directly to his head coach after the toss with an ear-to-ear grin, "Coach, we won the toss." Torchy followed, "Okay, you know what to do!"

The Hawks received the kickoff and ran the ball to the 27-yard line. Xavier first and ten. Full house at the City Stadium. And it's time for the *The Big Play* that only works on Thursdays.

Torchy described the action as if it was in slow motion, frame by frame: "Who am I watching? The first thing I see is Steinhorst, our quarterback, is protected and is going to run safely for his life before throwing the bomb to Bartosic. Then, I looked directly at the defensive back Canadeo. Why didn't I look at Bartosic? Because I've already gone eyeball-to-eyeball with him in Monday's practice. Bartosic will remember me when he's 75 years old!

"Bartosic was beautiful! Step one, step two—but Canadeo, whom I was watching, wasn't buying it the first two steps! Bartosic took step three. Canadeo was smart and stayed.

"Bartosic took step four. Canadeo came up—Bartosic took step five and Canadeo was out of position. The Hawks receiver then sprinted downfield like the winning horse in the home stretch of the Kentucky Derby. Then Steinhorst let it fly! Bartosic grabbed the pass and ran it to their two-yard line! Premontre was stunned!" remembered Torchy with great pride and satisfaction.

"I was ecstatic! I couldn't believe the play only worked on Thursdays and Saturdays. Our fullback, Jerry Rankin, punched it in on the next play for a touchdown. We kicked the extra point and led 7–0," he added on the lightning-quick momentum his Hawks gained early in the contest.

Xavier then kicked off to Premontre. The Cadets fumbled the ball on the return as the Hawks recovered and drove for another touchdown to lead 13–0. Xavier won the game 20–13 and never lost to Premontre in Torchy's tenure. Twenty-three wins in twenty-three games over an eight-year period in football and basketball.

Torchy proudly recalled his 1967 Xavier football team: "I loved that team. They were extremely coachable with a great spirit. Congrats to you guys! *The Big Play* worked! And the execution, the blocking, and the attention to detail was absolutely perfect. I'll never forget Shakespeare's touchdown pass to Millner in 1935. But sometimes in life things are like vapors: here and then gone. But the memories remain."

CHAPTER 15

Torch Will Never Go Out

I n the post-Rocky Bleier era, Torchy's football Hawks entered the
1964 season with an amazing 31-game winning streak over a three-
year period. The streak ended with an emotional loss to a tough and
physical Milwaukee Francis Jordan 26–12 at Appleton's Goodland
Field before a capacity crowd of 3,100.

The Hawks returned to their winning ways; however, several weeks
later, they ran into a confident, upset-minded St. Mary's in Menasha's
newly built Calder Stadium. The loss to the tough and gritty Zephyrs
was Xavier's only conference loss in 1964. Despite the loss, the Hawks
were still co-FVCC football champions with St. John's Little Chute
having identical 5–1 conference records.

Xavier kept rolling and repeated as FVCC Champions in 1965
and 1966 behind great interior line play, disciplined offensive execution, and a physical defense. In 1967, they finished 6–3 and lost two
conference games, the first time in the Torchy Clark football era. The
Hawks finished second to conference champions, St. John's.

Under the leadership of coaching guru Bill Fitzpatrick, a Notre
Dame graduate and respected comrade of Torchy's, St. John's was
consistently tough. "Bill Fitzpatrick's teams always executed and were

fundamentally sound. Every football game with the Dutchmen was a dogfight. The coaching in the FVCC was excellent and experienced. Don LaViolette, Larry Van Alstine, Ralph McClone, Avitus Ripp, Jim Kersten, Ted Fritsch, Donnie Gosz, and Marty Crowe were not only inspirational leaders, but also good friends," humbly recalled the Xavier mentor.

The Hawks rebounded from a second-place finish in 1967 to win another conference football championship in 1968, adding another shiny gold football to the almost-full trophy case. The 1968 Hawks were led by Brad Graff, Tom Thomson, Bill Pfefferle, Mike Barras, Ralph Kessler, Tom Putzer, Pete Hahn, Richard Koller, Ted Wenning, and Nick Heinritz. All were key players that led the Hawks to an 8–1 conference championship. Lineman Pfefferle and tight end Barras played college football at Xavier University.

In the 1960s, Hawks' basketball players began practice each day to the beat of the Globetrotters' theme song, "Sweet Georgia Brown," piped into the gym's P.A. system. Torchy liked the song so much, it became a Xavier basketball tradition as the players shot and warmed up. Why "Sweet Georgia Brown"? He simply explained, "I liked the song's energy, its familiarity, and I was a big fan of Brother Bones."

Torchy's practices were seldom over two hours. There were no sprints, suicides, or extra running. Every practice drill was game-specific with game-like intensity. Practicing the full-court press over and over again was his method of training his players into superior condition. The practices were demanding as he worked the Hawks relentlessly with the goal of "winning each practice."

For 38 years, Torchy's managers lined up 14 folding chairs out-of-bounds near center court for his players to sit during practice. The veteran coach addressed his team before and after practice as players sat in chairs. During scrimmages or a 5-on-5 full-court press segment, the subs were close to the action, simulating a game setting.

The veteran coach always wrote his practice plan on an envelope using both sides. This was not fancy Xavier or UCF letterhead stationery, but rather a plain white letter envelope. Each night after the day's practice, he would meticulously plan tomorrow's practice using another envelope. Was he organized? Extremely.

The basketball Hawks in 1964–65 were led by Mike Heideman, Tom Rankin, Paul Rechner, Paul Springer, Dan Hardy, Tom Heinritz, and Paul DeNoble. With the high expectations of excellence Torchy established early in his tenure, Xavier continued their Fox Valley supremacy, having a sensational 23–2 season and winning a fourth straight conference title.

"That team had a tough act to follow after our first three years," Torchy said of his 1964–65 team. "We had won 49 of our last 50 basketball games the prior two years, but that team was special . . . hard-nosed, tough mentally and physically. They had no quit in them. After three years of winning, we became the *bullseye* for many conference and statewide schools. That always comes with success," he explained how the Xavier game was highlighted on each opponent's calendar.

With victory after victory, Hawks' fans in the thunderous Xavier Gym proudly began to chant, *"The Torch Will Never Go Out! . . . The Torch Will Never Go Out! . . . The Torch Will Never Go Out!"* when the win was in hand. Xavier's engaged, passionate basketball fans loved their Hawks and wore white buttons with a blue "X" that read "The Torch Will Never Go Out," pinning it on sweaters and jackets. The Xavier pride and school spirit was second to none.

The pep band, under the leadership of Dutch Schultz, became one of the best bands in the country. The Hawks sprinted out for pregame warm-ups as the band enthusiastically played the school's fight song (founded by Claire Clark/via Xavier University/via Father Stan) to fire up the home crowd.

Mike Heideman, a six-foot-two junior forward who also played tight end in football, led the Hawks in scoring, averaging 13 points per game. "Mike was solid, smart, and tough," noted Torchy. "When I heard he went into coaching, it didn't surprise me. You love coaching guys like Mike Heideman. He was selfless and always had a team-first attitude."

After playing college basketball at UW-Lacrosse and coaching high school basketball in Augusta, Wisconsin, Heideman returned to Xavier in 1974, five years removed from the Torchy Clark era (1969). The young coach took the reins as head football and head basketball mentor quickly, picking up where Torchy left off. His basketball Hawks in eight years were a phenomenal 147–42. The ultra-successful Heideman left Appleton to become the head basketball coach at St. Norbert College in De Pere, Wisconsin, from 1982–86 before becoming an assistant to the legendary Dick Bennett at UW-Green Bay (UWGB) for nine years. Heideman, a Bennett disciple, became the head coach of the Phoenix for seven outstanding seasons. The consistent, solid guard play from Paul Springer and left-handed Paul Rechner sparked Xavier's up-tempo, full-court press system. "Paul Rechner was unselfish, a true winner, and one of my hardest workers. He was the nicest kid I coached at Xavier," remembered Torchy.

Tom Rankin, an undersized post player at six-foot-two, had an excellent career for the Hawks, averaging 11 points per game. "Rankin's scoring and rebounding helped us win the conference all three years. He was relentless every night and a warrior on the boards," added the Hawks' coach. Rankin recalled playing for the spirited Xavier catalyst: "Our team relied on each other. We were perfectionists and would not let any team beat us! Torchy was intense! That's where the perfection came from. He did not accept anything less than our best. The reason our teams were successful was a gentleman by the name of Torchy Clark."

Another key contributor was sixth-man Paul DeNoble, a solid player off the bench. The unflinching veteran did whatever was necessary for the (23–2) Hawks to win. His clutch jump shot at the buzzer was the difference in a huge road win at Milwaukee's Francis Jordan his senior year. "Paul embraced his role and had a "teachable spirit," recalled Torchy. DeNoble, like Heideman, coached at the college level (St. Norbert) after stops at St. Mary's Grade School, coaching Torchy's sons Tom, Bo, and Bob, and Tomahawk High School in Wisconsin. Paul DeNoble had a terrific run at St. Norbert for 18 years, inspiring and impacting many lives.

Under Torchy's leadership, Xavier's athletics flourished year in, year out in the 1960s, both on the gridiron and the hardwood. The model of consistency was unmatched as each season became an "instant replay" of the prior season's success. Winning conference championships and making State Tournament appearances became the norm as the Hawks continued their mastery in the state of Wisconsin.

On February 4, 1966, the basketball Hawks hosted the Don Goszled (4–6) Fond du Lac St. Mary's Springs Ledgers in their second FVCC regular season matchup. The Hawks in December had pounded Springs, 67–46 on the Ledgers' home court. Xavier was riding a 53-game conference winning streak going into the game.

Torchy's cousin Frank Shaw and his wife Virginia were in the hot, SRO Xavier Gym that night in Appleton with four of their five children: three sons, Tom, Tim, and Kevin (Torchy's nephews) and daughter Mary (niece). His oldest son Tom was St. Mary's Springs' best player. Tim Shaw was a sophomore on the team. A six-foot-two guard and an FVCC All-Conference player, Tom Shaw also competed in football, track, and golf for the Ledgers. The Shaw family sat five rows behind the Springs' bench as youngest son Kevin, an eight-year-old, was there to watch his idol, his older brother Tom try to defeat the indomitable Hawks. The Ledgers were huge underdogs and had never defeated Xavier in any athletic competition.

Kevin Shaw remembers the game's exhilarating atmosphere: "The Xavier Gym was deafening to the very end . . . and this visit to the Hawks' nest was no different than any other. On any night, playing at Xavier was like being chased by a bear! Torchy was so intense. He had such great respect from his players, and his team always played so hard. It was the game I'll never forget."

Xavier led 29–27 at halftime as Hawks' fans yearned for win number 54-in-a-row. With 1:58 in the fourth quarter, Torchy called a timeout to regroup his Hawks with Springs leading 54–53. During the timeout, an ecstatic Joe Goeser, the St. Mary's Springs radio play-by-play announcer broadcasting the game back to Fond du Lac, took a deep breath and said, "Can the 'Springers' do it tonight? They are trying to snap Appleton Xavier's 53-game conference winning streak. The 'Springers' are within 1:58 away from pulling the BIGGEST upset of the twentieth century."

At the 1:18 mark, Springs' Bob Johnson missed the front end of a bonus free throw. The Hawks then took the lead on a Steve Schmeider corner jumper to go up 55–54 as the Xavier Gym roared like a jet engine. Springs then scored with 52 seconds remaining as Jimmy Harbridge scored on a power layup and was fouled. He connected on the free throw to put the Ledgers up 57–55. With 49 seconds left, Xavier's Don Hurley, a tough, hard-nosed guard, missed the front end of a one-and-one free throw. Springs rebounded and Xavier's Mike Heideman fouled the Ledgers, stopping the clock. Mike Flasch hit two crucial free throws as Springs led 59–55 with 45 seconds to play. On the next possession, Xavier, scrambling for a quick score, was called for an offensive foul. Springs held on to win and pulled off the gigantic 60–57 upset!

Tom Kohl (1966) of the *Fond du Lac Commonwealth Reporter* (Wisconsin) summarized the miraculous accomplishment: "Holy Cow! St. Mary's Springs stole a whole trunk of Houdini's tricks and pulled the utter fantastic of this or any other cage year in stunning Appleton Xavier, 60–57, Friday night on the Hawks' home floor.

"Gene 'Torchy' Clark and his cagers had not known defeat in a conference game for over three years and were riding a tidal wave of 53 straight FVCC victories before the Ledgers floated into the Hawks' gym like a wayfarer and left like a volcano."

Yes, on February 4, 1966, the Shaws had a spectacular night. Torchy was naturally disappointed in the loss, but was proud and genuinely happy for the Shaw family, who he was extremely fond of. Tom scored 15 game-changing points for St. Mary's Springs in ONE of the Ledgers' greatest victories in school's history. Kevin had unforgettable lifetime memories as an eight-year-old . . . of his hero, his brother Tom, and his energetic Uncle Torchy.

Adrian Martin in *Marty: The Man Who Refused to Punt. The Life and Times of Legendary Coach Marty Crowe* emphasized "during the 1960s to beat Xavier and Torchy Clark was a *cause* for celebration." Beating the Hawks in football or basketball was like winning the Wisconsin Lottery. "The Miracle Xavier Win" was the motivational title of a gloried sports memory for a young 17-18-year-old St. Mary's Springs Ledger, Marinette Central Cavalier, or Manitowoc Roncalli Jet who did the unthinkable—and that is defeat the mighty Hawks.

Each monumental upset against a Torchy-led team was worthy of a rumored Hollywood movie deal or a potential book proposal from a leading publisher. The FVCC teams never discussed the numerous losses to the Hawks over the period, but rather, *proudly* reminisced through storytelling to grandchildren of the epic stone they slung to kill the "giant" (Xavier). Yes, Torchy had built a monster of success and a decade of dominance.

In 1966–67, the "culture of excellence" continued in Appleton as the basketball Hawks won their SIXTH straight FVCC Conference Championship, finishing 23–2. They were led by sharpshooting guards Pat Fitzgerald and Gene Jack. As in many years, Torchy's use of role players was like a maestro conducting his orchestra in perfect harmony. The instrumental role players included: six-foot-three center Dan Hardy, five-foot-ten guard Tom Heinritz, and six-foot-one guard Terry Graff. All were crucial to the uncanny success of the Hawks.

Fitzgerald, a six-foot-two guard, was a scoring machine in his three Xavier years (1965–68). The All-State selection could not only shoot, but had multiple explosive moves driving to the basket. Nicknamed "Fitz," he could stop on a dime, releasing his effortless and accurate pull-up jumper.

The Hawks' coach remembered his outstanding player's ability: "Fitz was quick as a cat. He had a dynamite first step and just knew how to score. The fans loved him . . . on any night he could score 30." Following his Xavier career, Fitzgerald signed a scholarship at Florida State University.

Jack, a six-foot guard and another pure shooter, bolstered the high-scoring Hawks with his patented jump shot. The confident shooter hit clutch shot after shot in many Hawks' victories. After playing at Xavier, Jack played baseball and basketball at Division II Rollins College in Winter Park, Florida. "Pat Fitzgerald and Gene Jack (besides Kip Whitlinger) were two of the purest shooters I coached," reminisced Torchy.

In the 1968–69 Xavier basketball season, the Hawks' magnificent run of success continued, winning the FVCC. They finished the regular season with a perfect 22-0 record. Eight conference championships in eight years! A remarkable accomplishment! The Hawks were led by the big three: six-foot-ten center Bob Fullarton, six-foot-one guard Mike Clark, and six-foot-one guard

Brad Graff. The trio knew and understood the Hawks' system of play. As sophomores all three played sparingly on the varsity, but gained valuable "Torchy" experience.

"Fullarton was the best big I coached, including UCF," noted the veteran coach. "He was an excellent rebounder, shooter, passer, and had a great feel for the game. Fullarton was a big-time player who could step out and handle the ball," remembered Torchy. Bob Fullarton had a stellar career at Xavier University (Cincinnati) and was drafted by the Buffalo Braves in the ninth round of the 1973 NBA draft. He then played professional basketball in Spain (Breogan Lugo and Basquet Manresa) for eight years. "My UCF team in 1974 played his pro team in Barcelona on our overseas trip to Spain. I was very proud of him," Torchy said of his special player. Fullarton and Torchy's son Mike were two of the top scorers in the FVCC as seniors.

Mike Clark was one of the starting guards for the Hawks in 1968 and 1969. "Mike was smart, a gifted driver, and a clutch player. He was a gamer!" reflected Torchy. The pair were a father-son duo for *seven* straight years . . . three at Xavier (1966–69) and four at UCF (1969–73). Mike was inducted into UCF's Athletic Hall of Fame in 2001, joining his dad and brother Bo, who were both inducted in 1998. "I count my blessings each day Mike chose to play at UCF. I was lucky to have him," the proud father added. The younger Clark gave the Knights instant credibility, consistent scoring, and helped build a solid foundation.

Brad Graff was one of Torchy's best athletes in his ten years. He recalled Graff's athleticism: "Brad was the second-best athlete I coached at Xavier, besides Rocky. He was cerebral, had great hands, quick feet, and tremendous instincts. I often wonder how good he could have been if he wouldn't have injured his knee [junior year]. He was a big key to my success at Xavier." Graff played college baseball and basketball at Xavier University. The two other starters were Tom Thomson, a six-foot-five forward, and Tom Vandenelsen, a five-foot-eleven point guard, who both played significant roles in the team's phenomenal success.

In 1968–69 the undefeated Hawks were one of Wisconsin's finest teams. It may have been Torchy's *best* basketball team at Xavier in the 1960s. St. Catherine's of Racine was also one of the top teams in the state that year. They were led by future Marquette University and NBA star Jim Chones.

During the regular season, Xavier had already beaten Manitowoc Roncalli twice in FVCC play. The two teams had played 10 days prior as the Hawks soundly defeated Jim Kersten's Roncalli Jets 88–48. They would play a third game, this time for the Regional Championship at Green Bay's Brown County Arena. The winner would advance to the 1969 WCIAA Catholic State Tournament in Milwaukee.

The Hawks lost 53–52 to Roncalli on a cold February night in Green Bay as the Jets pulled out the historic win. Yes, Jim "The Jet" Kersten had pulled off the 53–52 *miracle* upset of Xavier. Kersten, an ex-Marquette University basketball player (1956–60), graciously recalled with great emotion a moment still close to his heart: "Right after the awards ceremony and celebration my team went to our locker room inside the Brown County Arena. The first one to greet and congratulate us was Torchy Clark. That meant the world to me," added Kersten, a dear friend of the Xavier coach.

Torchy had a great relationship with many of the faculty members: "Dave Hussey was a trustworthy comrade who I refereed and coached with. Dave was a devoted educator and dynamic role model for our Xavier students. Other key lay faculty included: Bob Pliska, Giles Clark, Goose Gosling, Bob Strick, and Bill McGinnis." Harry Nelson, Torchy's highly respected assistant football coach in the early 1960s, said, "There will never be another Xavier!" Torchy added, "It was a once-in-a-lifetime situation: the timing, wisdom, administrative direction, players, teachers, and coaching staff all united perfectly!"

Having the sensational Rocky Bleier unquestionably skyrocketed Xavier's athletic early beginning. In his three varsity years, the Hawks never lost a football game. However, according to Torchy, "Rocky wasn't alone. Xavier was blessed with names like Whitlinger, Weisner, Rechner, Kornely, Rammer, Calmes, Helein, Schueppert, Werner, Peeters, DeBruin, Rankin, Boots, Heideman, and the Heinritzs' (18 children). I apologize to anyone I've missed, like Floyd Slayton, Greg Steinhorst, and all of you like Mike Gregorius whose names still echo in the Xavier hallways."

Upon departing Wisconsin in 1969 for UCF, Torchy reminisced on his cherished time at Xavier: "I'll never forget our tough basketball loss at home to St. Pat's of Chicago in 1966 which snapped our 62-game regular season winning streak. St. Pat's was an excellent team. Xavier had the greatest fans! I still get goosebumps thinking about Rocky's incredible Premontre run in 1961, the unbelievable football crowds at Goodland Field, Kip's 26-point clutch performance against Marquette in the 1963 State Championship, the ear-splitting roar of the Xavier gym, Bob Lloyd (WHBY) broadcasting the games, and John Paustian reporting the games in the *Appleton Post-Crescent*. It brings me great pride that 50 years later, Xavier's *spirited* and *national reputation* still lives on today. But sometimes in life things are like vapors: here and then gone. But the memories remain."

CHAPTER 16

Meeting Lombardi

Torchy created a sports dynasty at Xavier in the 1960s. Hired by Brother Peter in 1959, he was appointed to help build Xavier into one of the finest high schools in the nation, and that he did.

Vince Lombardi, 30 miles north of Appleton, began his Green Bay Packer legacy the same year that Torchy began building his foundation at Xavier. Lombardi assumed the head coaching duties from Packers' Head Coach Raymond "Scooter" McLean, who finished 1-10-1 his last season. Hired from the NFL's New York Giants, Lombardi had served as an offensive coordinator under Coach Jim Lee Howell.

The Packers won five NFL Championships including two Super Bowls (I and II) during his eight years as head coach (1959–67). Lombardi's dedication and commitment to excellence made the Hall of Famer one of the greatest coaches in sports history.

Lombardi and Clark would meet nine years later in Green Bay. In 1968, the University of Wisconsin-Green Bay (UWGB) administrators got the "go-ahead" to implement a men's intercollegiate basketball program which would begin competition at the NAIA level in the

1969–70 season. Torchy applied for the position and was fascinated with coaching at the college level. The new university was keenly interested in the highly successful Clark who had built an impressive resume at Xavier. Ed Weidner, the Chancellor of UWGB, was in charge of hiring the coach. Early in December, he made the short trip to Appleton to meet with the Xavier coach in his home. Weidner was intuitively aware of Torchy's mastery of local Premontre High School in football and basketball.

Lombardi, after ending his fabulous career as Packers coach in 1967, remained with the storied organization as the general manager. Under new coach Phil Bengston, the 1968 Packers were 6–7–1 and finished a disappointing third in the NFL's Central Division.

Shortly after Weidner's visit in Appleton, Torchy went to Green Bay for the formal interview. The Xavier coach was scheduled to meet with the school's ad hoc committee; however, Weidner first took him to meet Packer icon Vince Lombardi. The former coach served as a consultant for the position. The UWGB used Lombardi's expertise and insightful wisdom to assist them in the basketball hire.

On the drive to Lombardi's office through the beautiful suburbs of Green Bay, Weidner said to Torchy, "Oh, by the way, this subdivision is where you will want to look for a house." The two arrived at Lombardi's Packer office and Torchy reminisced, "The NFL legend greeted us with a handshake and gave us that warm, Italian tiger-tooth smile. I was a little nervous . . . but I only have *hero* worship for Christ. Besides, Lombardi and I were coaching peers . . . in a way. I had been a head coach for 18 years, and we both taught and coached at Catholic high schools [Lombardi at St. Cecilia and Torchy at Xavier]. *But, I knew I was in a presence!* And frankly, in meeting him, it was hard not to think of the Super Bowls, the Ice Bowl, the Dallas Cowboys, Tom Landry, Jerry Kramer, and Bart Starr."

Torchy continued the details of the meeting: "Lombardi's office was plain and unpretentious . . . typical of a humble, simplistic giant." Lombardi dove right into the interview, with Torchy's Xavier High School resume in his hand, and said, "I can't believe your records—they are unbelievable!" Torchy followed humbly, "Thanks, Coach." Some light conversation and small talk took over the exchange. Ten minutes later, Lombardi slapped his hand assertively on his desk, repeating, "Coach, your records at Xavier are just incredible!" The Oshkosh native responded to Lombardi's second definitive compliment, "Coach, I'm supposed to say that to you." Lombardi then chuckled.

In the middle of the interview, Lombardi inquired, "What do you think your attrition rate will be at UWGB?" The Xavier coach answered quickly, trying to somewhat deflect the question by saying, "You know, Coach, that's a profound question, no one has ever asked me that before." (He had absolutely no idea what the word attrition meant. The only thing he could think of is the word "contrition," which means sorrowful). Lombardi jumped in for the rescue and said, "About 15 percent, don't you think?" Torchy added without hesitation, "That sounds about right, Coach."

As the meeting came to a close, the three men stood up, shook hands and wished each other luck. The purpose of the Lombardi face-to-face was for the Packers legend to meet the short list of candidates. Torchy summarized his experience in Titletown: "I rated my interview a 'B'—I knew he was the king and he certainly was." Below are the records that impressed Lombardi on that December day in 1968:

Xavier High School, Appleton, Wisconsin Enrollment: 950 (1968)
   Winning streak of 62 regular season basketball games
   Winning streak of 53 conference basketball games
   Winning streak of 49 overall basketball games
   Winning streak of 31 football games

Torchy Clark's Xavier High School Overall Records

241 wins—22 losses—1 tie   15 Conference Championships
in 16 tries

- (Xavier did not compete as a four-year school until the 1961 season)

Torchy Clark was head football coach and head basketball coach. His specific records broke down like this:

Football Record	Basketball Record
63–8–1	178–14
7 Conference Championships	8 Conference Championships
(8 years)	(8 years)

The UWGB hired Dave Buss as their basketball coach, and began play in the 1969–70 season. Buss had a fabulous run at the school. Torchy looked back at the UWGB scenario and said, "One of my coaching peers asked, 'What about your interview with Lombardi? You had to be disappointed you didn't get the job.' I responded, 'What does a coach have to do in his career?'"

Buss' college experience as an assistant played a significant role in the new coach being hired. Torchy remembered, "Buss did a magnificent job with the UWGB program. He was an excellent coach who recruited 'tough' kids for his disciplined system. After a defeat in the Division II Final Four, his players carried him off the floor."

During the media friendly-era of the 1960s in Wisconsin, Torchy emphasized: "Lombardi and I got all the publicity in the Fox Valley. Granted, 90 percent was for the Packers." After the Lombardi interview, Torchy wrote a short note thanking him for his time. Below is Lombardi's honest reply to that letter:

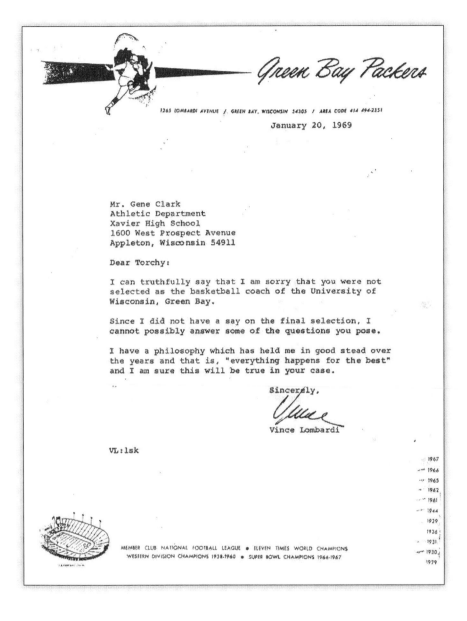

Green Bay Packers

1265 LOMBARDI AVENUE / GREEN BAY, WISCONSIN 54305 / AREA CODE 414 494-2351

January 20, 1969

Mr. Gene Clark
Athletic Department
Xavier High School
1600 West Prospect Avenue
Appleton, Wisconsin 54911

Dear Torchy:

I can truthfully say that I am sorry that you were not
selected as the basketball coach of the University of
Wisconsin, Green Bay.

Since I did not have a say on the final selection, I
cannot possibly answer some of the questions you pose.

I have a philosophy which has held me in good stead over
the years and that is, "everything happens for the best"
and I am sure this will be true in your case.

Sincerely,

Vince Lombardi

VL:lsk

MEMBER CLUB NATIONAL FOOTBALL LEAGUE ● ELEVEN TIMES WORLD CHAMPIONS
WESTERN DIVISION CHAMPIONS 1938-1960 ● SUPER BOWL CHAMPIONS 1966-1967

1967
1966
1965
1962
1961
1944
1939
1936
1931
1930
1929

The Xavier legend remembered the January 1969 letter: "Lombardi was absolutely right. I liked his letter and his sincerity. I took the job at the University of Central Florida (UCF); at that time it was called Florida Technological University. My family and I moved to Orlando,

Florida, 'The City Beautiful.'" UCF became one of the Top 10 Division II basketball programs in the country under Torchy's leadership.

Remarkably, Dave Buss' UWGB Phoenix and Torchy Clark's UCF Knights had historic seasons in 1977–78. UWGB, UCF, Cheyney State, and Eastern Illinois would all meet in the 1978 NCAA Division II Final Four in Springfield, Missouri.

Lombardi left the Packers in 1969, two months after the Torchy interview, and returned to coaching as the head coach of the Washington Redskins. Lombardi would coach the Redskins for one year before dying of colon cancer on September 3, 1970.

In retrospect, on Lombardi's life philosophy of "everything happens for the best," Torchy used those inspirational words to guide his life. The Wisconsin Basketball Coaches Association Hall of Fame coach articulated his thoughts on his 20-minute audience with ESPN's Greatest Coach of the twentieth century: "Lombardi was a man of faith, and I was too. Everything does happen for the best. *God had a plan for me.* I always believed when the Green Bay door closed, another would open. That other door was UCF. One of my favorite Bible verses comes from Jeremiah 29:11, 'For I know the plans I have for you not to harm you, plans to give you hope and a future.' But sometimes in life things are like vapors: here and then gone. But the memories remain."

Torchy Clark's UCF College Basketball Accolades

274 Wins - 89 losses (14 years) / UCF's leader in career wins (274)
5 Sunshine State Conference Championships in 8 years
College Coach of the Year—4 straight years in Florida
24 consecutive wins (1977–78) /Member of 7 Halls of Fame
NCAA Division II Final Four (1978)
Teams were nationally ranked in NCAA II 7 straight years
Voted Coach of the Decade by the Sunshine State Conference

CHAPTER 17

Humble Beginning

U CF opened in 1968, offering classes as Florida Technological University (FTU) with the mission of providing personnel to support the growing U.S. space program at Cape Canaveral on "Florida's Space Coast." As the academic scope expanded beyond engineering and technology, "Florida Tech" was renamed the University of Central Florida (UCF) in 1978. To ease any confusion for the reader, the author respectively refers to the university as UCF through most of the book, despite its 10-year history as FTU (1968–78). UCF is the largest college by enrollment in Florida and one of the largest universities in the nation.

In 1969, the university's desire to start an athletic program began with a search for a basketball coach/physical education professor. This new coach would establish a basketball program with the goal of the team becoming a "spirited" rallying point for the young school. Dr. Frank Rohter, the school's first athletic director and head of the Physical Education Department, was in charge of the hire.

Bob Willis, Torchy's close friend, was the general manager for the Orlando Twins of the Class A-Florida State League. Willis had tried to lure Torchy from Wisconsin to Florida twice before with opportunities to be the football or basketball coach at Orlando Bishop Moore Catholic High School. The valiant effort to bring the successful coach south continued by Willis through many lengthy and persuasive conversations with Rohter regarding the basketball opening. Willis thought UCF would be a perfect fit for his friend, with the limitless potential of the new university located 20 minutes from downtown Orlando.

On the strong recommendation of Willis, Rohter flew to Appleton in January of 1969 to meet and interview Torchy, who had built a sports juggernaut at Xavier. Rohter attended his practice, talked to his players, surveyed the community, and visited the Clark family at their home. The athletic director took Torchy's evaluation to a rather unconventional method when in Appleton he dined at a downtown hamburger joint. And then asked the cook, spatula in hand flipping burgers, "Who's the best coach in the state?" The burger flipper said, "Torchy Clark," without even looking up at Rohter.

A Chicago native and DePaul University graduate, Rohter did not know Torchy; however, his brother Norm attended Marquette, played football for the Hilltoppers, and knew him. After visiting Appleton, Rohter stopped by his alma mater in Chicago. He had played freshman basketball and boxed for the Blue Demons. While on campus, he hunted down Hall of Fame basketball coach Ray Meyer (724–354 record, 42 years) and asked him his candid opinion of Clark from Xavier. Meyer without hesitation said, "Torchy Clark is a winner!"

Rohter's sincerity and integrity convinced Torchy to take a hard look at the budding school. During his formal interview in Orlando, the young coach was impressed with the UCF Physical Education faculty of Frank Rohter, Lex Wood, Gerry Gergley, Ken Renner, Troy Cleland, John Powell, Pat Higginbotham, and Dick Hunter. It was a spirited group with high energy who had an excellent mix of academia, class, and experience. No one did it better than the Physical Education Department with Rohter as chairperson.

The Oshkosh-born Torchy also had a strong desire to live near his brother Jim, who now lived in Altamonte Springs outside of Orlando. The challenge of coaching at the college level and starting a program intrigued Torchy. Orlando as a city was an easy sell, and UCF's untapped potential was enticing.

The College of Education served as home to UCF sports from 1970–78. Calvin Miller, who was hired as the first dean of the College of Education, remembered when Rohter approached him about hiring Torchy. With extreme confidence, Rohter said, "The guy we need to develop our program is currently teaching and coaching football and basketball very, very successfully in Appleton, Wisconsin." Miller then asked Rohter if Torchy had a master's degree, which he did not. Torchy accepted the job with the condition he would enroll in the master's program and earn his degree in three years. Torchy delivered on his promise.

On August 1, 1969, FTU/UCF formally hired Gene "Torchy" Clark as its first basketball coach and tenured physical education professor. "It was one of the finest decisions we ever made," Miller said of hiring Torchy. "I guess I would say he's one of the finest individuals I've had occasion to work with professionally. He's very different and had his idiosyncrasies, but to me they were all good."

The Clark family was reluctant to leave the coziness and comfort of the Midwest, not to mention friends and Little League teammates. But the father of five insisted the family would enjoy the Central Florida area and its fabulous weather. "It was a humble beginning at UCF from my previous job at Xavier with the great tradition and culture we had established," said the eager, but overwhelmed Torchy. In August of 1969, the Clark family arrived in Orlando.

UCF gave the 40-year-old the opportunity to implement his own program from scratch. And scratch is an understatement! The infant school with 2,500 students had no gym, no equipment, no schedule, no assistant coaches, and worst of all no players for the team that would start practice in less than two months.

The beginning of UCF's basketball program had a starting point. And in 1969, both Rohter and Clark were at the sprinter blocks ready to run. The Knights' basketball coach recalled, "My job was to get the program up and running. I only knew the right way, which was through hard work, humility, and integrity. I had to find a team from the student body. We had no scholarships, and it was too late for any recruiting."

Torchy got a big-time break when son Mike decided to join the family in Florida and play at UCF in the inaugural season. Mike originally committed to play basketball at St. Norbert College, near Green Bay, but had a change of heart and came to the Sunshine State.

The humble beginning was taking shape; however, now the coach had to find 15 more players that could play college basketball. Torchy began watching UCF intramural games on the outdoor basketball courts on campus or at Lawton Elementary in nearby Oviedo. "It was recruiting at the *one* level on a scale from one-to-ten with ten being the highest, but it was necessary to find players. Plus, it was cost saving!" he humorously added of the unconventional recruiting. "I just walked over to the courts and watched the games. I did not have to rent a car or get on a plane. If the games were at Lawton, I drove five miles."

One of the first people Torchy encountered "recruiting" the intramural games was Russ Salerno. A senior five-foot-eleven guard, Salerno was a gifted three-sport letterman (football, basketball, and track) at Orlando Maynard Evans High School, graduating in 1961. Salerno, 26, was married with a child and had one more year of school at UCF before receiving his B.A. degree in Physical Education. Salerno remembered, "I had heard through the grapevine the school was thinking about starting a basketball program."

Torchy attended one of Salerno's games. Shortly afterward, he approached the intramural player, introducing himself as the new basketball coach. He told Salerno the school was starting up a team this year. The former Evans Trojan asked, "You mean 'a real team'?" Torchy followed, "Yeah, a 'real team,' and we will play other colleges and programs."

The senior was excited about having the golden opportunity to play college basketball. Salerno then introduced Torchy to several of his intramural teammates, all excellent players: Don Mathis, Rudi Jessee, Don Lilly, and Earl Stokes. The five, including Salerno, played on UCF's first team.

Another way to recruit on-campus players for Rohter and Torchy was from the Class Registration line at the library. As students waited to register for classes, the athletic director and coach looked down the line for any tall, physically fit-looking players. One such player was Bob Jenkins, a six-foot-three power forward who had played a little basketball at Cocoa High School.

Jenkins attended UCF and had no intention of playing basketball, but became a valuable reserve and rebounder for the Knights. Jenkins and Torchy had a strong player-coach relationship.

The school's nickname in 1969 had not been established yet. Rohter, however, wanted the new university to be called the "Mickey-Naughts." In Rohter's vision, the logo for the "Mickey-Naughts" was Mickey Mouse on a rocket. It represented both Disney World and Cape Canaveral, both 45 minutes from the campus. The "Mickey-Naughts" lost the nickname vote and UCF became the Knights of Pegasus.

Torchy fondly remembered, "The rumors of a basketball team spread like wildfire on campus. I selected 16 players for the first team. I was fortunate to have Mike Clark, Rudi Jessee, Don Mathis, Russ Salerno, Earl Stokes, Skip Repass, Don Lilly, Bob Jenkins, Don Jacobs, Don Hill, Jay Daugherty, Mark Thornton, Wayne Bennett, Bobby

Cooper, Bob Phillips, and Vince Bralts. I used Russ, being the elder statesman, to help drive vans to practice." Salerno and Torchy would become lifetime friends.

The Knights (not "Mickey-Naughts") in the first season competed in 14 games as a club team. UCF was able to schedule Palm Beach Atlantic, Fort Lauderdale University, Patrick Air Force, and New College. Home games were played at Winter Park High School about 15 minutes from campus. The team used several different gyms for practice the first year, including the Naval Training Center, Bishop Moore Catholic, Oviedo, Winter Park, and Lawton.

Torchy kept two bags of basketballs in his car, along with the medicine kit, as part of the traveling show for practices. The team took full advantage of reversible practice jerseys which doubled as game uniforms. The black side of the reversible had gold numbers, and the gold side had black numbers. It worked perfectly for home and away games, as the Knights did not have ample time to order game uniforms for the first season.

"One game we came out for warm-ups wearing the black side of the jersey. We saw the other team had navy blue uniforms . . . we easily switched to the gold side with a quick change," laughed point guard Mike Clark. Claire and Russ' wife Mazie took turns washing the jerseys at their homes. Much of the UCF basketball equipment was stored in the Clarks' garage.

Torchy introduced his full-court face guard press and transition game the first UCF practice. The players took notice immediately of the driving intensity of their "hot-shot" coach from America's Dairyland. His oldest son Mike was immune to the passion and fire after three years at Xavier.

On November 21, 1969, the Knights of UCF played their first-ever game against Massey Tech in Jacksonville, Florida, winning 99–38. The next night, November 22, the Knights hosted Palm Beach in their first home basketball game in the school's history at Winter Park High School in front of 1,220 fans. President Charles Millican, FTU/UCF's first president, was given the game ball by captain Russ Salerno. The president was proud of Torchy and the first team. Millican tossed up the honorary jump ball against Palm Beach as UCF won, 93–71.

Torchy used his press to change the tempo and hound the Sharks' (Palm Beach) guards into turnovers just like Rocky Bleier hounded the Marquette guards in Xavier's 1963 State Championship. His winning formula of success continued as the Knights won their first eight games. Mike Clark averaged 24.4 points per game for the first team. Mathis, a sophomore center who played with a contagious enthusiasm, led the team in rebounding for the 11–3 Knights. Jessee, a sophomore guard, was a confident, skilled shooter as Stokes, Phillips, Jenkins, Salerno, and Lilly all played key roles.

It was a humble beginning but a successful and strategic basketball season for the young university. A dynamic coach was hired in 1969 to build a program; and good things were on the horizon for the fast-improving Knights. Torchy remembered the first year: "I trusted Dr. Rohter in making the move to Florida. I believed in my heart UCF was a sleeping giant. But sometimes in life things are like vapors: here and then gone. But the memories remain."

CHAPTER 18

New York City

In the second year of UCF basketball (1970–71), the Knights competed at the NCAA Division II level, offering partial scholarships. Torchy had sufficient time to order uniforms, complete a schedule and recruit players. Russ Salerno served as graduate assistant coach, attended classes to complete his master's, and taught several courses in the Physical Education Department.

One of the Knights' starters was Jim Flanagan, a six-foot-four, 245-pound bruiser who was an excellent shooter and rebounder. As loyal soldiers, Salerno (1970) and Flanagan (1971) remained close to their UCF mentor; both would play pivotal roles in Torchy Clark's life.

Flanagan played one year of college basketball at Orlando Junior College before transferring to UCF. Flanagan fondly recalled, "I learned more basketball in one year with Torchy than I did in my entire life." Flanagan averaged 8.8 rebounds per game, ranking him in the UCF record book (Top 15) for rebounds per game average in a single season. He also corralled 20 rebounds in a game.

UCF's 1970–71 team finished with a 17–9 record, playing the likes of Georgia Southwestern, Florida Institute of Technology, North

Georgia, Palm Beach Atlantic, SUNY New Paltz, and Greensboro College. School spirit had picked up significantly, and the Knights played in front of many avid, energetic UCF crowds, using nearby Oviedo High School as their home court.

Donald Clark (Torchy's father) said in the 1940s, "Your team is only as good as your guards." That adage played out as the Knights were led by leading scorer Mike Clark, "Fast" Eddie Smith, a five-foot-eight transfer from Valencia Junior College, and shooting dynamo, five-foot-nine Rudi Jessee.

The small line-up of three guards was ideal for Torchy's full-court press. The Knights played at a fast pace and pressed throughout the game; their lightning quickness created havoc for many opponents, the same *havoc* created by the young coach's St. Mary's Grade School and Xavier High teams.

Fans loved the Knights' style of play and enjoyed watching the animated Torchy. The intense motivator always felt the "duty" to give his team everything he had. "Once Torchy crossed the out-of-bounds line to start a practice or game, he became a different person—a competitive, emotional, and passionate coach bleeding for a win. Off the court, he was a great guy, but boy was he COMPETITIVE," strongly emphasized Russ Salerno.

Torchy reminisced on his second year: "Don Mathis was one of the hardest-working centers I ever coached. He battled every single possession. Our schedule was difficult the second year. We were able to recruit some good players, but most importantly, quality people."

Another solid player was Mike Lalone, a six-foot transfer from Valencia Junior College. Lalone was a former Orlando Maynard Evans basketball player coached by legendary Fred Pennington, one of the best high school coaches ever in the state of Florida. Torchy recalled coaching Lalone: "Mike was a pleasure to coach. What a great free throw shooter (84.5 percent career average)! He had a high basketball

IQ and was physically tough. But everybody that played for Pennington was a Trojan. I liked guys from Evans."

Besides Salerno and Lalone, Torchy had the privilege to coach several former Evans' players, one being Calvin Lingelbach (1973–77), who gave Knights fans an array of magical memories. Lingelbach became a UCF Hall of Famer in 2005. Five other Evans' stars played for Torchy: guard James "Beach" Beacham (1979–81), guard Dave Murray (1982–83), power forward Jeff Smith (1974–75), forward-center Kenny Allison (1980–81), forward Lem Reed (1982–83), and guard Bob Mitchum (1970–71).

The Knights' schedule included a five-day trip to New York City in December. As a college coach, Torchy liked to take his team on a fun, cultural trip as part of the "college experience." The Black and Gold were slated to play three games in three days against Maritime College, Rutgers-Camden (South Jersey), and Cathedral College. All three were formidable opponents for the second-year Knights.

Flanagan, Torchy's power forward, remembered the special time in the Empire City: "It was a great trip—we stayed on a ship for two nights as part of our game agreement with Maritime. We slept in the officers' quarters, but it was so cold on that ship. It's been almost 50 years, and I still remember that experience. That was a fun year."

The three games in three days began with Maritime. The Knights defeated a well-disciplined NCAA Division III team, 103–83. Sophomore guard Mike Clark scored a then-school record 41 points in the win against the Privateers. Maritime could not stop the high-scoring, acrobatic Clark as he hit clutch shot after shot, halting any Privateer rally in the second half. Clark scored an incredible 100 points over three games on the trip and was a constant scoring threat. Smith, a crowd favorite, added 15 points, seven assists, and six steals to secure the first win. Flanagan added 10 rebounds in the game.

The Knights faced a tough opponent in South Jersey against a physical and talented Rutgers-Camden team in the second game. The aggressive, trapping 1-3-1 zone of Camden stymied the Knights in the first half. But Torchy's critical halftime adjustment to overload the Camden zone with a baseline runner helped the Knights win 96–80. The torrid scoring pace of Mike Clark continued in the Big Apple. Torchy's oldest son had 33 points and eight assists in their second win of the trip. Don Mathis grabbed 12 rebounds against the much-taller Camden squad. The third and last game pitted UCF against Cathedral College of New York, a memory for the ages. In an early start time on December 23, the Knights had an unusual, but not too surprising chain of events that played out their last day of the trip.

The Cathedral game was scheduled for 6:00 p.m. to accommodate the Knights' travel itinerary, which included a late-night commercial flight to Orlando after the game. The players enjoyed seeing the city at Christmas, but were excited to get home and spend time with family.

The second-year Knights stayed at one of Midtown's iconic hotels, The New Yorker, the last three nights. Torchy was hoping for an undefeated 3–0 New York trip; it would have been an early Christmas gift for the 1951 Marquette graduate.

After flying into JFK, the Knights rented two Chevy Caprice vans to shuttle from game to game. Assistant coaches Salerno and Jack Pantelias (UCF head baseball coach) were the designated drivers of the vans during the Knights' five-day stay. The team departed for the Cathedral game at 3:30 p.m., receiving a late checkout from The New Yorker. Cathedral College was located approximately 45 minutes from the hotel. Torchy rode shotgun in the second van side-by-side with the easygoing, cigar-smoking assistant, Pantelias, behind the steering wheel.

The budget-conscious Knights traveled to New York with only ten players. The team's plan was to arrive at Cathedral by 4:30, allowing players ample time to get game-ready. Salerno's van led the UCF convoy and had the handwritten directions to the gym. However, the Knights ran into some unexpected weather as it began to snow in Midtown. The rush hour traffic was busier than normal with last-minute Christmas shoppers searching for the perfect gift. The second van missed a stoplight at a congested intersection, and the two vans were instantly separated. The first van plodded through the heavy snow and found the Cathedral Gym at 5:40, 20 minutes before tip-off. Salerno remembered, "I was so worried about being late and assumed the second van had already arrived. I thought I'd get *fired* and Torchy would be outraged. Much to my surprise, the other van wasn't there yet, and I really dodged a bullet." But Salerno still had other problematic issues to face.

First, where was the second van? Secondly, the Cathedral coach was "hopping mad" about the game scenario transpiring before his very eyes. And lastly, the Knights had no uniforms or gear, all of which were in the second van. The host team came to the rescue by letting the "Salerno Five" wear an old "crummy" set of Cathedral road uniforms. The five players quickly changed into their makeshift uniforms.

The second van of players, still stuck in holiday traffic, helplessly asked for directions from the bustling New Yorkers. No one had any idea on the exact location of Cathedral College. Most knew the directions to St. Patrick's Cathedral, but that wouldn't help the Knights on this snowy day in 1970.

Meanwhile, the "Salerno Five" stretched quickly to get ready to play. At 5:50 the two referees, following game protocol, checked the starters for each team in the official scorebook. Salerno's decision to pick his starters was relatively easy! He politely explained the Knights' dilemma to the referees. Desperate for some compassion, he got very little, if any. Salerno kept looking and looking at the gym doors, waiting for Torchy and the other five Knights to arrive. But unbeknownst to him the second van was still a city hour away.

At 6:00 as the game clock expired, the horn blared out in the small gym. The referees told Salerno he had 15 minutes, but sternly warned him that after the allotted time, the game would start, missing players or not.

With the second van still not in sight, at 6:15, the referees said, "Coach, we have to start." The hopeless assistant said, "Our guys are coming!! Give us a few more minutes." The head referee continued, "Coach, if we don't start now, it will be a *forfeit* for your team." Salerno pleaded one last time, but to no avail.

The game began with the "Salerno Five" against Cathedral, the best opponent UCF would play on the trip. Salerno now laughs at the game he will never forget: "I coached the first half, but I found myself looking at the doors more than the game itself." At halftime, the "Salerno Five" trailed the home team.

FINALLY, the second van arrived at the Cathedral Gym as Torchy and his players hustled inside. They anxiously looked up at the gym's poorly lit scoreboard with 7:36 on the halftime running clock and the visitors down 12. The frustrated Torchy found his way to the Knights' locker room and barked at Salerno, "Why did they start the game? Russ, you guys should have waited." Salerno shot back quickly, "Torchy, I tried to get them to wait. I really tried, but they said it would be a forfeit, so we started."

All ten players changed into their UCF uniforms faster than the speed of light for the second half to play against a tough, scrappy, and excellent-shooting Cathedral. Torchy was fuming over the situation, but also realized that anything can happen, especially during rush hour in New York City. The Knights lost to Cathedral, 87–85 in a game that went down to the last possession. The home team hit several key free throws to seal the win against the *tardy* Knights.

UCF went 2–1 on their whirlwind New York trip. At JFK after the game, as the Knights waited for their flight back to Orlando at the terminal gate, Torchy jokingly poked (Russ said Torchy was not joking) at his trusted confidant, remarking, "Russ, that's your loss!! I was 2–0 on the trip and you were 0–1. That's your loss!!"

Torchy recalled the 1970 adventure: "It was a great trip and an unbelievable experience for our players. My UCF teams were getting better and better each game, each season. But sometimes in life things are like vapors: here and then gone. But the memories remain."

CHAPTER 19

Common Denominator

In 1973, the 37th President of the United States, Richard Nixon, was the commencement speaker at UCF's Spring Graduation. The outdoor ceremony, near the reflecting pond in front of the beautiful library, was a great moment for the university. After Nixon finished his speech, Torchy, dressed in cap and gown as a member of the faculty, began to walk toward the presidential limousine. "I really wanted to meet the President. As Nixon walked by, I extended my right hand hoping to shake his hand. The Secret Service hovered around the President and wasn't too happy with me," recalled the former history teacher.

Nixon shook Torchy's hand. "Hello, Mr. President, I'm the basketball coach here at the university," said the eager Torchy. Nixon asked, "Where did you go to school?" Torchy replied, "Marquette." The President continued, "Oh, Milwaukee is a great city! I love the state of Wisconsin! Fine state!" The proud father added, "My son [Mike] graduated today." Nixon followed up and said, "Congratulations!"

Looking back on graduation day, Torchy often wondered, "If I had told the President I was from Idaho . . . would Nixon have said that Idaho is a great state? But nonetheless, it's not every day you get to meet the President of the United States." Richard Nixon delivered the commencement speech on UCF's campus three weeks after the nationally televised Watergate Hearings (1973) began in our country.

One of Torchy's goals each season throughout his career was to teach his system so well that his players could also teach it, know it, and operate freely in it. Torchy's philosophy and system remained constant at all his stops as he stayed true to his core teaching principles.

In his outstanding career, each team he coached had different personalities, different strengths, different weaknesses, and different levels of talent. But the common denominator of Torchy's magnificent success was his consistent teaching of his trademark press, trusted 2/3 zone, and "short-half" court traps (blitz) out of the zone. His defense became his offense.

Offensively, the coaching guru taught the three-man weave, five-man weave, and ran only three or four offensive plays with isolation options. Torchy wanted his team to play 94 feet; however, he did implement a freelance motion which allowed "disciplined-freedom" offensively. His stall, executed meticulously in games, became an offense in itself, developing its own distinct identity. Using valuable game time, the stall created opportunistic driving gaps for layups, pull-up jumpers, and drive and kick rhythm jump shots.

The Hall of Fame coach taught his teams to look to score immediately after an opponent's score. Torchy called this the "lull period." He believed this was the time to go . . . the offense becomes complacent after scoring, relaxing briefly, creating a short window of opportunity to look long. This "lull" lasts only three to four seconds. And according to Torchy, "You must do it quickly, like a thief in the night, in a good way."

In his successful system, the "lull" was the most potent time to strike opponents with the long baseball pass leading to a layup. Torchy invariably preached the importance of the easy basket to his teams.

In his eyes, there was no substitute for the easy basket. Frequently, the concept is an overlooked strategic key for basketball coaches at all levels. The UCF mentor remembered, "Fans watch our games and think it's unbelievable how many layups we get. They say it looks so easy. But this is our style, we get them because we work at it."

The Xavier icon seldom talked to his players about Vince Lombardi, but was influenced by the Packers' system of the individual commitment to a group effort. Torchy's attention to detail was different than most coaches. It was not the information on an eight-page scouting report or the three ways to front the low-post defensively. In his 38 years, Torchy seldom handed out written scouting reports. Rather, it was his attention to detail of the "total committed effort" from each player—the complete understanding of one's ROLE within the team—and how that basic understanding leads to the team's ultimate success. The buy-in of each player was an absolute.

At St. Mary's Grade School, Xavier, and UCF, the high benchmark of winning through hard work and obligation had been established early in Torchy's tenure at each school. He was able to create his *culture of excellence* immediately, building a foundation for future success and championships.

Despite being a group of basketball nomads without a home gym, Torchy nonetheless led the Knights to continued success in the program's third and fourth seasons. The teams in that era (1971–73) were led by Mike Clark, Arnett Hall, Eddie Fluitt, and several junior college recruits.

Mike Clark passed up three scholarship opportunities at UW-Green Bay, Rollins, and St. Norbert to play for his dad with no scholarships the first year. He would help Torchy launch the UCF program in 1969. As a junior, Clark averaged 23.3 points per game; his senior year, the crafty point guard averaged 15.0 points per game in his Lou Gehrig-like UCF career.

The Knights' talent was boosted tremendously with Assistant Coach Russ Salerno's strong recruiting classes. As scholarships increased, he reeled in two blue-chip players: Arnett Hall, a six-foot-two transfer from Indian River Junior College in Fort Pierce, Florida; and big man Eddie Fluitt, a six-foot-seven center transfer from Lake Sumter Junior College in Leesburg, Florida.

Hall, mentored by Indian River coaching legend Mike Leatherwood, averaged an eye-popping 20.2 and 20.7 points per game in his two years at UCF. "Arnett could really play and had a great shooting stroke. On any night, he could score 25–30 points. Our schedule got tougher and tougher each year, and I'm glad we had Arnett. He was quiet, but so confident. Torchy enjoyed coaching him," reminisced Mike Clark. After UCF, Hall played professional basketball in Spain.

Fluitt was a rebounding machine for the early Knights. "Eddie was an outstanding recruit and what a great guy! He was a Division I rebounder," added Salerno. Fluitt presently holds the UCF record for the best rebound average per game for a single season (14.0 rebounds per game in the 1971–72 season).

Three other quality recruits for Salerno were Zettie McCrimmon, Angelo Callins, and Bob Jones. McCrimmon, one of the many talented players from the McCrimmon basketball family of Kissimmee, Florida, was a six-foot-four forward who had two great years after transferring from Valencia Junior College in Orlando. "I liked Zettie. He was an experienced veteran and had a good feel for the game. He was important to us in the early years as we tried to establish a winning tradition," said Torchy.

Angelo Callins, a five-foot-ten transfer from Pensacola Junior College in Pensacola, Florida, was a jet-quick combo guard and an excellent addition to the Knights' firepower. Hall and Callins teamed together in the backcourt to lead UCF to a 16–8 record in 1973–74. Jones, a six-foot-five power forward also from Valencia via Bishop

Moore, had a deadly mid-range jumper and a blue-collar work ethic in two solid years.

John Smith, a six-foot-five center, was a strong physical rebounder and a great team player. Smith, a transfer from Hillsborough Junior College in Tampa, Florida, had two outstanding seasons for UCF. "John Smith was a trench guy who worked relentlessly to get every rebound. He was a beast on the boards!" recalled Torchy.

On February, 3, 1972, the Knights beat Biscayne College 73–60 in a monumental win at the Lake Highland Gym in Orlando. Three years later, both UCF and Biscayne would be co-members of Florida's new Sunshine State Conference. The Bobcats, coached by Ken Stibler, played several high-major Division I schools every year. Stibler believed in "toughening up" his team by playing superior opponents. The Knights beat Biscayne in a hard-nosed battle from start to finish with 1,057 fans in attendance. The win proved the Knights could play with anyone. Torchy was at his best as he utilized his full-court press to force three Bobcat turnovers which led to six consecutive points late in the second half. The spurt kept Biscayne at bay: The Bobcats could not get any closer than five points. Torchy's defense once again became his offense.

Mike Clark scored a team-high 28 points in the program-changing win. His floor game, poise, and decisive baskets helped the Knights defeat the aggressive and well-coached Bobcats. "The Biscayne game was definitely a turning point for the program. We finally beat a talented and experienced Division II team. It was a far cry from that humble first year of reversible jerseys," said Mike Clark, who scored 2,085 career points as a Knight.

The 1971–72 season was the first year UCF played local Rollins College, a well-established Division II basketball program. It was the beginning of an intense and entertaining rivalry. Rollins beat UCF, 83–72 at Enyart Alumni Fieldhouse in the inaugural game.

Torchy advised young coaches, "Stay with simplicity; many coaches complicate the game with too much strategy." The founder of UCF's basketball program looked back proudly and remarked, "Our up-tempo style and system helped us sign several program-changing recruits. During this period, the Orlando community jumped on board as UCF fans. But sometimes in life things are like vapors: here and then gone. But the memories remain."

CHAPTER 20

The Dragon Slayer

I n the Spring of 1975, UCF announced they were joining the Sunshine State Conference, a new NCAA Division II league, along with Rollins College, Florida Southern College, Biscayne College, Eckerd College, and Saint Leo College. UCF was the only state school in the Florida private colleges' newly formed league. The Sunshine State Conference was the "brainchild" of Saint Leo Athletic Director and Head Basketball Coach Norm Kaye. Dick Pace, the Maitland-based Southeastern Conference official, served as the conference's first full-time commissioner (1976-85).

Torchy was in favor of joining the conference with the possibility of basketball rivalries emerging into intense and highly competitive games. The coaching in the Sunshine State from its inception was phenomenal; every conference game was a "white knuckler" which immediately captured the "fancy" of college basketball fans in the state.

Bill Beekman, aka "Hoops McKnight," a 1975 FTU/UCF graduate, has written extensively and chronicled the history of UCF basketball and football. His series of articles called "Dribblings Including the Adventures of the Disco Winnebago and Blocked Punts . . . Fond and Foggy Memories from the Early Days of Knights' Athletics" is an excellent read. Beekman is such a passionate Knights fan that when he cuts his finger, he bleeds black and gold. He is a true Knight through and through, still proudly cheering for his alma mater faithfully at many basketball and football games.

On January 31, 1976, in an 8:00 p.m. standing-room-only Sunshine State showdown, the embryonic Knights faced the experienced, Jim Jarrett-led Moccasins of Florida Southern. Both the upper and lower levels of the gym were filled to capacity; UCF athletic officials and administrators were beaming. What a grand idea to start a conference in Florida!

Beekman remembered the galvanizing Homecoming contest: "It was the first big game that unranked UCF ever hosted. Florida Southern swaggered into the Winter Park High School Gym, unbeaten and boasting the nation's top NCAA II ranking. To boot, the Winter Park Gym was the high school home of Florida Southern's All-American six-foot-nine center John Edwards. Woefully undersized, conventional wisdom said that Torchy's (12–3) Knights were doomed. It was conventional wisdom that was doomed from the opening tip.

"The sell-out started with six-foot-six UCF freshman jumping jack David Lewis, an Indianapolis, Indiana, native, soaring over Edwards to get the opening tip. UCF got the first bucket of the game. Lewis packed Edwards on his first shot, setting the tone for the rest of the game.

"The bigger Mocs were no match for the Knights' speed and quickness that night in 1976. Bennie Shaw and Bo Clark were the scoring heroes, but it was All-American Jerry Prather's three consecutive steals that sealed the game. In a basketball version of 'No Mas,' Florida Southern let their No. 1 ranking die as Calvin Lingelbach dribbled the last 70 seconds away. The Knights dominated their first-ever BIG home game, winning 92–76 as 3,100 Homecoming fans stormed the court in jubilation, chanting, "WE'RE NUMBER ONE!"

After the mad rush, Knights fans hoisted Torchy on their shoulders and carried him victoriously to UCF's locker room. The Knights had just defeated the No. 1 team in the nation rather convincingly, as Torchy's press and Jerry Prather were the true heroes of the dragon slaying.

In 1965, Boston Celtics' beloved radio announcer Johnny Most made his famous, "Havlicek stole the ball" call. Havlicek's steal in the Boston Garden with five seconds left in Game 7 of the Eastern Conference Championship against the Philadelphia 76ers sealed the Celtics' 110–109 win, leading them to the 1965 NBA Finals against the Los Angeles Lakers. The Florida Southern-UCF game 11 years later was UCF's basketball rendition of "Havlicek stole the ball." This time the call was "Prather stole the ball," and not only once, but three straight Mocs' possessions.

UCF had a slim 61–58 second-half lead as fans sat restlessly watching the Knights battle the best team in the land. With 8:40 left in the game, Prather picked off a pass from Florida Southern's Mike Spatola to the right wing. He then fired the ball to teammate Bennie Shaw for an uncontested layup. At 8:19, Prather scored himself after he picked off the same-type pass. This time he fed Shaw, but Shaw fed back for an equally easy two-pointer. Eighteen seconds later, Prather repeated the routine and again set up Shaw. UCF now led 67–58, and the Knights were in total control of the game. Prather remembered his heroic second half against Southern: "I was just anticipating the pass. Torchy always teaches us to gamble and aggressively jump lanes in our zone. We were just trying to disrupt their offense."

Prather scored a team-high 25 points, but for all practical purposes the game was finished with his three "quick as lightning" steals. Lingelbach remembered UCF's historic night: "It was a fantastic game and an unbelievable atmosphere. The crowd was our SIXTH MAN!! They fell in love with our fight and heart. Torchy had us really prepared to play Southern. In his eyes, we were not backing down from anybody."

The Knights did a great job of shutting down Edwards, the Mocs' center who was held to only 14 points. The multi-talented Edwards had a terrific career for Southern and is the second all-time leading rebounder at the Lakeland college with 1,214 career rebounds. His 15.8 rebounds per game average as a senior is a school record. Edward's No. 41 was the first men's basketball number retired at Florida Southern.

Torchy and Edwards had tremendous respect for each other in the UCF-Southern battles. And their respect continued through Edwards' career coaching high school basketball. Both had a mutual friend in highly successful longtime Orlando high school basketball coach, Rudy Tapia, who was Edwards' coaching mentor at Orlando's Edgewater High School for several years. Tapia, one of the "best in the business," was an excellent coach and motivator in the Central Florida area. He was first introduced to Torchy early in his career as a young head coach at Lake Highland Prep when UCF used the Highlanders' gym as a practice and home court in the early 1970s during their gym-less years.

Seven days removed from the emotional Homecoming win, Torchy's Knights would face another arduous task. "The Game" (1976), as it was referred to by the media and fans, found UCF matched up *again* versus the No. 1 team in the country, Rollins College. Two Mount Everest climbs for Torchy and his team in a week. Almost unimaginable: a rare occurrence in college athletics.

The *Orlando Sentinel* depicted "Rollins as a cool, calm, experienced and unshakeable team coached by the famous Ed Jucker of the University of Cincinnati fame. The hype for 'The Game' created a healthy, rambunctious fan base and a spark of alma mater pride for both institutions." The schools were approximately nine miles apart, creating a local, intimate and spirited rivalry similar to a small college version of Duke and North Carolina.

"The Game" on February 6, 1976, at Rollins' Enyart Alumni Fieldhouse was only the second sell-out in the facility's storied history. The first sell-out was a 1974 high school matchup for the ages between two national powerhouses, Winter Park High School and Orlando Evans High School. The high school game was so BIG that if played today (2020), it would be nationally televised on ESPN. The game featured two future NBA players: Winter Park's Stan Pietkiewicz and Evans' Darryl Dawkins.

According to Larry Guest (1976), who wrote in the *Orlando Sentinel,* "There was the strong possibility of ticket scalping at the UCF-Rollins basketball game. 'Gee, I hope not,' mused Rollins' basketball coach Ed Jucker, grinning at the prospect that Orlando's interest in NCAA Division II basketball may have reached that unseemly plateau. 'Scalping isn't right," said a laughing Torchy Clark, 'but it's nice to hear the word.'"

Guest continued to expound that "Fans who show up without tickets may be forced to scan the faces outside the door in hopes of finding an enterprising soul who bought in bulk during Rollins' first-ever advanced ticket sale. The Central Florida area was grinning broadly over unprecedented fan support spawned by (1) glittering win-loss records, (2) national rankings, and (3) the special magic of a conference pennant race."

He went on to note that "when six Florida colleges banded together last off-season to form the Sunshine State Conference, the driving purpose was a guaranteed berth for its champion in the NCAA Division II postseason tournament. The founding fathers naturally assumed the attraction of a conference race would create a certain amount of additional fan appeal. But not in their wildest dreams did they imagine the series of sell-out crowds that would erupt in the league's inaugural season."

Prior to coaching at Rollins, Jucker coached the University of Cincinnati to three Division I Basketball National Championship

Games, winning two titles for the Bearcats, in 1961 and 1962, defeating Ohio State University both years. Ohio State's team, coached by Fred Taylor, was led by players Jerry Lucas, John Havlicek, and Bobby Knight. In addition, Jucker coached the legendary Hall of Famer Oscar Robertson as head coach of the NBA's Cincinnati Royals for two years (1967–69).

Of the UCF-Rollins emerging rivalry, Jucker recalled, "Yes, the league has stirred up some excitement among students. Our campus is buzzing." The Knights' Clark added his thoughts on the Rollins series: "Sure, rivalries are great and it's always exciting for the fan and player when the game means something, as with conference standings. It adds extra spice to the game."

Guest reported, "When Rollins traveled to Lakeland in 1976 to play Florida Southern, athletic administrators of the school had to lock the doors, turning away several hundred after some 3,600 fans squeezed into the 3,300-seat Jenkins Fieldhouse. A Rollins campus group organized student bus charters, with the goal of five busloads to Lakeland. They stopped at seven because they couldn't get any more tickets."

"It's a nice problem to have," said Jucker. "It forced us to meet as a staff and decide how many tickets should be allotted for UCF and how many we have to set aside for our students. We've never had to do this before." A big-time rivalry was starting to bloom.

Packed arenas were commonplace in the Sunshine State Conference in 1976. Each team played only 10 conference games, magnifying each game's importance. *For most games, an empty seat at Rollins, Florida Southern, and UCF was only a rumor.* "I think people are starting to realize that they don't have to go to Florida or Florida State to see good basketball," said Jucker. Good basketball it was. "The Game" had skilled Division I-caliber athletes on both teams. For the spectator, it was basketball heaven . . . like watching a Division I Mid-American or Big South Conference showdown in your backyard.

The Knights were led by senior stalwart Bennie Shaw, a six-foot-one left-handed scoring machine who averaged 26 points per game his senior year. The blue-chip recruit was a transfer from local Seminole Junior College in Sanford, Florida. In 1974, Torchy's assistant, Ben Meixl, his longtime chum from his childhood days in Oshkosh, recruited the outstanding Shaw. Oddly, the smooth point-maker competed every practice and game with a straight pin in his mouth. Teammates claim Shaw never swallowed one!

The scoring gem loved playing for Torchy. He became an unstoppable force in his system which allowed him plenty of freedom offensively. And nobody did it better than Shaw! The Orlando Boone High graduate was a Small College All-American. Bennie Shaw was a ninth-round draft pick of the Milwaukee Bucks in the 1976 NBA Draft.

The Knights had two other superb guards in Calvin Lingelbach and Jerry Prather. Lingelbach, a six-foot-two point guard, was a floor general, scorer, and quarterback for the pesky Knights. An exceptional athlete who also had a stellar career as a Knights' baseball shortstop, Lingelbach, according to Torchy, "may have been the *toughest* leader in UCF basketball history." Torchy continued his praise for his point guard: "I loved his grit, determination, and focus. If Calvin Lingelbach was *stock*, I'd buy it out."

Prather, a six-foot-three sophomore sensation, did it all for the Knights with his "electric" rebounding, scoring, passing, and defending. In countless eyes of UCF basketball fans, Prather was not only the most underrated player, but without a doubt the most valuable in Torchy's 14 years. Prather averaged 21.5 points per game his senior year in 1977–78, leading the Knights to college basketball's Promised Land, the NCAA Division II Final Four. He was the best of the best!!

The Rollins' Tars were led by the three "Cincinnati Kids" Jucker recruited from his hometown: seniors and four-year players Bruce Howland, a six-foot-six forward; Tom Klusman, a six-foot-one point guard; and six-foot-seven center Steve Heis. The Tars also had sophomore future All-American Gary Parsons, a six-foot-six athletic power forward.

Klusman, Rollins' current basketball coach, has been the head coach for 40 unparalleled years. He ranks fifth among active NCAA II coaches in victories and tenth all-time. The former Tar, a heady tough competitor (1972-76), has had a spectacular career, winning 717 games at his alma mater. Torchy, after retiring from coaching in 1983, became a confidant of the then-young Rollins' coach, developing a close relationship, attending several Tars' home games each season.

"The Game" was the first meeting of the 1975–76 season between the top-ranked Tars against the unranked paupers of UCF. "The Game" was a sellout and televised live on Orlando's Channel 24 WMFE TV. The 3,000-seat Enyart Alumni Fieldhouse was packed at 7:00 p.m., 30 minutes before tip-off. No seats were available for late-arriving fans.

The crowd was split 50/50, with fans from both schools ready to cheer and simultaneously taunt opposing players with plenty of tricks in their bag. The fans at Enyart were right on top of the live action. A player taking the ball out-of-bounds on a side-out was two feet away from rowdy fans from either team. An *Orlando Sentinel* reporter asked Torchy, "What's the difference between the two schools [Rollins and UCF]?" Torchy sarcastically responded, "Their kids drink Heineken, ours drink Miller Lite." The humor was silly, but regardless, most fans at Enyart still believed the Tars had too much experience and size for the much smaller but quicker Knights. Most on either side agreed Rollins would win "The Game."

The young Knights' starting two freshmen jumped the Tars early with excellent perimeter shooting and easy transition baskets. Lingelbach was able to penetrate the Rollins' paint (lane) at will for drive and kick opportunities to the confident-shooting Knights. The Knights' quickness and pace bothered the Tars from the start. Shaw hit several pull-up jumpers against the Tars' man defense, as the Knights led 38–29 at the intermission. Most of the 3,000 fans at halftime did not want to leave their seats for fear of losing them.

Bolstered by a strong defense, transition game, and uncanny perimeter shooting, Torchy's Knights jumped out to a 54–36 lead early in the second half. The UCF crowd roared loudly! Jucker, hastily, called a timeout to calm and regroup his struggling Tars.

Both coaches dressed dapperly: Torchy was wearing a leisure suit, and Jucker wore a conservative blue blazer and yellow Rollins tie. Jucker had coached on the national stage many times in his illustrious career and was a seasoned veteran of big games. Torchy had coached in many big games too, but not the same magnitude as Jucker. The Jucker-Clark dynamic was always interesting to observe in the Hatfield-McCoy series. Fans and players did not know what to expect from the two; however, both had a deep respect for the other.

The senior-laden Tars chopped UCF's lead to six points, 62–56, with 9:36 to play in the second half, as the boisterous Rollins' faithful were now alive with the Tars back. This time, it was Torchy who called a timeout to settle his anxious Knights, amongst the sea of blue and gold Rollins fans standing and cheering. The Tar fans had awakened from their *Knightmare* of the first hour of UCF's dominance. Enyart was rocking!

After Torchy's timeout, the Knights ran a set play hitting a clutch driving basket and free throw to push their lead back to nine points, 65–56. The UCF faithful at "The Game" went ballistic on the three-point play! With UCF up 14 points late in the second half, Torchy decided to pull the ball out, running his "triangles-delay" the last four minutes. This was the same strategy he used against Marquette High and Abbot Pennings coaching at Xavier. Torchy's "Triangles-delay" was decidedly effective and created strategic mismatches for the upset-hungry Knights . . . it also used valuable clock time.

Shaw led UCF with 26 points, and freshman Clark hit several key free throws down the stretch to keep the Tars from rallying. The Knights won 94–77 in the first game of the 1975–76 season series. "I was happy the way we did it," remarked the triumphant Torchy. "We needed scoring from Shaw and Clark, rebounding from Lewis and Belotte, and the floor game, control, and leadership of Prather and Lingelbach. And that's what we got!"

UCF shot a flaming 65 percent from the field on 33–51 shooting in the contest. Torchy's game goal of shooting more free throws than the opponent was clearly evident in the box score. The Knights shot a sizzling 28–34 from the free throw line; the Tars were only 17–23.

"I thought we had 'em," said a surprised Jucker of the Tar comeback that cut the Knights' big lead to six at the nine-minute mark. "But we came up with a bad defensive play, they made the shot and then pulled away again."

The Knights won their 12th consecutive game and stood 5–0 in the Sunshine State Conference. Guest (1976) of the *Orlando Sentinel* reported the morning after "The Game" in jest: "The Tars, like any self-respecting college basketball team, have to duck under the door facing as they enter the gym. UCF's Knights, who don't even have a gym of their own to enter, are just tall enough to keep their wallets from scraping. The Knights, Rollins' fans haughtily suggested, would have better odds tied to a railroad track. The paupers made prince. The peasants overran the palace. The hoboes are now riding in the Pullman. They did it with speed and heart."

The ultra-competitive Jucker, a two-time NCAA National Basketball Championship coach, met with reporters after the 94–77 loss, and had his eyes instantly on the rematch two weeks away, three miles up the road at UCF's home court. "We'll be ready next time, I promise. We're not worried about having to play on their court. In a crosstown rivalry like this, it doesn't make much difference. The crowd will be equally divided. I'm looking forward to it." SO WAS CALVIN LINGELBACH!

Torchy humbly recalled the dreamlike week and the slaying of two dragons (No. 1 teams in the country): "Both Southern and Rollins were outstanding college basketball teams. That may have been the best Rollins' team ever. Our quickness and our pace were huge factors in the big-time wins. The UCF crowd was absolutely fantastic! But sometimes in life things are like vapors: here and then gone. But the memories remain."

CHAPTER 21

Rollins—Down 22

In the biggest game of the 1975–76 season, UCF trailed Rollins 56–34 with 12:03 to play in the second half. "The Rematch" of the UCF-Rollins series this time was on the Knights' home court, Winter Park High School. Sophomore Gary Parsons of Rollins hit an 18-foot jump shot that put his team up 22 points.

After hitting the jumper, the Division II All-American pumped his fist as the exuberant Tar confidently ran past the UCF bench. There was some arrogance to his fist-pumping, but Parsons was ecstatic about the enormous lead the Tars had built with 12 minutes to play. Rollins had complete control of the game, and things were looking pretty darn good for the Blue and Gold.

"The Rematch" was an 8:00 p.m. tip-off, which was the earliest availability of the facility. The 3,000 fans in the hot and noisy gym were 60 percent Knights and 40 percent Tars. The game featured No. 7 nationally ranked UCF against No. 9 Rollins. Tickets for the game sold out a week in advance; however, it was a problem both institutions enjoyed having.

Plenty was at stake in the "The Rematch," and most Knights' and Tars' fans were aware of the game's consequences. The Knights were

19–3 (9–0 conference record) riding a 16-game winning streak; the Tars came in with a 17–4 (8–1) record. The only conference loss for Rollins was to UCF two weeks prior, a game in which the Knights shot a blistering 65 percent to crush the host Tars, 94–77.

If UCF defeated Rollins, the Knights would win the Sunshine State regular season outright. If the Tars won, they would gain a share of the conference title with the Knights, having identical 9–1 records. More importantly, both teams were playing for potential NCAA tournament berths. Rumors had the NCAA taking two Sunshine State Conference teams, but the tournament committee can be a fickle bunch, and both coaches knew nothing was guaranteed.

Rollins slowed the smaller and quicker Knights by controlling the tempo from the start with a disciplined shot selection. The game's pace in the first half favored the Tars as they led 29–26 at halftime behind the strong play of Gary Parsons; Ed Lake, a six-foot-two shooting guard; and veteran playmaker Tom Klusman. The Tars played with tremendous confidence and poise in Jucker's well-executed game plan. The "Cincinnati Kids" understood the urgency and championship significance of the game, leaving everything on the floor in the last Sunshine contest of their celebrated Rollins career.

A Winter Park High graduate and basketball sensation, Parsons was playing "The Rematch" in his home gym. Gary Parsons is the father of Chandler Parsons, a six-foot-ten small forward, who had a sensational career for Billy Donovan at the University of Florida. As a Gator, he was named Southeastern Conference Player of the Year in 2011. The gifted athlete was drafted in the 2011 NBA Draft by the Houston Rockets as the 38th pick. Currently, Parsons is in his ninth year in the league with stops in Houston, Dallas, Memphis, and Atlanta.

Rollins came out of the locker room "on fire" the first five minutes of the second half behind the shooting of Parsons and Lake. The Tars' quick passing against the Knights' 2–3 zone created several high-post and short-corner opportunities which led to easy baskets. With the Tars up, 41–34, Rollins went on an explosive 15–0 run against the cold shooting and flat-footed Knights. Yes, the Tars scored 15 consecutive points to take a commanding 56–34 lead. UCF literally "hit the wall" struggling to score possession after possession. And bad offense led to poor defense as the hapless Knights faced tremendous adversity.

Turnovers and missed jump shots buried the Knights while UCF fans sat shocked in silence. This was not supposed to happen to one of Torchy's teams; not on the biggest sports stage in the university's young history.

The sheer domination by the Tars included a gigantic 27–8 run to start the second half with Klusman running the show. The Tars' comfortable lead of 22 points was humongous; in 1976, college basketball did not have a shot clock or a three-point shot. It was almost time for the Tars to light up the Ed Jucker (Red Auerbach) cigar as sweet revenge and a conference championship were near.

A few Knights' fans pondered the idea of leaving early—Rollins' 22-point lead looked insurmountable for UCF to overcome. But the consolation was, despite a loss, the Knights would still share a Sunshine State Championship.

The Tars' complete manhandling of the Knights forced the irate Torchy to call a timeout. With his players expecting to hear it, he emphatically ripped into his squad: "I'm not losing. I'm not losing this game." This was Torchy's *obligation*, his duty—to give his team every ounce of energy and emotion he had to bring them back within striking distance. And then somehow miraculously find a way to win, despite the Grand Canyon-size hole his Knights had dug. This PRECISE moment is why Torchy Clark won 82.2 percent of his football and basketball games in his career. For him the obligation was not just talk. It was REAL. It was SERIOUS. The passion . . . the drive . . . and the obligation were all major components of his DNA.

Torchy intensely DEMANDED in the huddle, "Nobody is going to do this to us. We are going to PRESS and PRESS and then PRESS some more. We are going to face guard and cut this lead to eight with four minutes left." Calvin Lingelbach remembered the most important timeout of the Torchy era at UCF: "He always tells us when we're going to press, that if you're gonna lose by two, you might as well lose by 40, so we're gonna press our guts out."

The Knights' comeback began with freshman Bo Clark's 20-foot jumper to cut the lead to 56–36. Behind the incredible defense and scoring of Jerry Prather and Calvin Lingelbach, the Knights quickly scored the next six points to cut the lead to 56–42. The Tars' leading scorers Bruce Howland and Gary Parsons had been saddled on the bench with four fouls. Meanwhile, Bennie Shaw, UCF's leading scorer at 26 points per game, was also in foul trouble. Shaw was forced to sit most of the second half before fouling out at the 4:15-minute mark.

With 7:06 to play, the Tars still had a comfortable 61–46 lead; however, the Knights *refused* to quit and stormed back *again* behind the gutsy play of Prather and Lingelbach, who scored seven straight to trim the Rollins' lead to 61–53. As the Knights chipped away, UCF fans became more and more *engaged* with each basket. The fans' frenzy provided a bolt of energy for the Knights as they pressed and pressed; exactly like their coach DEMANDED at the timeout. Torchy remembered the last 12:03 of the game: "We scored off traps, deflections, steals, and in transition. It was vintage 'Rat game' . . . the same 'Rat game' I used at St. Mary's and Xavier. And we had our crowd in the palm of our hand. They were a HUGE part of the comeback!"

Lingelbach's competitive leadership was unrivaled, but in this game he was a five-star general. The point guard did everything humanly possible to bring the Knights back. He was all over the floor at both ends—making plays, defending, scoring, and leading. Torchy reminisced, "Calvin took the team on his back. He never took his foot off the pedal. He believed me when I said in the timeout, 'I'm not losing this game.'"

Shaw's substitute, senior backup combo guard David Green, a six-foot chiseled guard from Chicago, finally got his opportunity. Green added backcourt depth to the Knights' arsenal and accepted his role as a "microwave-scorer off the bench" like a champion.

A tenacious presser, Green couldn't score like Shaw (nobody really could), but he could defend and "get to the rim." The chance to play and be a part of the Knights' attempted comeback excited Green. This was his opportunity to win a championship for Torchy in front of the now re-energized UCF faithful. The Knights were back! Rollins began to fatigue from the up-tempo style—the opposite tempo played in the first half. Defense created offense as the Knights scored easy basket after easy basket. UCF's confidence soared; and with 2:15 left, stunningly, the score was tied 69-all. Prather hit two free throws to put UCF up 71–69 with 1:54 to play.

After Claire recorded Prather's free throws on her plain envelope, she briskly retreated outside to the gym's parking lot—no longer able to handle the game's roller-coaster ride of emotions: "I just couldn't take it anymore and wanted to get away from the pressure," said Claire.

Rollins' Bob Morris, a six-foot-five forward, scored off a rebound to tie the game 71-all with 1:36 to play as the crowd stood anxiously the remainder of the game. The SRO crowd was being entertained by a fervid, passionate level of basketball. But the true barometer of enjoyment was in the eye of the beholder. For UCF fans, they were witnessing a classic game that will forever be etched in their minds and hearts. For the shell-shocked Rollins' fans, they were hoping to wake up from another terrible *Knightmare: Part 2*. They couldn't fathom what had just transpired the last 10–11 minutes of game time.

After the Rollins' basket at the 1:36 mark, UCF's Willy Belotte, a six-foot-seven center, was called for charging as Rollins regained the possession. Belotte, a Milwaukee native, one of Torchy's favorite players, shared time with freshman starter David Lewis.

At the 1:20 mark and the score tied 71-all, the Tars threw the ball away, nervously forcing a pass inside. The Knights now had the possession as Torchy called a timeout. He decided to milk the clock: The plan was to attack the basket at the five-to-seven-second mark. The Xavier legend called for an isolation for Prather—with Lingelbach as the second option. But more importantly, he wanted the Knights to take the last shot. Win the game or win it in overtime.

As UCF ran their "triangles-delay" game, Lingelbach penetrated and threw the ball to an open David Green with four seconds left. Green, who played incredibly in Bennie Shaw's absence, attacked the basket and drove squarely into a Rollins player who drew a charge with two seconds left. After a Rollins' timeout, senior Tar center Steve Heis inbounded the ball full-court, passing to guard Ed Lake, who fired a quick lob to Tars' "leaper," six-foot-five Dirk Twine. As Twine went up to catch the lob, he collided with Lingelbach after the horn sounded as game official Wayne Smith swallowed the whistle. There was no foul called on the play.

The game was tied 71-all. It was OVERTIME with the Sunshine State Conference Championship on the line. UCF had outscored Rollins an amazing 37–15 in the last 12:03 of regulation.

Immediately after the horn expired, a frustrated Ed Jucker walked on the court protesting the no-call. He vehemently argued a foul should have been called; and the NCAA Championship coach was assessed an "unsportsmanlike conduct" technical foul by the other official, Jack Wise. Both Smith and Wise were NCAA Division I (Southeastern

Conference) officials who been assigned the Division II Battle of the Titans. To start the overtime, UCF would shoot a free throw and get first possession as a result of the technical.

Lingelbach shot the free throw. Bill Buchalter of the *Orlando Sentinel,* who covered the game, called Calvin Lingelbach "Calvin Cool." Lingelbach had made 29 consecutive free throws without a miss. "Calvin Cool" made it 30. The Knights were up 72–71.

On the Knights' first possession, it was "Calvin Cool" again who, after 16 seconds, drained an adrenaline-filled 12-foot left-wing jump shot to put the Knights up 74–71. Rollins missed a shot, and 24 seconds later, UCF's Belotte scored off a rebound, which put the Knights up 76–71 as *pandemonium* set in.

By the time the Tars finally scored in the extra session, the Knights had assumed a 78–71 lead, and the turnabout was just beginning. It was Knights' eighth man David Green's turn to take over the overtime. And that he did!

"Mister Overtime" aka David Green was all over the court, trapping, stealing, and slashing as he scored 11 *consecutive* points in the extra session. Rollins did not score during Green's scoring barrage. Recalling his clutch performance of 1976, Green said, "This is my biggest thrill at UCF. Being a senior, I'm just glad I could do so well in one of my final games." Torchy joyfully summed up his senior's outstanding play: "David Green is the best overtime player in the country."

Incomprehensibly, the Knights outscored the Tars in overtime 24–7. UCF defeated Rollins 95–78 in thrilling fashion as Green (11) and Lingelbach (9) scored 20 of the Knights' overtime points. Green's 11 straight points in overtime were more points than the entire Rollins team (7) had scored in the extra period.

For the game Lingelbach (24 points), Clark (22 points), and Prather (16 points) led the Knights' scoring attack in the *epic comeback*. BUT

TORCHY

IT WAS TORCHY'S TIMEOUT, CALVIN LINGELBACH, DAVID GREEN, AND THE FRENZIED UCF CROWD WHO WERE THE TRUE HEROES!

"Calvin Cool's" determination and perseverance emotionally propelled the Knights to win. Calvin Lingelbach—unheralded, unsung: Calvin Lingelbach—the man who gave UCF the 1976 Sunshine State Championship and a ticket to the NCAA South Region Tournament.

Larry Guest (1976) of the *Orlando Sentinel* wrote, "This time (game two) the hero was Calvin Lingelbach, a scrawny, loose-jointed, disheveled guard who surely must be Raggedy Ann's older brother. 'Lingle Dingle,' as colorful Coach Torchy Clark has dubbed him, could take a shower in a drain pipe. Like so many of Torchy's rag-tag collection of undersized runts, you're not sure whether those are his ribs or if he's wearing a herringbone suit.

"But he must have looked like Mean Joe Greene to the Rollins' Tars in the stretch Tuesday night as he led a disrupting full-court press that kept picking Rollins' pockets and breaking Knights for repeated lay-ups as that marvelous 22-point lead steadily vanished" (Guest, 1976).

Ray Ridenour, UCF's assistant, remarked after the game, "We had one goal in the game when we found ourselves down 22. We wanted to be down by four buckets with four minutes to play. And when that four-minute mark hit, we were down four buckets. That's what won it for us" (Coble, 1976).

After working for Torchy several more years, Ridenour became the head basketball coach at Daytona State in 1980, averaging 24 wins a year in 13 phenomenal seasons. He was one of the best ever at Daytona State. The loyal Ridenour played a titanic role in Torchy's success at UCF with his fabulous recruiting—signing several talented blue-chippers each year. No one did it better than Ray Ridenour.

Glenn Wilkes, the legendary Stetson University basketball coach for over three decades, witnessed the UCF–Rollins game that night as a spectator and said, "It was an unbelievable comeback, one of the greatest I've seen."

Lingelbach, deservedly so, cut the championship net that night, symbolizing a conference basketball championship, the first ever in school's history. Bo Clark summed up the wild sequence of events after the game: "Calvin is the best pressure player I played with in my career. When the pressure is on, Calvin comes through."

Torchy recalled his team's relentless spirit: "Calvin was terrific. He hit clutch shot after clutch shot. That was the most amazing comeback I've ever seen anytime, anywhere—under any circumstances. We were picked fifth in the Sunshine State preseason basketball poll. And we won it!!"

Bill Buchalter (1976) of the *Orlando Sentinel* wrote, "The game was two . . . no make it three games in one. Three distinct battles between two of the nation's best Division II basketball teams. Rollins was the winner of the first game, running off a 22-point lead in the first 28 minutes (20-minute first half, first eight minutes of second half). Then UCF won the next two games, a full-court press and Calvin Cool blitzing the Tars in the final 12 minutes of the second half, followed by the five-minute overtime session to pull off the victory."

President Charles Millican of UCF was uplifted by the fascinating turnabout in momentum. He was uplifted a second time to help cut the championship net in celebration of the never-to-be-forgotten blockbuster win. "The Rematch" of Rollins-UCF on February 24, 1976, according to many basketball aficionados, fans, coaches, and players, was "one of the greatest games ever."

Larry Guest (1976) of the *Orlando Sentinel* concluded, "that anyone who didn't get excited at this game could get himself declared legally dead. And anyone who didn't extend at least a silent salute of admiration to those big-hearted little guys in their black and gold underwear, don't even register on the compassion scale." Guest summarized UCF's unbelievable feat rather fittingly: "The stunning comeback was a work of art. It was pure Carnegie Hall. It should be framed and hung in the Louvre alongside Rembrandt, Caruso, the Hope Diamond, and Jonas Salk."

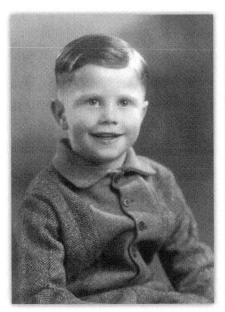

Eugene Allan Clark at age three
(Clark family photo)

Torchy's younger brother Jim at
age 30 (Clark family photo)

1949-50 Marquette University basketball team. Torchy (#37) is in front
row center. (Marquette University Raynor Memorial Libraries Archives)

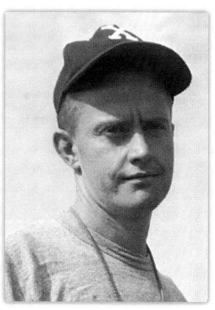

St. Mary's Grade School
Basketball Team (1953)
(Clark family photo)

A young Torchy coaching Xavier
football (Xavier HS photo)

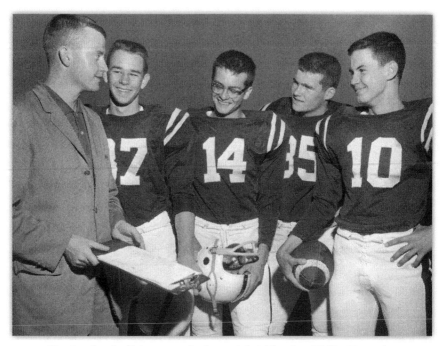

Xavier football in 1960. Left to right, Torchy, Kelly Kornely,
Dick Rankin, Tom Peeters, and Dick Weisner (Xavier HS photo)

Xavier High School—1962 Wisconsin Football State Champions (9-0)
(Xavier HS photo)

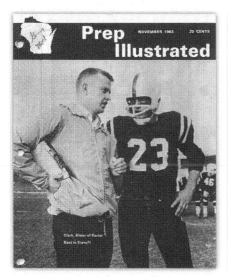

Torchy and Rocky Bleier on
the cover of *Wisconsin Prep
Illustrated* (1963).

Bleier played for the Pittsburgh
Steelers (1968, 1970–80) and won
four Super Bowls.
(Xavier HS photo)

Xavier scoring sensation Kip Whitlinger drives to the basket against Marquette High. (*Appleton Post-Crescent* photo)

Xavier High School—WCIAA 1963 Basketball State Champions (25-0) (Xavier HS photo)

Torchy clutches the 1963 state championship trophy with Dick Weisner and Kip Whitlinger (left to right). (Xavier HS photo)

Torchy hoisted by the champion Hawks (1963) after defeating
Milwaukee Marquette 71–66 (Xavier HS photo)

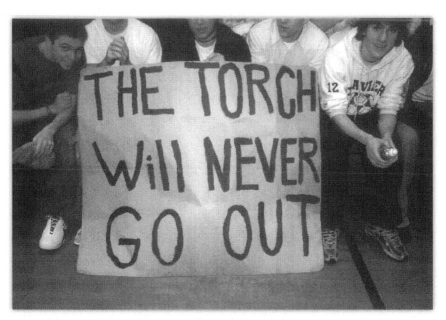

Xavier fans chanted "The Torch Will Never Go Out" when the game
was in hand (Xavier HS photo)

Post-Crescent Magazine
Sunday, March 22, 1964

The devoted Claire cheers on the Hawks in
Milwaukee (*Appleton Post-Crescent* photo)

Torchy is presented a clock by Hawks seniors Mike Heideman
(far left) and Paul Rechner (center) in commemoration of his 100th
conference victory (1966). (*Appleton Post-Crescent* photo)

FTU/UCF's early Department of Physical Education headed by
Dr. Frank Rohter seated fourth from left to right (Clark family photo)

Torchy huddles with the first UCF
team (1969) that finished 11–3.
(UCF photo)

UCF Hall of Famer Mike Clark
(UCF photo)

Torchy celebrates a 1980 win at
Rollins with Appleton native
Paul Haas (#55). (UCF photo)

Torchy and assistant Russ Salerno
(1971) coaching the Knights
(UCF photo)

Torchy is carried off the court (1976) after the Knights' upset of
#1 nationally ranked Florida Southern. (UCF photo)

Torchy in his office. Picture of brother-in-law, Jim Bunning, Baseball
Hall of Famer, behind Torchy's right shoulder. (UCF photo)

The 1978–79 (19–7) UCF Knights and Torchy in front of the school's
reflecting pond (UCF photo)

Torchy's *"greatest player at UCF,"* NCAA II All-American Jerry Prather, shoots a jumper. (UCF photo)

In a rare moment, a calm Torchy (1975) watches as assistant Ray Ridenour jumps for joy. (UCF photo)

Torchy's *greatest* UCF team, the 1977–78 Final Four (26–4) Knights that won 24 consecutive games (UCF photo)

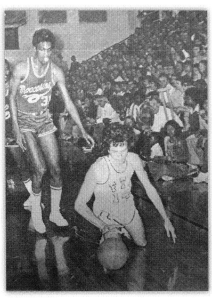

Torchy: "If Calvin Lingelbach was stock, I'd buy it out." (UCF photo)

Torchy's favorite part of coaching was teaching the game. (UCF photo)

Torchy juggled the coaching duties of both football and basketball at Xavier. (Clark family photo)

Torchy works his bench (1980) in a sold-out UCF Gym. (UCF photo)

Torchy and Claire with their children and grandchildren (2003)
at Orlando's Amway Arena (Clark family photo)

Three generations of coaches: Left to right, JP (grandchild),
Bo, and Torchy (1997) (*St. Augustine Record* photo)

Torchy and lifetime friend Bob Willis at Tinker Field (1980)
in Orlando (Photo by Bob Watson)

Torchy and Claire at her St. Margaret Mary (Winter Park, Florida) retirement party (Clark family photo)

Gene "Torchy" Clark Gym at Xavier High School in Appleton, Wisconsin (Xavier HS photo)

UCF's leader in career wins (274–89) (UCF photo)

Torchy and Bo banners hang from the rafters
at UCF's Arena. (UCF photo)

Torchy in front of his tribute display at the Florida Sports
Hall of Fame (Clark family photo)

Claire was a constant ray of sunshine who brightened the day
of anyone she met. (Clark family photo)

CHAPTER 22

Family

Torchy and Claire were proud parents and raised five children: Mike was born in Milwaukee during their Marquette days, and Tom, Bo, Bob, and Patty were all born in Appleton. The devoted dad loved his family and spending precious time with them. Many Appleton days, Torchy would allow one or two of his boys to tag along with him to Hawks' football or basketball practices. At Xavier, he was deeply immersed in his multiple roles as teacher, athletic director, and coach.

Surprisingly, the busy redhead also worked as an official for ten years, refereeing high school football and basketball games throughout the snowy roads of Eastern and Central Wisconsin. The extra money supplemented his family's income, allowing Claire to stay home with the children. Torchy recalled, "Many nights I would referee with Bob Willis or Dave Hussey—make $25 for the game and spend $5 for a beer and a sandwich on the trip back. I would put the other $20 on the kitchen counter for Claire to buy groceries for the week."

Claire steered the ship in the Clark household. She was a gentle soul. Torchy emphasized, "To my way of thinking, the man should be the head of the family and the woman the heart. We go to our strength. We have been given strength by God." Torchy added, "I was stronger at discipline than Claire. I also handled the pressure in the family. Claire gives the charity, the love, and the little services."

The Hawks' mentor continued to expound on his foundation for life: "When I first heard Lombardi on TV, in the early 1960s, he emphasized the three most important things in his life are God, family, and the Green Bay Packers. I shouted to Claire in the kitchen that I said the same thing eight years earlier. But my version was, God, family, and your occupation [pharmacist, certified financial planner, coach, real estate agent, bricklayer]. Think about it . . . start with God and keep him No. 1," continued the coaching lifer. "Follow with No. 2, which is your family, and then No. 3 is your life's work. It's so simple, but you have to work at it. Good things come hard. But remember, I operate off of simplicity, and it's easy."

Claire handled the money and the checkbook. "Why?" said Torchy. "Because that's her strength. It's old-fashioned, I know, but that's the way we did it for 57 years. We worked together as a team. Troubles popped up like technical fouls, and we weren't immune to arguments and flare-ups."

Blessed with a marvelous Oshkosh sense of humor, Torchy laughed at his handyman abilities around the house: "I never had a callus on my hand from a tool or hammer in my life! I wasn't proud of it, but I wasn't good at fixing things. I didn't know the difference between a Phillips screwdriver or flat-head. Claire repaired the little things and sometimes one of the boys helped. In a few scenarios, we had to bite the bullet and bring in a professional."

UCF's first basketball coach jokingly reflected, "As a fun way of poking at my lack of handyman skills, Claire developed a scoring system for me:

CLAIRE'S SCORING SYSTEM

16 points	If you cut the grass
8 points	If you say "please" and "thank you"
1 point	If you win a conference championship in basketball or football
2 points	If you are selected "Coach of the Year"
18 points	If you help paint the master bathroom
2 points	If you win 24 consecutive games
15 points	For washing the car
1 point	For 40 years of teaching
25 points	If you repair a leaky toilet
1 point	If you give a banquet talk or write a book
2 points	For never missing a paycheck in 41 years

Torchy strongly emphasized, "Claire is still Division I!!" On his good fortune of marrying his beloved Claire, the outstanding teacher advised his UCF students by saying, "It's all about the draft! It's all about the draft! That's the one thing you can control in your life is—who you marry. I always said I was blessed to have Claire. For me, she was a high draft pick. And I signed her to a lifetime contract!"

The father of five discussed his life goals: "After we got married, we wanted a family, and I wanted to be a coach. I had four specific goals which all came true: (1) I got married, (2) I raised a family, (3) I got the opportunity to coach and work with young people, and (4) I got the opportunity to coach my sons. Teaching and coaching has been a beautiful way to make a living. My joy was my family," said Torchy.

The caring and loyal father continued: "I enjoyed bringing my sons as kids to practice. They were able to shoot baskets on the side goals or throw the football on the sideline. It is one of the great perks of coaching—to have your family involved. Looking back, it allowed me to spend precious time with my kids . . . an innocent, fast-moving period of their lives you can never get back. Many times watching them . . . brought me back to my childhood in the late 1930s shooting baskets at Oshkosh State.

"My father [Donald] said to us growing up, 'find a job in your life that you enjoy going to work each day. Do something that makes you happy,'" recalled Torchy. "I was truly happy teaching and coaching. We did not have a lot of money, but the little things were important."

Torchy remembered his special touch of heaven: "Happiness for me was going to basketball practice on Thanksgiving morning in Wisconsin and come home to my wife and five children. The fireplace is glowing, my wife is cooking the turkey, it's snowing outside, the T.V. is on, and the Packers are kicking off to the Lions."

Not having a lot of money didn't imply that the longtime coach couldn't enjoy the finer comforts of life every so often. Of course, they were less frequent and more on the humble side. But that was okay, money was not important to Torchy—happiness was.

The teacher and coach at St. Mary's in Appleton recaptured another life lesson he learned, whether rich or poor, from the late 1950s regarding the *simple* pleasures of life. He recalled a trip to the Windy City four hours away: "I drove to Chicago to see the White Sox and the Tigers play at Comiskey Park to watch Jim [Bunning] pitch. Rocky Colavito, the All-Star outfielder, and Jim were roommates while playing for the Tigers. Both were class guys."

After the game, Rocky, Jim, and Torchy got a bite to eat. The three walked to a pub a few blocks from the hotel where the Tigers were staying. Torchy recounted, "Colavito ordered a chopped sirloin, so did I. Colavito ordered a bottle of Hamm's beer, so did I. He owned a Cadillac. I owned a Ford. He had a beautiful wife named Carmen. I had a beautiful wife named Claire. Outside of Colavito hitting the long ball and having a better throwing arm, we were the same. You don't need a lot of money," stressed Torchy.

In the Clark household, sports played an integral role, especially attending Torchy's football and basketball games. For the Clarks, the social calendar always revolved around his games in Appleton or Orlando.

Torchy illustrated a typical game-day routine in the Clark household: "Before each (UCF) home basketball game, I always took a shower at 6:00 p.m., when I would hear my wife and daughter, Patty, talking about what they are going to wear to the game. Bo, who lived at home his freshman year at UCF, is getting his ankles taped by Tom. Bo is a player, and Tom is the manager/trainer. As part of his pregame ritual, Bo wants his ankles taped at home, allowing Tom more time when he arrives at the gym.

"Tom and Bo leave first; my other two sons, Mike and Bob, leave next. Patty, Claire, and I all go together. We all have the same *cause*. It is clean and honest fun. When the game is over, I don't go to parties. I'm too exhausted; I have put everything I have into the game. We usually all meet at the house around 10:30 or 11:00 p.m., watch the local sports and talk things over for 15 minutes. And then the independence starts," continued Torchy. "Claire and I go out for a pizza, and my kids divide with each other or friends. We were truly blessed as a family," he added of his endearing memories.

Some nights after UCF games, Torchy's daughter Patty, the youngest and a cheerleader at Bishop Moore, walked with her dad in the neighborhood, trying to help him unwind from an emotional game. Torchy proudly added, "These are the real fringe benefits of coaching, and yes, it was a family affair. At least it was for us!!"

Torchy liked to tell the story of his two sons, Mike and Bo, who together at UCF scored almost 5,000 points (without a rebound). But the most valuable player in the Clark family was Claire. And second-oldest son Tom received votes for MVP. A six-year team manager for Torchy at UCF, Tom began his "labor of love" while in high school. The grateful father reminisced about Tom's blue-collar and humble work ethic: "He does everything for me, including lugging team uniforms, washing and cleaning equipment, training (in the beginning), and virtually everything. He has been my MVP at UCF. I don't know what I would have done without Tom."

In 1974, the UCF Knights traveled to Spain on their once-every-four-years NCAA-allowable foreign tour. Tom, the smartest student in the Clark family, was forced into playing action with a shortage of UCF players that summer. "Tom is six-foot-two and played high school basketball at Bishop Moore. He has flat feet, plays hard, but isn't the greatest player," explained Torchy. "But everybody loves Tom . . . he is likeable and has an engaging personality. Tom was really sharp."

UCF was in Barcelona to play three Spanish teams in exhibition games for the week, and Torchy remembered the irony of the scenario: "We were practicing in an arena that sat 8,000. I called Tom over to center court and privately said to him, 'What the heck are you doing playing basketball in Barcelona, Spain?' Both Tom and I had a good laugh."

Regarding that same trip, the UCF coach reminisced about a funny incident: "One night during one of the games in Spain, I could not handle the horrible officiating any longer. I don't speak Spanish, so I started yelling, 'El Stinko, El Stinko, El Stinko' on every poor call. The next day my interpreter said the referee asked him, 'Why is the American coach [Torchy] yelling 'El Stinko' all the time?' The interpreter told the referee not to worry . . . "El Stinko" is one of his [Torchy's] players."

One of Torchy's refereeing partners was Bob Willis, who became a lifetime confidant. Willis owned a successful dry cleaning business in Appleton. Torchy and Willis developed a friendship over the years. On a visit to Willis' shop to pick up his clean shirts on a hot summer

Appleton day, Torchy smelled the tremendous solvent in the store. The Xavier coach squawked at his friend, "Bob, these fumes are going to kill you someday. I don't know how you do it. I could not handle this every day."

The Baltimore Orioles had a Class-A Midwest League team in Appleton, the Appleton Foxes, who played at Goodland Field. The general manager position became available, and Torchy recommended his buddy Willis. Leaving the dry cleaning business and the solvent, Willis became the new general manager of the Appleton Foxes from 1958–63. Ironically, the farm team was managed in 1960 and 1961 by a young Earl Weaver who was working his way up to the Major Leagues. Willis would play transformational roles in the lives of Harry Nelson, Jim Clark, and Torchy Clark, recommending all three for coaching positions in Florida. And Willis batted a thousand at the plate, as all three close friends were hired and moved to the Sunshine State.

Bob Willis also played an instrumental role in the life of one of MLB's greatest, Rod Carew. When Carew was playing with the Class A Florida State League Orlando Twins, Willis was the general manager of the ball club. Larry McCarthy (1988) of the *Orlando Sentinel* reported, "Rod Carew, prone to moodiness, was in his first season of pro ball and one night walked off the field in the middle of a game, went into the clubhouse and began taking a shower. Manager Harry Warner was livid! Willis, watching from his box seat at Tinker Field, wondered what was going on and rushed to the clubhouse. The first thing he saw was Carew taking a shower.

"Willis read Carew the riot act. Carew said, 'The players don't like me. They're on my case and I'm quitting.' Willis said, 'There are only two people you listen to—me and the manager. If you leave, you are going to have to do it over my body.' Carew regained his composure, dressed back, and went back to the bench.

"Willis saved Carew's career and later delivered a future Hall of Famer [1991] to the Minnesota Twins. 'That was one of the biggest things in my life, making sure Carew didn't get out of that clubhouse,' Willis said. "Carew a few years later said, 'If it weren't for Bob Willis, I'd be riding a subway now and carrying a lunch bucket.'"

Rod Carew was an 18-time MLB All-Star with the Minnesota Twins and the California (Los Angeles) Angels. His lifetime batting average was .328, and seven times he led the American League in hitting. Carew's jersey No. 29 is retired by both the Twins and Angels organizations.

Torchy shared a story called "You Figure this One Out." He remembers the 1970 game in Atlanta when he was coaching his son, Mike, at UCF in the early years. About an hour before the game Torchy was sitting with the opponent's assistant coach in the first row of the bleachers in the small gym. The two began to visit as the opposing players came strolling in across the hardwood floor.

The assistant said, "See our kid in the red sweater? He can really fill it up!"

"Good shooter?" Torchy asked.

"Deadly," the assistant said.

"See the kid behind him—he can really fill it up too!" added the assistant.

Torchy followed, "You've got a couple of good shooters, huh?"

The assistant replied, "The big guy sitting in the bleachers is also one of our top shooters—he really fills it up!

"And one more thing—the last guy coming into the gym with the green hoodie, is lights out our best pure shooter. He can really fill it up too."

The Knights' coach thought to himself . . . WOW! They have FOUR guys that can shoot it. Torchy noticed he said or asked nothing about his (UCF) team. He then reminded himself the words of wisdom from a wise friend who said, "You don't learn anything with your mouth open."

Torchy said nothing, but observed, "Now, I began watching and listening to their handsome and polished head coach. He was six-foot-two with an outgoing and bubbly personality. He was greeting all the parents and showing them their seats." Torchy thought, "Boy, what a nice person! Plus, he had four guys who could *fill it up*. Reflecting, I envied him with his class and kindness. And his elite shooting team!"

The game started as Torchy recalled, "We are beating the four sharpshooters by eight points at half. They played a rough, physical style of play. With 2:30 left in the game, we were up 10 points. They began to undercut our players, including my son, Mike, as he drove to the basket several times.

"'Fast Eddie' Smith, my excellent 28-year-old guard, came over to me and said, 'Coach, get Mike outta there before they hurt him!' I immediately got Mike out like 'Smitty' had said. We won by 12 and Mike had 43 points. On leaving the gym after the game, I heard the voice of the cocky assistant who said, '*Hey, Coach, your son—really fills it up!!*' I knew that and laughed. Remember these four things:

1. We won.
2. Mike had 43 points.
3. We kept our mouths shut before the game.

"What's number four? You guessed it! *Answer:* If their head coach is such a nice guy, polite, and courteous, then why didn't he control his team when they undercut our players three or four times? Sometimes, what we see and hear can be deceiving."

Another family story is called "Claire's Bracelet." Torchy tells it: "When I was coaching in Appleton in the 1960s, Vince Lombardi was in our backyard. Lombardi gave his wife Marie a bracelet with seven miniature silver footballs on it from two Super Bowl Championships and five Conference Championships. I said to myself, 'Great, I'll give Claire a bracelet with our 15 conference championships and two State Championships.' So, I had a beautiful 17-ball bracelet made up . . . yes, a combined 17 miniature silver footballs and basketballs. A year later, I said to Claire, 'You never wear that bracelet I bought you.' She said, 'Torchy, it's too heavy!' *Remember, winning is hard!!"*

To the 1951 Marquette graduate, coaching was important, but more meaningful was his role as a husband and father. As the oldest of Torchy and Claire's five children, Mike, remembered, "Torchy took his parenting very serious. If you had a problem or needed advice, he was always there. He was a good listener . . . one of the best. That's probably a side of his personality that a lot of people didn't see. He loved being around his family."

Fishing was one of Torchy's favorite hobbies. Many Sundays, Torchy would bring the kids to Lake Poygan, near the charming village of Winneconne 30 minutes from Appleton to fish. "I remember him smoking his corncob pipe, fishing, and relaxing. It was his escape from coaching. For a few hours, he didn't have to worry about the excellent shooting of St. Mary's (Menasha) Mike Heroux or the missed extra point in the loss to Bill Fitzpatrick's Dutchmen. Those were special childhood memories," said Bob of the days at the pristine lake in lovely eastern Wisconsin.

As a parent of four sons who played in the talented Appleton Little League and basketball at St. Mary's Grade School, Torchy was far, far away from being a helicopter parent. The dad let his sons' coaches . . . coach. "He probably only went to two or three Little League games each year. And would sit on a park bench by left field keeping his distance. I think being a coach himself, he fully understood his role as a parent: to take a step back," Bob concluded.

An absorbing game Torchy taught his sons was his version of dice baseball. The game itself only required two dice, pencil, paper, and MLB box scores or rosters to write the starting lineups. For the Clark boys growing up in the 1960s, dice baseball became an enjoyable and cheap form of entertainment. Torchy's simple game that he passed on to his sons became precious "memories for life."

In his travels, Torchy found the secret of happiness was to live moment by moment, thanking God for what He is sending us every day in His goodness. The veteran coach loved the quote from St. Francis Assisi, a saint he greatly admired, who said, "We have been called to heal wounds, to unite what has fallen apart and to bring home those who have lost their way." St. Francis continued by saying, "*Faith* is an adventure, a march through a wilderness of doubts." In closing, Torchy remembered, "Appleton was a tremendous place to raise our family. When we left in 1969, we gave our bobblehead collection to the McGinnis family. And one more thing, always remember the draft! But sometimes in life things are like vapors: here and then gone. But the memories remain."

CHAPTER 23

Real Pressure

In 1977, the (23–3) UCF Knights were joined with Armstrong State University, Valdosta State University, and host, University of Tennessee-Chattanooga (UTC) at the NCAA Division II South Region Basketball Championship in Chattanooga, Tennessee. To say the least, it was a brutal region to survive and advance. UCF was matched up against Armstrong State (15–13) and a front line made up of seven-foot Crow Armstrong, six-foot-seven Dennis Davis, and six-foot-five Henry Wright. Host UTC (22–5) would play Valdosta State (22–5) in the second semifinal game.

Before leaving for Chattanooga, UCF's basketball coach spoke briefly to the *Orlando Sentinel*: "This regional is much stronger than last year's. All four teams are excellent and UTC is absolutely loaded with talent."

According to Larry Green of the *Chattanooga News Free-Press* (1977), the beat reporter for UTC covering the NCAA tournament who dutifully observed, "Torchy Clark is another basketball coach. Like most he has the rudiments of his craft mastered. He knows about every zone defense devised. And he can call the corresponding offense to overcome it. He understands weak-side cuts, triangles, box-and-ones, four corners, the works. *But Torchy Clark is not just another basketball coach.* At UCF, an island of higher education on Orlando's hemline, he coaches basketball without the benefit of a classroom.

"Every day he spends hours fighting Orlando traffic to meet the team at practice as his players ride in two vans driven by assistants to a high school gym on loan, where Torchy will probably be faced by unimaginable practice situations his team will have to deal with." Larry Green continued, "When the school where his team is practicing has a dance scheduled, his team fires jump shots around crepe paper decorations and dribbles through homecoming throne rooms of cardboard. Luckily, Torchy is a man of patience.

"Once the game starts he rants, he raves, he squats in front of his chair, he encourages and he motivates his players to greater things. That is a part of his obligation to his team—coach to players. Along the way he built a reputation as a man who adequately befit his nickname. 'Torchy' burned brightly with enthusiasm, intensity, and candor. It wasn't an act, but rather an approach that came quite naturally. 'After a game a fan said to me "that was quite a show you put on tonight," said Torchy. UCF's coach responded, 'That wasn't a show. We were coaching. I think when you're animated and you're involved, you really don't care, and I really didn't. In my way of thinking, it makes a difference. Anyone who has a little *tornado* in them, their team is going to play better ball,' strongly emphasized Torchy." Green (1977) described the UCF coaching icon through the lens of life's BIG picture: "He is short physically. With an even shorter fuse. But he knows the game, knows its place in his life and has a philosophy that has to be inscribed on a stone tablet somewhere."

UTC hosted a pre-tournament banquet-luncheon for all tournament coaches and fans (mostly UTC boosters) at the Chattanooga Tip-Off Club. It's customary for the NCAA host school to hold a banquet before a qualifying postseason tournament. Each of the four participating coaches were scheduled to speak and give a brief synopsis of their ball clubs. All praised the unbelievable hospitality and class of Chattanooga. But the several hundred people in attendance were curious to hear how each team matched up against their beloved Mocs. And the fans of Chattanooga had an undying loyalty and passion for their hometown team!

It was tournament time, which means regular season records are thrown out the window. A good record doesn't help anymore. Torchy was the last coach scheduled to speak at the March 1977 luncheon. Thirty years prior he had graduated from St. Mary's Menasha High School and lived in Oshkosh. But now Torchy listened to each coach talk of pressure: pressure of tournament play, pressure of winning, and the pressure to make your college, alumni, and community proud.

"We lost eight games by a total of 15 points," said Armstrong's boss Bill Alexander. "We haven't jelled yet, but we have won some big games in the last few weeks, when it came down to nut-cutting time. You can bet these two games up here will be close ones." The Pirates were the dark horse. UTC's Coach Ron Shumate was very worried. "I'm as scared going into this regional as I've been going into a tournament." Shumate continued, "Last year we played inspired basketball and won. We have to do that this time, and I'm not sure we are capable. We've won a regional before. Maybe it just doesn't mean as much to us now. It seems like all we think about is the nationals. Well, while we're thinking about Springfield [Final Four]—just winning this regional means more to Valdosta State, UCF, or Armstrong State than anything in the world. They've never won one and they want it bad."

Valdosta was coached by the veteran James Dominey, who played a demanding schedule against the likes of Division I schools: Middle Tennessee State, Tennessee Tech, and Georgia Southern. The Blazers had Mark Patrick, Jackie Manuel, and Bruno Caldwell to draw points and rebounds. Guard Larry Miller was a steadying influence for an excellent, well-coached Valdosta team.

FINALLY, it was Torchy's turn as he stepped to the podium as the emcee introduced him. The crowd was anxious to hear about the all-around play of the gifted Jerry Prather, the brilliant leadership of Calvin Lingelbach, the pure athleticism and rebounding talents of Lee Riley, the consistency of UCF's glue guy, Tyrone Sparrow. And Torchy would briefly recognize his sophomore starting guard and son Jim, nicknamed "Bo."

UCF was the highest-ranked team at the South Region with a 23–3 record and a No. 7 national ranking. But the best team was the host, UTC. Most attendees were Mocs' fans who came to hear UTC's Ron Shumate, an excellent strategist and recruiter who had an incredible run in Chattanooga. The fans had wanted to hear his mini-scouting report of the three other teams.

Torchy seemed nervous, and many of his friends thought he was beginning his "afternoon worry" on game day, thinking about Armstrong's State's redwood tree-sized frontline, sheer athleticism, and innovative coaching. But as he spoke, he surprisingly first wanted to *clear* the air of any basketball talk.

The Knights' coach adjusted the height of the microphone. "You know, my little brother Jim was a coach, too, and one day he called me and said, 'Torchy, I'm ready to start a new career and enter the business world. I need a change, a spark.'" Torchy continued, "My brother said he was going to take a job with the Gillette Corporation. A year later, on another call, Jim told me he just got a huge territorial promotion. And he would now be moving into a higher position with the company in Denver. He told me he was the head coach of Gillette, covering the West region. My brother was happy, and I was so proud of him! (Like I was with Sister Joseph Mary at St. Peter's in 1939.)

"After that, Jim, 36, made a couple business trips to Los Angeles and then started having problems with headaches. The doctors told him it was nerves, the pressure of big business. Jim told them it wasn't. He went to another doctor and learned he had a malignant brain tumor. They operated. He died," Torchy sadly explained.

The people at the banquet sat stunned and speechless by the coach's revelation. After 20 seconds of uncomfortable silence, Torchy, now choked up, struggled to say, "A little later Jim's wife Diane called me and said she thought she was pregnant with their *sixth* child. Pressure? That's real pressure." The audience continued to listen and was captivated by this *different coach* who wasn't worried about his matchup against Armstrong State, Valdosta, or UTC or his team's lack of focus or lack of concentration.

Torchy stayed on track by saying, "Every day I pick up the newspaper, and I read about people dying and being killed. And I say a short prayer: God protect his or her soul. I turn the page and there are the obituaries. And I say a prayer for each one: God protect his or her soul. Sometimes you say so many prayers it takes a long time to get through the newspaper.

"And then, I finally come to the sports page and it's hard to take a game serious, to think there is really pressure." Torchy's intimate speech at the tournament luncheon sent a powerful message to all attendees that afternoon. He spoke from the heart. He put things in perspective: Basketball is just a game. An important game, but still only a game.

Green (1977) wrote of the UCF coach: "Thursday night, as Torchy roamed through the Sheraton Downtown (Chattanooga) in between cups of coffee with a friend from Orlando, he decided to buy a chance with a gumball machine. 'It will be a yellow,' he said sternly. 'Well let's make it an omen for the tournament then,' said the friend. 'It will be yellow or blue,' said Torchy, deciding to help his chances, but finally settling for his original choice when pressed. He put the penny in the slot and pulled the handle along the track. And nothing happened. He reached up into the outlet and worked for his prize, his omen. At last, one round ball of sugar slid out and landed in the stop. It was *yellow*. It is highly doubtful that men like Torchy Clark need omens, harbingers of fate's favoritism. A man armed with a realistic outlook on his world doesn't need that to get by."

In the loud and boisterous Maclellan Gym (Big Mac), the Knights defeated Armstrong State 91–82 in the first round of the NCAA South Region behind a combined 58 points from Jerry Prather and Bo Clark. Prather added 12 rebounds in the win. Calvin Lingelbach, playing with a painful knee the entire second half of the season, was courageous and tough as the Knights' quarterback. Lingelbach was at his best as usual during *crunch* time—the last seven minutes against Armstrong. Lee Riley and Tyrone Sparrow were terrific on the boards against the much taller Pirates in UCF's first-ever NCAA Basketball Tournament win. Host UTC defeated Valdosta 92–76 in the second semifinal.

The Knights would play the home team (UTC) in the South Region Championship Saturday night in front of a SRO crowd (4,177). In the title game, Torchy screamed and pleaded with his team as the Chattanooga crowd unmercifully taunted him. They weren't obnoxious, but rather rabid, fanatical college basketball fans urging their Mocs to win a championship for the right to move on to the NCAA Division II Elite-8 in Grand Forks, North Dakota.

Green (1977) summarized his final thoughts on Torchy Clark: "If he won, he could be happy with a job well done, just like another coach. If he lost he will suffer, but it won't crush him. He's not at the bottom of a mine in Pennsylvania, laboring to breathe beneath a pile of rocks. Or fighting to stay alive on small bits of food in some foreign land. *Either way, Torchy Clark is a winner, not just another coach.*"

—Contributions from Larry Green,
Chattanooga News-Free Press, 1977.

CHAPTER 24

Memphis—Lonely Bench

The fog comes on little cat feet. It sits looking over harbor and city on silent haunches and then moves on.

—Carl Sandburg.

In 1973, Memphis State University lost the NCAA Division I Championship Game to John Wooden's UCLA Bruins 87–66. The Gene Bartow-coached 24–6 Tigers were led by Larry Finch, Larry Kenon, and Ronnie Robinson. In the 1976–77 season, Torchy's Knights faced Memphis for the second consecutive year at Mid-South Coliseum in Memphis, Tennessee. In the prior year (1975–76), the Tigers defeated the Knights 76–57. Memphis was a member of the talented Metro Conference and was coached by Wayne Yates. The high-flying Tigers were coming off a 21–9 record and a 1975 NCAA Tournament appearance.

On Friday night, November 26, 1976, UCF defeated Flagler College, 89–62 at home. The next day, Saturday, November 27, the Knights were matched up against powerhouse Memphis on the Tigers' home floor.

The game was scheduled for 8:10 p.m. at Mid-South. Ten thousand tickets had been sold for the 10,815-seat venue.

The scheduling of back-to-back nights was unavoidable, as Flagler and Memphis were unable to change the date of their game with the Knights. Torchy decided to roll with it, assuming there would be no travel hiccups. It was not a standard practice for UCF to travel by plane on game day, gambling with flight delays. The scenario was indeed rare.

The Knights' Saturday itinerary included a 9:00 a.m. commercial flight to Atlanta, a connecting flight to Memphis, a shootaround at Mid-South, the Memphis-UCF game, and then fly back to Orlando the next morning. The hiccups were ready to start.

Torchy remembered the hectic day: "It was foggy as Claire drove me to the Orlando Airport that morning at 7:00. I was a little concerned with the fog, but didn't think it was thick enough to cause any delays. From my frequent trips to the airport, I knew the fog usually lifts by mid-morning." The Knights would face the omnipotent Tigers in 12 hours.

The veteran coach arrived at the airport and headed to the Delta terminal to meet up with his team. "The fog was still bad as we checked in. I thought to myself, we might catch a break and the game may be canceled. We were *only* a 35-point underdog. But games like that always seem to be played," said Torchy with a twist of sarcasm.

The official party included 17 people: 12 players, two coaches, trainer, athletic director, and team manager Tom Clark. The weary UCF players were tired from the previous night's game. The itinerary had the Knights arriving in Memphis at 12:20 p.m. A Mid-South 3:00 shootaround had been scheduled.

The Knights' traveling party was scattered near Gate 11 waiting for the boarding announcement. Jack O'Leary, the loyal UCF athletic director, made the trip to support and assist the team. The first sign of a travel glitch came at 8:45 a.m. as the Delta gate attendant announced the 9:00 flight had been delayed. Strangely, the fog had not lifted, and the delay continued through 10:30. Meanwhile, trainer Ron Ribaric and O'Leary began to explore other flight options out of Orlando.

O'Leary found a flight that bypassed the fog and traveled west instead of north. The available flight took the team to Mobile, Alabama, and then connected to a flight to Memphis. But the next hiccup for the Knights was fast approaching—there were only *seven* seats available on the Mobile-bound plane.

"Torchy, what do you think?" asked O'Leary.

The coach responded, "It's simple, Jack. We'll take the starting five, Ray (assistant coach) and I, so our starters can get some shots up and get a feel for Mid-South. We'll meet you at the arena or the hotel. I'm sure the fog will lift soon and you guys will be there by late afternoon." O'Leary said, "Sounds like a great plan, Torchy!"

After meeting with the entire party on the status of the flight to Atlanta, the team split into two groups. The "Lonely Seven" (five starters and two coaches) hustled to a different gate to catch the Mobile flight; the rest of the traveling party remained at Gate 11 with O'Leary. Unfortunately, the Knights' team equipment and uniforms were on the Atlanta-bound plane on the tarmac entrenched in a deep fog. There wasn't enough time to transfer the gear to the Mobile flight, which had already been delayed 20 minutes.

The "Lonely Seven" arrived in Memphis at 1:30 p.m. As the team was leaving for shootaround, Torchy got a call from son Tom at the front desk of the Memphis-Marriott with the latest 2:30 update: "Dad, we are badly fogged in at Augusta." Torchy questioned his son's response, "Augusta?" Tom continued on the oddity, "We circled Atlanta, but we couldn't land, so they rerouted us here."

O'Leary verified Tom's account of the situation and thought they may get out of Augusta within the next few hours. The Knights' AD told

Torchy to call the Memphis coach and athletic director immediately, explaining the bizarre predicament. The first call was to Memphis Head Coach Wayne Yates, a former six-foot-eight Memphis Tigers superstar (1959–61) and a 1961 NBA first round pick (fifth pick). Yates had short stints in both the NBA (Los Angeles Lakers) and the ABA (Oakland Oaks). The Tigers coach was infuriated, understandably so, with the events that were playing out on game day. Torchy reminded him the Knights played a home game last night and were supposed to land in Memphis today at 12:20 p.m.

Yates didn't want to hear about the travel hiccups and decisively said, "We have to play this game. This is our home opener! We have 10,000 people coming tonight." Torchy's *obvious* concern was having only five players. And the possibility of someone fouling out or an injury forcing the team to play with four. He also reminded Yates pointedly the Knights had no gear and no equipment. The frustrated Memphis coach concluded the heated conversation, "You better call our athletic director."

The Memphis AD, too, was terribly flustered. But as athletic directors do, he wisely suggested a remedy to the once-in-a-lifetime scenario. The AD informed Torchy that they (Memphis) would provide UCF with game gear—a set of road Memphis uniforms, shoes, and any game necessities. The game time would be pushed to 9:00 p.m., hoping the other UCF players would arrive by then. Torchy bravely asked, "How about if we play tomorrow night?" The AD, now angry, shot down his request for a game postponement and said, "That's *impossible*, we rented Mid-South Coliseum for tonight, and we have to play!"

Torchy's next call was to his Knights' boss, who was still stranded in Augusta. "What do you think, Jack?" said UCF's coach, knowing well the situation was uncontrollable.

"Play 'em," O'Leary replied with no uncertainty.

The five Knight players wore street clothes for their team's shoot-around at the Coliseum. Each player was issued a new pair of white high-top Converse Chuck Taylor All-Stars by the Memphis equipment manager for the night's game. Right out of the box!

During the one-hour walk-through, Torchy laid out his game plan meticulously. His blueprint was to spread the floor offensively against the taller Tigers using valuable clock time on each possession. There was no shot clock in college basketball at this time. According to Torchy, the less Memphis had the basketball, the greater chance his Knights had to win. His strategy sounded familiar—almost identical to Marinette Central's in the 1964 Wisconsin Basketball State Championship.

After shootaround, Torchy got yet another call: The remaining UCF players would be arriving at 7:30 for the now-9:00 p.m. start. "At this time, we thought our other players would meet us at the Coliseum," said the relieved coach.

As the "Lonely Seven" prepared to leave for the game from the Marriott, a giant 56-passenger chartered bus authorized by the Memphis Athletic Department pulled up near the hotel's front entrance. "Heck, we didn't need a bus, we could have taken a minivan," recalled Torchy. On arriving at Mid-South, the players went directly to the equipment room. Each player was given a navy Memphis jersey and game pants, two pairs of white socks, tights, and a towel. The seven-year-old uniforms were embroidered with large scripted "Tigers" in white with a tint of orange trim.

At 8:15, as the five Knights took the floor for pregame warm-ups, Torchy and Ray Ridenour were told by a Memphis assistant AD the other group of Knights did not make it out of Augusta. They were not coming! It would be a lonely bench. But Torchy still had a game plan to beat Memphis with five players.

According to Brandon Helwig (2012) the publisher of UCFSports .com, the game was special for Knights' junior standout Jerry Prather, who grew up in New Albany, Mississippi, located 80 miles southeast of Memphis. "I was excited to play in front of the hometown fans, at least a few from New Albany," Prather said.

MEMPHIS vs. UCF (November 27, 1976)
(from Bobby Hall [1976], *The Commercial Appeal*, Memphis Tennessee)

Memphis Starting Line-up
F–James Bradley, 6'8, sophomore
F–John Gunn, 6'9, junior
C–John Washington, 6'11, senior
G–Dexter Reed, 6'4, senior
G–Alvin Wright, 5'11, junior

UCF Starting Line-up
F–Jerry Prather, 6'3, junior
F–Tyrone Sparrow, 6'3, senior
C–Lee Riley, 6'4, junior
G–Bo Clark, 6'1, sophomore
G–Calvin Lingelbach, 6'2, senior

RESERVES: Rodney Lee, 6'7, sophomore
  Smoke Holliman, 6'2, junior
  Steve Meacham, 6'8, sophomore
  John Kilzer, 6'6, sophomore
  Buster Hancock, 6'0, junior
  Lee Saunders, 6'1, freshman
  Dennis Isbell, 6'7, junior

RESERVES: NONE

RADIO: WMC-AM 79; TELEVISION: WKNO-TV (Channel 10), replay at 10:15 PM

"We had no subs. Memphis wore their home jerseys, and we wore an old set of their road uniforms. Each of us could pick any number. In the locker room, we all laughed at wearing Memphis' jerseys. At least for one game, we could tell our kids we played Division I basketball," reminisced Bo Clark.

Prather, the best player in the Torchy era, remembered the 1976 night in Tennessee: "I think it was a huge surprise to the fans when we walked out on the court looking like Memphis. That was the big joke in the Coliseum. They thought it would be a blowout with us being NCAA II. It was definitely humbling."

On paper, the high-flying Tigers held every advantage over the shorthanded and much smaller Knights. Lee Riley, a six-foot-four center and transfer from Polk Junior College in Winter Haven, Florida, was the starting post. A rebounding machine, Riley had a spectacular career and was a walking double-double. His all-around play, unselfishness, and athleticism helped the Knights to two incredible seasons with records of 24–4 and 26–4. Riley was a key player on Torchy's greatest at UCF—the 1977–78 Final Four team.

Senior starting forward Tyrone Sparrow was a six-foot-three "tweener" who rebounded like he was six-foot-seven. The 26-year-old, an Orlando Jones High School graduate, had already served in the military as a U.S. Marine before coming to UCF. "He's one of my favorite people; he's an adult. He is a very, very unselfish ball player. He's a team player, and that says it all," said Torchy about his unsung player he had the privilege to coach.

As tip-off began, Torchy's players knew they had no substitutes; but his Knights played hard and battled every possession. Despite the daunting odds, the Knights made a game of it. Riley and Sparrow battled toe-to-toe against the Tigers' front court of six-foot-eight forward James Bradley, six-foot-nine forward John Gunn, and six-foot-eleven center John Washington. Lingelbach and Prather penetrated the lane easily for pull-up jumpers. The dynamic duo played with Division I confidence; and both looked like All-Metro Conference guards against the mighty Tigers.

Torchy used every delay game in his bag of tricks: triangles, oranges, and five-men out, forcing the Tigers to extend their defense and guard the quicker Knights. The outmanned UCF hit shot after shot, handled Memphis' pressure, and completely stunned the 10,518 fans.

"I think the whole arena was surprised. The game went back and forth as we matched Memphis basket for basket. Yates (Memphis' coach) was astounded by our speed and shooting," said Prather. UCF kept it close throughout the first half and trailed only 38–32 at the intermission. The crowd themselves were dumbfounded, but impressed by the swagger of the small-college Knights.

The 38–32 Memphis halftime lead was a sweeping testament to Torchy's master coaching, motivational ability, and strategic expertise. The first half was sheer coaching brilliance as his fire and obligation gave his spunky Knights a chance to upset the Tigers. The next day, in *The Commercial Appeal* (Memphis) sports section was the feature game story accompanied by a photo of UCF's *lonely team bench* with only Torchy and Ray Ridenour in the picture.

The Florida Hall of Famer fondly recalled a touching moment of the 1976 game: "After returning to the court after halftime, the 10,000-plus fans gave us a beautiful round of applause that traveled like a wave around the arena. Yeah, I got a chill from the kind gesture and appreciation from the Memphis fans. They truly respected our great play and effort.

"With a minute left on the halftime running clock as our players were warming up, I walked over to the long Mid-South scorer's table and said, '*Mister Scorekeeper, we'll start the same five as the first half.*'" It brought down the house!

The Knights could not keep up with Memphis in the second half. "We ran out of gas the last 8 to 10 minutes of the game. Memphis took control during this tough stretch. We played so hard, and tonight, it was with only five guys," said Torchy of his team's gutty performance.

Luckily, UCF did not have anyone foul out. "Jerry (Prather) got his fourth foul in the second half and we were worried he'd get his fifth," remembered point guard Lingelbach. Memphis beat the short-handed Knights 84–53. The Tigers were led by James Bradley who scored 18 points, and John Gunn chipped in with a double-double with 15 points and 10 rebounds.

UCF's Prather said that he never played in front of more fans. "It doesn't matter who they play, Memphis always supports their basket-ball," Prather noted. "The biggest thing in Memphis has always been the Tigers. I think the game prepared us for the rest of the season. It gave us confidence. We thought, if we can hang with Memphis, we can play with anybody on our schedule," continued the talented Prather. His quote was prophetic.

Three days later, the Knights played on the road in Tampa against Division I South Florida (USF). The Knights defeated the Bulls, 66–57, at downtown's Curtis Hixon Hall. After the game, Torchy, surrounded by the press, well-wishers, and family remarked, "Our guard play was terrific tonight. That was the difference in us beat-ing USF. We have to be the best no-gym team in the country! But sometimes in life things are like vapors: here and then gone. But the memories remain."

CHAPTER 25

Final Four

The year was 1978. "When you come this far," said UCF Sports Information Director Neil Labar, "all the teams are tough." The Torchy-led Knights were 26–2, riding a remarkable 24-game winning streak and very much aware of that fact while taking nothing for granted. The UCF Knights earned their way to the 1978 Division II Final Four Basketball Championship in Springfield, Missouri, along with Cheyney State University, Eastern Illinois University, and the University of Wisconsin-Green Bay.

The UCF 1977–78 team was led by senior and four-year player Jerry Prather, who averaged 21.6 points, 9.3 rebounds, and 3.6 steals per game. Having a record-breaking year, Prather shot a jaw-dropping 59.5 percent from the field. A long, bouncy defender, he was one of the rare UCF players who could guard all five positions. Prather did it all, but most importantly, led with a humble yet warrior mentality.

A Mississippi native who prepped at W. P. Daniel High School in New Albany, Prather was recommended highly by Don Rowe, a Clark family friend and former teacher/basketball coach at St. Margaret Mary Catholic Grade School in Winter Park, Florida.

Rowe had relocated to Aberdeen, Mississippi, and was the assistant basketball coach at Aberdeen High School, 50 minutes north of Starkville.

The basketball Bulldogs of Daniel (1974) were playing Aberdeen as Rowe sat on the opposing bench. The basketball guru was in awe of the slender, pogo-stick Prather who was the "real deal" for Daniel that night. He made a huge impression on Rowe—scoring, defending, rebounding, and making plays at both ends. After the game, Rowe approached the senior All-State player, inquiring about his future. He asked Prather if he had ever heard of UCF in Orlando, Florida.

The next day, Rowe called his longtime friend and strongly endorsed Prather for the Knights. Rowe not only discovered an incredible person, but also discovered the best player at UCF in the Torchy era from 1969–83. With tremendous pride, Torchy articulated, "The three most influential and program-changing players in my fourteen years at UCF were Jerry Prather, Calvin Lingelbach, and Mike Clark. We wouldn't have accomplished what we did in the growing stages of the program without their powerful contributions."

Rowe's tip to recruit the Mississippian was exactly what the doctor ordered for Torchy's Knights. His presence in all four years was critical, but his da Vinci-like impact his last three years led UCF to an amazing record of 70–13. Prather's athletic ability and basketball savvy changed Torchy's teams from a good program to an *elite* national program.

UCF's basketball mentor referred to Prather as his "Ernie Banks." Banks was an 18-year Major League Baseball veteran and Hall of Famer (inducted 1997) for the Chicago Cubs. The humble and friendly Banks was nicknamed "Mister Sunshine," and Cubs fans adored him. UCF's loyal followers loved the easygoing Prather and his exciting, selfless, and passionate spirit. Torchy affirmed, "Never has there been a better guy (maybe Rocky Bleier). He gives you all he's got, and then some. And he's the most coachable kid I've ever had. Jerry did it all with genuine humility and a team-first attitude. When he was on the floor, he made the other players better. I never heard anyone say a bad thing about Jerry."

The 1977–78 season started in an unexpected way. Five days before the home opener in a NCAA-closed scrimmage at home against Division II Bethune-Cookman, Bo Clark, a junior and the previous year's leading scorer from a 24–4 team, broke his foot (fifth metatarsal). With an eight-to-ten week recovery period, Torchy decided to redshirt Bo for the season, preserving a full year of eligibility. This became an epic opportunity for Prather to grab the baton as the main anchor of the mile relay—and take full reins of the team.

The Knights opened the season at home against Flagler. Prather scored 28 points, grabbed six rebounds, and added six steals in an 84–56 win. Torchy recalled the first regular season game: "I'm just glad we got the first one! Jerry had his hands full, but he can handle it." Torchy's up-tempo system was efficient as the Knights scored easy basket after easy basket from the press and fast break.

Three days later, the Knights (2–0) beat a disciplined, physical Benedictine University 64–61 at home. The starting five were Jerry Prather, Lee Riley, Mike Spivey, Cleveland Jackson, and Pete Krull. Will Nix was the valuable sixth man, along with thousands of UCF basketball fans!!

Jackson, a five-foot-eight point guard, was one of assistant coach Ray Ridenour's big-time recruits. A transfer from Shelby State Junior College in Memphis, Tennessee, Jackson was a constant scoring threat. He thrived in Torchy's transition system, averaging 18.7 points per game. "Cleveland had two outstanding years for us. He had an intense passion to win and was the heartbeat of the team," said Torchy.

Spivey was a six-foot-three guard-forward on the prior year's Sunshine State Championship team (1976–77). Blessed with an engaging and dynamic personality, Spivey was thirsty to improve as a player. "Spive was an unbelievable teammate and all about winning. He slid in for Bo at the two guard and also played point guard. Our defense and rebounding improved with him in the lineup," said Torchy.

The 2–0 Knights traveled to Texas to play back-to-back Division I games in consecutive nights against Lamar University and Rice University. The Billy Tubbs-led Lamar Cardinals in 1978 finished 8–2 in the Southland Conference and 18–9 overall. Tubbs had a phenomenal 80-home-game winning streak during his tenure as the Cardinals' coach. With Lamar's home court advantage and greater size, Torchy tried to control the tempo with a patient, disciplined offense using valuable clock time on each possession. The Knights still fell, 65–62, to Lamar in an overtime heartbreaker.

The second night of the back-to-back was against Rice in Houston, about one and a half hours away. The Owls of the Southwest Conference were coached by Mike Shuler, who would later become the head coach of the NBA's Portland Trail Blazers and the Los Angeles Clippers, coaching in 338 NBA games. On Saturday night, Rice beat the Knights 65–63 in a dogfight. UCF now was 2–2 in their young, *unraveling* season.

Four nights later, the Knights matched up at home against Lawrence University, a Division III school located in Appleton, Wisconsin, the city where Torchy and Claire raised their family for 16 years.

The Knights answered the bell against Lawrence, winning the game 100–77 with Prather leading the team with a triple-double stat line of 25 points, 14 rebounds, and 11 steals. New Albany's pride and joy began his first stride of the relay leading the Knights.

Lee Riley, UCF's undersized center, added 15 points and 11 rebounds for a double-double in the Lawrence win. Riley, the gentle, soft-spoken center, did it all for Torchy in his two years. The true unsung hero, Riley, to some UCF fans, may have been the most valuable. The Knights were back on track with a 3–2 record.

UCF then traveled to Columbus State University in Columbus, Georgia, to play in the Cougars' four-team tournament. The Knights beat Knoxville College 95–86 the first night. The championship game matched UCF against the host team, No. 13 nationally ranked Division II Columbus State. Jackson played a spectacular championship game leading Torchy to a 74–62 victory. He was named MVP of the tournament.

The Knights were 5–2 riding a three-game winning streak. "The two wins at Columbus were huge! Our confidence as a team to win on the road was momentous. We were finally able to establish roles within our team and got it together [at Columbus]," noted Torchy.

Krull, a six-foot-six versatile forward with great shooting range and rebounding toughness, had a superb year for the Knights. A prized recruit, Krull was a Wisconsin All-State standout at Wittenberg-Birnamwood High School. Torchy used his home state of Wisconsin as a fertile recruiting ground several times in his 14 years. "We were fortunate to sign him, and the 'Florida Factor' helped. His steady, consistent play and decision-making helped us get to the Final Four."

Nix, a six-foot-five power forward from Cincinnati, Ohio, was a four-year player who Torchy trusted with his experience. Adding veteran depth, Nix was an excellent rebounder and big spark off the bench. The senior played a major role in the Knights' historic run, averaging 6.9 points per game and 5.3 rebounds per game. "Will was a committed teammate and one of our true warriors," added the championship coach.

The Black and Gold kept rolling, winning four straight non-conference games at home to raise their record to 9–2, riding a seven-game winning streak. The players began to believe in each other, but most importantly began to trust Torchy and his system.

UCF roared through the tough Sunshine State Conference unblemished with a 12–0 record! The season was a validation of the team's blue-collar work ethic, the total buy-in, and the absence of any egos. Torchy was three-for-three with Sunshine Regular Season Championships. And in two of the three years his Knights were undefeated in conference play. Yes, the torch was burning brightly on the UCF campus as the hungry and humble cagers now had a magnificent 19-game winning streak!

In Lakeland, the Knights won the Conference Tournament, beating Saint Leo 89–60 in the semifinals and then pounding Rollins 103–66 in the tournament championship game, running their winning streak to 21 games. "I don't know if we can play any better. Mark Freidinger [Rollins' head basketball coach] always does a super job with his kids and always has them ready to play," said Torchy.

After the championship game, Freidinger, in his first year as Rollins' boss, commented on the Knights (1977–78): "It's still Coach Clark's philosophy. They are going to play the way he wants 'em to—just without Calvin (Lingelbach) and Bo (Clark)." Freidinger continued, "Cleveland Jackson has done a great job of stepping in for Lingelbach. He's making things happen, too. He fits right into their style."

Jackson, nicknamed "Pee-Wee," was a one-man wrecking crew against Division I USF in Tampa. Torchy's point guard was 13–14 (FG-FGA) from the field against the Bulls. His 30 points helped the Knights hammer their future in-state rival 79-57. Jackson's play was astonishing to Torchy: "I'm not sure if I have ever seen a better individual game performance than Cleveland's against USF. He scored on everything . . . 20-footers, driving floaters, and transition pull-up jumpers.

"For the first time in all my years of coaching, I felt like the *chaperone* who turned six Frankensteins loose. The kids kinda let me know, 'We understand you and what we have to do.' I've never seen anything like what this team is doing," said Torchy. "But, that's what makes this bunch so special. They are good people. Everybody knows

Prather is the franchise. Jackson is fabulous at stopping and popping. And Riley, he's just been like Abraham Lincoln—darn humble and he boards with the big guys," the coach added proudly.

Hal Wissel, head coach at Florida Southern from 1977–82, a huge rival of UCF, complimented the Knights after a 1978 Mocs loss in Lakeland. "When I was coaching at Fordham University in New York, we played Marquette, and UCF has the same talent and quickness as Marquette. We played 35 super minutes tonight," said Wissel, "but UCF is really good. When they go up, they really go up. I mean their elbows are over the rim. You can't play a disciplined ball control style against them, because they're so quick. You have to shoot it out with those guys."

Torchy and Wissel (UCF-Florida Southern) coached against each other in many intense, high-level Sunshine State games. There was tremendous mutual respect between the coaches and players of each institution. Under Wissel, the Mocs made three straight trips (1980, 1981, and 1982) to the Division II Final Four, winning the National Championship in 1981. Wissel is a published author of two highly successful basketball coaching books: *Basketball: Steps to Success* and *Becoming a Basketball Player*.

John Ebeling, a six-foot-eight power forward who played for Wissel at Florida Southern (1978–82), battled against Torchy's UCF teams each year for Sunshine State supremacy. A three-time Division II All-American, Ebeling was highlighted in Jay Bilas' book *Toughness: Developing True Strength On and Off the Court*. According to Bilas (2014), "In my rookie year in Italy, I played in a road game against Liberti Firenze, an Italian pro team in Florence. In that game, I was matched up against perhaps the toughest player I had ever suited up against. His name was John Ebeling."

The Knights rode a 21-game winning streak when they hosted the 1978 NCAA Division II South Region with Florida A&M, Livingstone, and Augusta. With another standing-room-only crowd at the UCF Gym, the Knights defeated Augusta 86–66 in the second semifinal.

The next night, UCF faced Florida A&M and Clemon Johnson. A six-foot-ten, 240-pound center, Johnson later played in the NBA for 10 seasons. He carried the Rattlers to the South Region finals after defeating Livingstone in the semifinal. The Knights defeated A&M 85–78 in the championship game at the loud, pulsating UCF Gym. Jackson was again sensational, scoring 48 points in the regional tournament, and was named Most Valuable Player.

In the quarterfinal, the Knights hosted the West Region champion, the University of San Diego. The winner would advance to the NCAA Division II Final Four in Springfield, Missouri. Torchy's Knights had overachieved, and the buzz on the national stage was extraordinary: winners of 23 consecutive games with a sterling opportunity to reach the Final Four. It was a proud moment for the university and the city of Orlando. Under the tutelage of Coach Jim Brovelli, San Diego had a 22–6 record. It had been the best year in the school's history. The high-scoring Toreros (88.3 points per game) were one of the most explosive teams in the nation. Yet the Knights defeated San Diego 77–71 and were headed to Springfield!! Despite a 2–2 start, and gut-wrenching losses to Lamar and Rice, Torchy's team was headed to the Show-Me State and the 1978 Division II Final Four.

1978 NCAA II MEN'S FINAL FOUR
Springfield, Missouri
March 17, 1978

7:00 PM	UCF (26–2) vs. CHEYNEY STATE (24–2)
9:00 PM	UWGB (29–1) vs. EASTERN ILLINOIS (21–9)

The (26–2) Knights were matched up with (24–2) Cheyney State in the first semifinal game. The Wolves were coached by the legendary John Chaney. Before coaching at Temple for 26 years, Chaney coached at the Division II school in Pennsylvania for 10 years (1972–82). Similar to Torchy, Chaney had coached at many levels—junior high, high school, and college. Both coaches shared similar core values of accountability, gratitude, and humility. And neither forgot their heartfelt appreciation of their deep roots, their humble coaching beginnings in Philadelphia for Chaney and Appleton for Clark.

Torchy was coaching in a Division II Final Four, the pinnacle of his college coaching career. Xavier's State Championships in both football (1962) and basketball (1963) were incredible milestones for the father of five. In the second semifinal game, UWGB played Eastern Illinois in the 9:00 p.m. game. Ironically, the Xavier legend was interviewed for the vacant UWGB head coaching position by Vince Lombardi in 1968.

The Pennsylvania State Athletic Conference (PSAC) power was one of the nation's best rebounding teams. The much taller Wolves ran Chaney's potent match-up zone aggressively with intense ball pressure and great length. Chaney was demanding, and his teams played with resilience, physicality, and mental toughness. Torchy was also demanding, and his teams played with single-mindedness fueled by quickness, full-court transition, and the obligation—to teammates and coaches.

In the first half, the Knights struggled against the Wolves' match-up and trailed 20–8 after the first seven minutes. Cheyney State overmatched UCF with pure strength and uncanny perimeter shooting against the Knights' 2/3 zone. The Wolves were able to dominate the boards against the smaller Knights, leading to many second and third shot opportunities. Cheyney State led 40-28 at the half.

The Wolves handled Torchy's full-court press effectively, as the Knights fought and clawed, trying to get back in the game. Andrew

Fields, Cheyney State's six-foot-seven All-American center, scored 17 points and corralled 18 rebounds for a double-double to lead the Wolves' attack. Cheyney State defeated UCF 79–63 as the 24-game winning streak came to a halt. The Knights had not lost a game since losing to Rice, 65-63—stunningly three months ago!!

The quickness, tenacity, and heart of the Knights that electrified UCF's basketball fans throughout the season could not overcome the athleticism and discipline of the Wolves. Torchy recalled his thoughts on the Cheyney State game: "You can only out-quick people for so long. Fields (Cheyney) and Johnson (A&M) were the two best bigs we played all year. It was a clean and consistent game. We lost as a team. Cheyney State's size was the difference. This was a SIZE tournament."

Prather scored 27 points in the losing cause for the Knights. He quickly added after the loss, "We were midgets here today. Cheyney State's length really bothered us. We had to hit shots and we couldn't. Their match-up was tough." UCF's cold shooting in the first half buried the Knights early, creating a huge hole that was tough to dig out of against a Chaney-led team.

In the third-place game, the Knights lost to Eastern Illinois 77–67 to finish the season with a program-best 26–4 record. The Cheyney State Wolves beat UWGB 46–40 to win the 1978 Division II Men's Basketball Championship and claim the school's first national title. The Knights had lost to the National Champions for the second consecutive year! In the prior year (1976–77), UCF lost in the South Region Championship to eventual 1977 National Champion UT-Chattanooga on their home floor 88–79.

Spivey, the talented transfer from Miami-Dade Junior College in Miami, Florida, concluded, "It's kinda hard being a senior to go out with two losses in a row. I think we only played up to our capabilities in the first half of the Eastern Illinois game. That 24 in a row was a long streak, and we can always be proud of it."

Jaffe (1978) summarized, "That Jerry Prather—you can't say enough about him as a person and player. He's super as both. He was hailed as the No. 1 Division II player in Florida. Prather was also named as an NCAA II All-American by the National Association of Basketball Coaches (NABC). He did everything that was asked of him and did it well. It's fitting that he was a part of UCF's greatest season. The year that was UCF's greatest in the Torchy Clark era.

"Nobody expected it. Not faculty, not students, not even the coaches. But UCF's basketball team made believers of them all. Clark had built a basketball program at a school that had nothing. Coach Torchy Clark, a quiet give-all-the-credit-to-the-players-type person, deserves recognition for the way he molded the team together. With the loss of Calvin Lingelbach and Tyrone Sparrow, the outlook was still bright. But the loss of Bo Clark complicated matters. People were ready to forget this season and look forward to the next. Torchy Clark wouldn't let it happen. He held the team together.

"For his efforts, Clark was named Florida Division II Coach-of-the-Year. He was selected as the Sunshine State Conference Coach-of-the-Year for the third straight year. Credit goes to the team. All contributed. That's the way Torchy wanted it. A super season was a year that will be remembered by all, especially those we faced." (Written by Rick Jaffe, *UCF Future*, March 31, 1978.)

CHAPTER 26

Tap Your Emotions and Intensity

For 38 years on the football and basketball sideline, the successful mentor coached with relentless emotion and intensity. According to Torchy, "Emotions can be tricky. There are negatives such as fear, anger, agitations, disturbances, and disgust; but let's remember emotions also include joy, yearning, surprise, and strong feelings . . . so it's not all bad.

"An emotionalist, by definition, is one who endeavors to arouse emotions in others and use it as an art. I'm an emotionalist by nature. I see it as my duty to use the gift. It is spurred by duty and obligation. Complicated? Not really. Most people do not tap into this area. Most people think it's 'manly' to keep part of you controlled and not show your emotion. Personally, I believe this limits you . . . especially in sports."

Torchy reminded us of two baseball greats when describing intensity and emotion: "Ty Cobb and Pete Rose were not blessed with raw ability, but had the quality and discipline of watching every pitch, concentrating on every phase of the game.

"More importantly, Cobb and Rose concentrated on every movement of the game," said Torchy. "That is 100 percent alertness, intensity, emotion, and singleness of purpose. A high price to pay—the *completeness* of the physical skills with mental skills."

In regard to emotions, he recommended strongly, "Instead of floating through life, try getting intense. Don't worry about the stress. What causes stress is sin. It might be pride." The King of Emotion (Torchy) elaborated, "By definition, intensity gives you a degree or amount of strength, force, and energy. I tapped into this and used it."

He laughed at his odd success at calling cards, hitting numbers, and calling roulette colors, red or black. "Sometimes, I felt like I should have gone to Vegas! I could hit fifty-foot shots in basketball and kick field goals beyond my distance when charged up."

In almost four decades of coaching, Torchy's phenomenal *82 percent winning percentage* is attributed (like Cobb and Rose) to his emotion, total concentration, and singleness of purpose. "That was my secret to football and basketball success. The concentration level of our players was always exceedingly high—engaged and attentive. Players not only understood their specific role but proudly embraced that role with the commonality of winning as the ultimate goal," said Torchy. "I realized I coached in a different era; however, 40 years later, well-defined roles and team chemistry are so important to a team's inner core. My teams always had the 'it factor' and bought into our winning culture," noted the 38-year veteran.

Success, tradition, players' leadership, and Torchy's personality were other essential components which assisted players in the "total committed effort." He was one of the best in getting the "buy-in."

Torchy remembered a specific coaching situation of how his intensity helped his team: "A good example is coaching the face guard press. The more intense I was, the better our press was. I saw this nightly in our practices; high intensity got results. Sure, you automatically assume kids are afraid to make a mistake. I don't think so."

Holly Criswell of the *FTU Future* (1975) wrote, "Red-faced, body shaking with half-suppressed emotion, the contrived excitement of UCF's Eugene 'Torchy' Clark can be an entertainment in themselves. But what sort of person is this flamboyant, intensely competitive man when he is outside the boundaries of a basketball court? 'I think I'm a pussycat,' said Clark seriously, 'but when that whistle blows you can bet, I'll be in the game!'

"Clark's self-definition seems incongruous (pussycat?) with the overzealous, fire-breathing coach he projects at courtside. 'I don't think any successful coach can sit there and watch the game go by,' said Clark when asked about his excessive emotional displays on the sidelines. 'It would be easier if I wasn't so emotional. Yet if I wasn't, I'd feel guilty,' he added.

"A glance at Clark's overall record shows his approach cannot be all wrong. According to Clark, coaching means more than simply teaching young men how to handle a basketball. 'I want to win, for sure. But I also want a kid to be a better person as a result.'"

Bill Buchalter (1979) of the *Orlando Sentinel* emphasized that "UCF's Torchy Clark credited his success in coaching to his negative approach: 'Defeat is right smack around the corner. But believe me, it's an advantage to be pessimistic. It's a constant reminder you're gonna be blown out. It makes you come out with intensity. We always had the built-in intensity factor.'"

On the front door of the small UCF basketball office in the school's Education Building, Room 173, was a magazine cut-out, white letters on black background that described his emotional intensity: *Clark gets it done.* Nancy Ridenour, wife of UCF assistant Ray Ridenour, remarked, "I just think of Torchy as 'electricity.' He's always turned on and tuned up."

A perfect example of his "pessimistic" approach was when in 1979 he reasoned there was no way his Division II Knights could beat Southern Conference power Furman in the season opener. Torchy was "negatively positive." He told his team, "They're better than we are. They are expected to beat us and should." Torchy then added, "But," he warmed to his negative charm, "if we can make them play OUR game, then we might make things go OUR way." Things went UCF's way. UCF 84, Furman 77. Bill Buchalter of the *Orlando Sentinel* (1980) wrote, "Incredibly, the strength of Torchy Clark and his program is also his Achilles heel. Critics decry his negativism, his crying towel propaganda. And Torchy laughs all the way to the victory bank."

Yvan Kelly, a dedicated team manager, recalled his responsibility at a 1977 UCF practice session: "It was during that time of endless practices prior to our first game, as I recall, that Torchy came to me with a clipboard and a piece of paper. He gave me the assignment that day to make a note of everything he said to his players during practice. He wanted all his statements to be categorized as either "positive" or "negative." It was going to be the "Torchy Clark Report." I dutifully paid close attention to all he said over the nearly two-hour practice and recorded them on the tally sheet.

"At the end of practice, Torchy came to me and asked for the clipboard. He wanted to see how things had turned out. I don't remember the exact numbers, but the positive comments outnumbered the negative comments by a 2 to 1 ratio. Torchy was happy with that outcome, and he often used the report over the years to show that he actually said more encouraging things to players than discouraging things.

"There was just one flaw in the report. There was no methodology to indicate the intensity of the comments. There was a big difference, from the recipient's perspective, between an almost offhanded 'Jerry, that was a good pass' comment and a very loud bark during a defensive press drill, 'CLEVELAND, THERE ARE FOUR OF THEM AND FIVE OF YOU. HOW COULD YOU LET THE BALL GET IN?'

"It was true on that day Torchy said *many* more positive things to his players than negative. And that day was not unique; that was Torchy's coaching style. He did say more positive things than negative things. It just always didn't feel that way."

Ray Ridenour described Torchy's intense practices: "Most coaches just practice for three hours, but Coach Clark's practices are designed with the goal of trying 'to win every practice.' I came from Ohio and I was a stickler for details. Torchy taught me there is more to basketball than details. He gets inside and gets the very best out of players. He repeats and repeats. For example, NO FOULING! After the fourth time of repeating NO FOULING, the players finally get it that he doesn't want them to foul."

Torchy Clark and Ray Ridenour's UCF teams over a six-year period from 1974–80 had a stunning (128–34) record. Ridenour emphasized, "I can remember the practice sessions before the NCAA tournament in Chattanooga. Or like when we played Furman in 1979. It's him. Intensity is too much overused, but he made it *important*. He brought the best out in an unbelievable player like Ruben Cotton or in the fringe players. It's what made us win." And win. And win.

Torchy recalled his passionate coaching style: "I want a player on his toes. It's my personality. It's the way I am. I wrote an article called 'Elimination of Fear.' It explained the coach-player relationship. Yes, I thought my players feared me like Lombardi's players feared him or Shula's feared him. It all goes back to intensity."

The former football and basketball coach reflected on his career: "Gosh, it's fun to look back, but it's dangerous, too. Maybe I did things wrong. My coaching life was so intense—my teams won so many times, that I even wanted to win the practices.

"My insecurity came in winning and my security was actually caused by my insecurity. I like people who are a little insecure: They are *hungry* and want to succeed. Someone asked me, 'Are you saying that many successful people are actually insecure?' Absolutely—it's their 'go' button! Hey, I thought Vince Lombardi was a little bashful. I loved to coach against secure and comfortable coaches," stressed Torchy.

The discussion of winning—serious winning—consistent winning was a hot topic in his UCF Coaching class. During a discussion, the great teacher remembered, "One of my students commented, 'Coach, it can't be all winning . . . it's got to be a lot of fun, too.' 'Winning is fun!' I responded. 'If you want the other kind of fun, you go to Chuck E. Cheese's!' [his class erupted with laughter]. It's a serious business: they fire high school football and basketball coaches."

Torchy continued his philosophical thoughts in his coaching journey: "As a young boy, I once asked Coach Bob Kolf [Sr.] at Oshkosh State how many years he had coached. Kolf responded, '34 years.' That didn't faze me—years mean little to a boy. But now I look back and I, too, followed a similar path coaching both basketball and football. I was never an assistant coach.

"For 58 consecutive seasons I've gone out on the field or on the court. That's a lot of football and basketball. This is all I ever wanted to do. Honestly, I don't feel like I know any more than anybody else; besides, the young coaches today are extremely sharp. Perhaps, I understand the emotions and feelings of the game as well as many. Words like anxiety, catharsis, and reality have not escaped me. Over the years, I've found that coaching really doesn't need you . . . it's BIG and moves on like life—with or without you," said the reflective Torchy.

"There are many great coaches and more potentially good coaches in a vastly over-crowded profession, that to coach and work with young people is an honor. Yes, I've worked hard physically and especially emotionally, but I repeat, it's still a *privilege* to coach. Usually, when a person quits a good coaching job, they won't replace that job. So stay with it and be humble!" he strongly recommended.

It was this personal intensity that helped Torchy survive during the early years of the Knights' program: the nomadic, no-gym existence and the struggle for community support. Torchy remembered, "When I first came to UCF, Dr. Rohter (my hero) told me, 'Al McGuire couldn't do this job.' I thought Rohter was kidding. But you know, after 11 years, he was right. It's been a different kind of job. One that needed patience, flexibility, a low profile, and a bucket of humility. And I loved it!"

John Valerino (1979) of the *Lakeland Ledger*, the beat reporter for Florida Southern, portrayed UCF's high-energy coach: "Clark is a fox. He's clever, very crafty and he knows how to get the most out of his players. He's a strategist. Clark doesn't like to lose. He'll do anything within the framework of the rules to reach perfection. He does, however, accept defeats graciously, although by his record at UCF, he hasn't had to do that too often."

As a coach, Torchy believed all great athletes need a motivator to inspire and push them to their limit. Even the best need that extra inspiration! To many outstanding athletes he had the *privilege* to coach at St. Mary's, Xavier, UCF, and Trinity Prep, Torchy was *that* motivator, that extra inspiration. In retrospect, he often shared this overlooked, urgent aspect of intensity: "I hear parents say, my son or daughter really loves the game! Does he or she really love it?"

Torchy assessed today's coaches: "Many coaches and people are afraid of emotions, intensities, and high motivation. I had to be intense . . . being normal doesn't work for me," said the coaching veteran. Here is a story that illustrates this clearly:

Dr. Ed Stoner, UCF's team doctor and a close friend, ordered an EKG test for Torchy during a routine physical exam. Stoner did not like what he saw; however, he said he wasn't a cardiologist. The physician asked, "Torchy, do you guys play tonight?" The coach replied, "Yes, we do." Stoner continued, "I don't like this EKG, but go ahead and coach tonight. But take it easy and don't run any steps."

Torchy recalled the (Stoner-EKG) game vividly: "I was scared. Claire and a good friend sat behind our bench during the game. We were huge favorites, but I was worried what Stoner strongly advised, so I took it easy. No emotion; no intensity, just coaching, and floor direction." At one point, Torchy turned to Claire in the stands during the game and said, "If this is coaching, I want no part of it! I felt like a robot! And yes, we got upset—by 30 points!"

After several more tests, Torchy was cleared to go by the doctors. In the next game he was his "normal" self and concluded, "I went back to coaching with emotion and intensity. We played the same team on the road and won by 35. That was a 65-point emotional swing. But sometimes in life things are like vapors: here and then gone. But the memories remain."

The following is written by Bill Beekman (FTU, 1975). "Dribblings Including the Adventures of the Disco Winnebago & Blocked Punts: Fond and Foggy Memories from the Early Days of Knights' Athletics."

"A funny, engaging and truly nice guy off the floor, the Torch was nuts once he passed through the arena doors. He'd walk to the bench with his sandy hair neatly combed and very dapper in a tweed blazer, university-striped tie, and an oxford shirt. Mere moments into the game, however, the jacket would hit the floor, with the tie askew and his rear shirttail hanging out.

"The sideline was his territory as he relentlessly paced the floor, barking at his players, muttering at the refs and shouting instructions to the floor, sometimes sitting on his haunches. He'd get wild-eyed at bad calls or bad play, pulling at his hair while his face turned a bright crimson.

"He played to the crowd, and the fans (often 3,000 of them) loved it. He'd pray, eyes heavenward on his knees pleading for divine intervention from the referees. While arguing calls with officials, the game ball would mysteriously wind up tucked behind Torchy's back, hiding under his jacket.

"Make no mistake, though, it wasn't just a show—Torchy was always in the game. His teams may (occasionally) have been outplayed, but he was never outcoached. Short on size, his teams compensated with speed, tenacity, and defense. They beat presses with long baseball passes, ran isolation plays ('Mississippi'), and used the outside shot to set up the inside play, and ran their fast break with abandon. The Torch was 'Run-and-Gun' before 'Run-and-Gun' was cool. If a bigger slower team played a zone defense, he'd stall until the opposition was shamed into a man-to-man where he had the advantage ('Oranges').

"Ask anyone that's taken one of his classes, and they'll tell you, he was the best professor they ever had (like Daunte). I only met Torchy a couple of times, and I loved the guy. He often said his life was about 'God first, family second, and basketball third.' If that's true, he's a lock for the Hereafter because he's a devoted family man, and the best damn basketball coach I've ever seen. Period."

CHAPTER 27

Champion of the Underdog

T orchy was always a "champion of the underdog." Mike Wood and Frank Bouressa have been underdogs most of their lives. Wood, 63, has been a high school assistant basketball coach in the Central Florida area for 27 years. He has worked under many outstanding head coaches in tradition-rich programs, including: Bishop Moore Catholic, West Orange, Evans, Lake Brantley, University, Apopka, Wekiva, and Winter Park. After eight long and tedious years of part-time classes, Wood graduated from UCF in 1990 with a degree in Physical Education and Sociology.

The bound and determined Wood loves coaching, loves the camaraderie of the game, loves the relationship with the coaches, but most importantly strives to be a role model of courage and fortitude for his players. He is a basketball coach today because of Torchy Clark's guidance and direction.

In 1956, Wood was born with cerebral palsy as his umbilical cord wrapped around his neck, cutting off much-needed oxygen to the brain during mother Roberta's delivery. He has been unable to walk his entire life without the use of two metal canes. Sometimes he crawls on the ground to move from one spot to the next. He walks, but know that every *single* step is a laborious struggle for Wood. Walking is something that many of us take for granted. But Mike Wood keeps walking and crawling and fighting.

At the age of 12, Wood developed type 1 diabetes. For the last 50 years he has taken four insulin shots a day. The diabetes has damaged his sight severely in one eye. The feisty underdog faces major obstacles each day, yet despite the physical roadblocks, he has won over 400 games in almost three decades of coaching.

Cerebral palsy has robbed him of all muscular strength of his lower body. However, cerebral palsy has not robbed him of his upper body strength, or his brilliant mind, or his heart, the size of Texas. Wood has an engaging laugh and a great sense of humor. And he knows the game of basketball.

If he had not been born with cerebral palsy, Mike Wood would have been the starting defensive back at five-foot-seven, 175 pounds for the 1974 Orlando Edgewater High School Eagles. And he would have knocked the "crap" out of opposing halfbacks tackling them. Wood would have been the toughest, most physical player on the team. His football coach would have used his tenacity of a bulldog and relentless grit as examples for his team to emulate. During practice, the coach would scream at his fragile linebacker, pleading for him to be *as tough as Mike Wood.*

Torchy and Wood first met at UCF in 1982. After getting his AA Degree at Seminole Community College, Wood began taking classes at UCF with his then-major of Liberal Arts. One morning on campus as he journeyed from class to class, he recognized Torchy outside the Administration Building. He immediately stopped his motorized scooter to say hello.

The two struck up a conversation, naturally centered around sports. They talked about Torchy's current UCF team that Wood had seen several times on local WFTV-Channel 9. Torchy wanted to hear about Wood's life, his goals, and his plans for the future. The coach invited him to his basketball office anytime he wanted to visit. And he did on several occasions.

A few days later, Wood showed up at one of the Knights' basketball practices, thoroughly enjoying the two hours of observation and learning. Soon, he was attending one to two practices a week. Torchy on many occasions gave Wood a ride home after practice to his home at that time in Lockhart (Orlando). The next semester, the UCF junior enrolled in his Coaching Theory class and took several more "Torchy" courses in the future. Wood became a basketball junkie and learned the game just being around him. He caught the coaching bug.

Torchy, the "champion of the underdog," thought Wood would be an excellent basketball coach. As his mentor, he advised Wood to pursue a degree in physical education and enter the coaching profession. Despite his cerebral palsy and his inability to physically demonstrate a basketball skill, Torchy *still* encouraged him to be a coach. He strongly suggested Wood attend Don Rutledge's officiating class at Valencia Community College to improve his expertise and rules of the game. Wood took the class four times. Rutledge was a close friend of Torchy's and refereed NCAA Division I basketball for 30-plus years. "As a competitor, teacher, coach, or person, Torchy Clark has few peers at any level," commented Rutledge, who officiated in an amazing six Final Fours. (Bennett, 1997)

The stouthearted Wood fondly remembered his mentor's impact: "Torchy never felt sorry for me. He was my *hero*. I am a coach today because of his belief in me. He inspired me to follow my dream of being a coach."

Wood added, "Torchy motivated me to finish my classes and get my degree despite my disability. He didn't see my weakness—he saw my heart and my strengths. *Torchy gave me hope.* Physically, I could only take a class or two each semester. I had to take three, sometimes four different busses to get from Lockhart to UCF. I spent a lot of time on a bus, as you can imagine."

After graduation, Torchy helped him secure his first coaching job at Good Shepherd Catholic Grade School in Orlando. Wood recalled his confidant's sincere endorsement: "He recommended me and went to bat for me. A lot of the principals were hesitant to hire me as a coach. Torchy became my biggest advocate. He also helped me land other coaching positions."

The Knights' coach thought Wood had a lot to offer and knew the game. He remembered Wood's relenting passion and spirit: "I love fighters. Mike is a fighter. He has a great athletic mind, but more importantly has a tremendous willingness to learn and improve as a coach."

One of Torchy's kind gestures of love was to write a letter to then-President Ronald Reagan, asking if the POTUS could write a note to Wood. Claire delivered the authentic, autographed picture of Reagan to Wood's home with the handwritten message, "To Mike, Keep Fighting! All My Best, Ronald Reagan." The picture meant the world to the young coach.

The thirst for knowledge motivated Wood to take part in several coaching clinics. He even traveled to Milwaukee, Wisconsin, to participate in a clinic with former UCF assistant Dave Shaw. Today, Shaw and Wood stay in constant touch and together attended The American Conference Basketball Tournament at Orlando's Amway Center in 2018. Shaw is a close friend of High Point University Basketball Coach Tubby Smith, after the two worked together at Virginia Commonwealth in the early 1980s. Several times over the years Shaw has arranged for Wood to watch a Smith-led practice and observe the future Naismith Hall of Famer.

Shaw reflected, "Tubby has been great with Mike and is one of his heroes now. Mike enjoyed following Memphis on their big run in the American Tournament. We stopped by the hotel to see Tubby. That meant a lot to Mike. He loves talking basketball and just being around coaches."

The Madison, Wisconsin, native has replaced Torchy as a mentor to Wood but lives 1,300 miles away. The two developed a friendship beginning in 1982 when Shaw assisted Torchy.

Mike Wood is truly an underdog. But he doesn't want compassion—he wants to talk basketball. And wants to teach other coaches Torchy's face guard press and its SIDE-MIDDLE-BASKET coverage.

Frank Bouressa was also an underdog who faced life-threatening adversity with powerful humility and a fearless perseverance. Bouressa was a tough, hard-nosed lineman who played football for Torchy at Xavier as a sophomore and junior in 1967 and 1968. He did not play for Torchy his senior year, as the Wisconsin Hall of Famer had already departed to Florida, starting the program at UCF.

After graduating from Xavier in 1970, Bouressa emerged from a pizza parlor in downtown Appleton after eating there. Outside the front door, he was approached by a drunk who asked him for a cigarette. "I don't smoke," replied Bouressa, the former 210-pound lineman. Angered and frustrated by the answer, the drunk severely punched and clocked Bouressa in the mouth as the lights went out immediately for the football player.

For six months, Bouressa lay in a coma in an Appleton hospital with no body movement. His brother Jerry, a Catholic priest, found that Bouressa could move his pinky finger slightly. This allowed Bouressa to communicate, and they were able to work up a set of yes and no signals. Even so, the doctors were all asked the same question: Did they really expect the young 18-year-old Bouressa to survive, let alone even speak a word, walk, smile, or raise his hand? The answer was always no.

When Torchy was living in Florida and coaching at UCF, he began to correspond with Bouressa, writing him letters. His brother, Father Jerry, read Torchy's letters to him in the hospital, hoping he would understand them. He wanted Frank to know his former high school coach was praying and pulling for him each day while attending daily Mass. Months after Jerry's discovery that Frank could communicate, he regained consciousness, but was still only able to talk slowly and move his hands. Torchy remained in contact with his former player through many long-distance phone calls to Wisconsin. In addition, the coach sent Bouressa a brand-new pair of Chuck Taylor All-Stars with a letter inside the box.

Six years later in 1976, Bouressa called Torchy to inform him he was coming to Orlando to spend a week with the Clark family. Bouressa was unable to walk, stand or raise his arm; however, he had the handshake of a weightlifter and a big-time smile.

When he visited the Clarks, he needed help getting in and out of bed and his wheelchair. For the entire Clark family, it was a labor of love. No one complained. But coming to Torchy's Florida home was the right place to go, with the young energy and spirit seeping from every nook and cranny. They set Bouressa up in their spacious family room to make him comfortable. The former Hawk had longed to spend time with his mentor, his coach, Torchy Clark.

"All of my kids were absolutely great with Frank. We had a routine going," said the appreciative dad. "The improvement in Frank's speech was unbelievable. The fact he was able to make the mental improvement he made was a miracle. He was really sharp," added Torchy.

Struggling to get the words out, Bouressa unmistakably said to his Xavier coach, "They never caught the man who hit me, but I hold no malice against him. You can't *hate* someone you don't know." Bouressa couldn't identify him anyway. The blow to the head by the drunk left him blind.

Torchy was not always the intense, fiery coach on the sideline that Xavier or UCF fans observed. Many Torchy fans arrived at UCF games early to sit behind the Knights' bench to watch the coaching ace close-up in action. His lasting and powerful influence goes well beyond what the average fan, former player, or opposing coach genuinely knows. Torchy was a champion of the underdog, believing strongly in compassion, loyalty, and love. One of his favorite quotes was from St. Andrew Kim Taegon, who said with mighty strength, the strength of both Mike Wood and Frank Bouressa, "I urge you to remain steadfast in faith, so that at last we will reach *Heaven* and there rejoice together." (Catholic Company, 2018)

In 1986, Frank Bouressa died in Wisconsin at the age of 34. Torchy has one of his toughest Xavier lineman in heaven. Frank's eyesight is 20/20. He can punt a football 70 yards. He doesn't have to play the line anymore. The angels moved him to wide receiver. He can run a perfect pass pattern and catch a perfect, spiraled pass from his old, but now young football coach, Torchy Clark. There are no pass interceptions in *heaven*. And Frank's smile is even greater, his suffering is over.

CHAPTER 28

Establish a Reputation

In 1979, *Sports Illustrated* assigned Roger Jackson to research the possibility of writing a feature story on Torchy and Bo Clark of UCF. Torchy remembered, "My teams had been mentioned a few times in *Sports Illustrated*. I was quoted in the THEY SAID IT column: 'All coaches, not just Division I coaches, can get high blood pressure, heart attacks, ulcers, and yes, fired too.'

"*Sports Illustrated* was a big thing for our university at the time. We opened our season upsetting Division I Furman 84–77 on the road in Greenville, South Carolina," noted Torchy. Pete Krull, a seasoned veteran and four-year player said, "If this isn't our biggest win, it's pretty close." A major cog on the 1978 Final Four team, Krull was the ultimate team player and became one of the Knights' true unsung heroes.

"Ruben Cotton was the difference in the Furman win. What an exhibition he put on tonight," said a happy Torchy. Cotton, a six-foot-one forward and transfer from Brevard Junior College in Cocoa, Florida, had 19 rebounds and dominated the glass against the much taller Paladins. The Knights outrebounded the home team, 44–34. Immediately, after shaking hands postgame with Furman Coach Eddie Holbrook, Torchy bolted for the closest exit. He then began to walk around Greenville's Coliseum, trying to unwind from the emotional upset.

When he returned from the cold, he proudly concluded to the press, "It wasn't the biggest win in my life . . . but it was the biggest mismatch win since I've been here." Torchy never expected his Knights to open the 1979–80 campaign like this, not against Furman, a squad returning nine lettermen. The Knights shot brilliantly from the floor, hitting 35 of 56 attempts for an "off-the-charts" 62.5 percent.

Gerald Jones, a six-foot-one, 180-pound guard from Kirkman High School in Chattanooga, Tennessee, and a fabulous Ray Ridenour recruit, was unstoppable against Furman, adding 16 points. The Knights led 44–37 at the half. The Paladins sliced UCF's lead to 74–73 with three minutes left. Jones took over, hitting a pivotal 3-point play on a 10-foot floater and free throw. The slick guard then added a fast break layup to give the Knights a 79–73 advantage. UCF ran Torchy's "triangles-delay" game the last few minutes, hitting crucial free throws to hold off the stunned Paladins.

Before coming to UCF, Jones was an Honorable Mention Junior College All-American at Dalton Junior College in Dalton, Georgia. The prolific scorer had two exceptional years as a combo-scoring guard for the Knights, graduating in 1980. "Gerald was tough, super skilled, and was a winner. He was so strong and a beast getting to the rim. Several Sunshine State coaches, including me, thought he was the *best* guard in the league," added Torchy. Furman's All-American Candidate and NBA prospect, six-foot-eight forward Jonathan Moore, was kept in check by the Knights' stingy 2–3 zone. The defense clogged the middle and denied Moore the ball. Amazingly, the vastly undersized Cotton outrebounded Moore 19–6 in the game.

Torchy recalled the huge win: "I believe *Sports Illustrated* now was a believer and sent Roger Jackson to write a story." Jackson was in Orlando to see the Knights easily handle Florida Memorial College

116–80 in the home opener. Again, it was Torchy's rugged defense that dominated play as his full-court press was a problem Florida Memorial couldn't solve. UCF's intense ball-trapping forced numerous Lion turnovers, leading to a plethora of *easy* baskets.

Despite scoring 33 points, Bo Clark passed the credit to Cotton, who had an unbelievable stat line against Florida Memorial. Cotton had a double-double scoring 25 points and collecting 12 rebounds. The Sanford, Florida, native also dished out four assists and had seven steals. "He did it all," Bo Clark recalled. "I'm glad Ruben is on our team. I wouldn't want to play against him. His athleticism is scary."

Ray Ridenour was the mastermind of Torchy's recruiting. His ability to sign Ruben Cotton and Gerald Jones was pivotal to the success of the 1979–80 Knights. Two other key junior college transfers that Ridenour signed were Roland Ebron, a six-foot-one forward from Broward Junior College in Fort Lauderdale, Florida, and Dean Rossin, nicknamed "The Enforcer," a six-foot-five center from Lake City Junior College in Lake City, Florida.

Earlier that year, *Sports Illustrated's* presence on UCF's campus was obvious quickly: "Roger Jackson began his research by interviewing Bo, Ray (Ridenour), Claire, my players, and I," said Torchy. "I thought it was odd *Sports Illustrated* didn't take any pictures after being on campus several days."

The (2–0) Knights next traveled to New Orleans to play Xavier University of Louisiana (NAIA). Jackson flew with the team on their commercial flight to the "Big Easy."

Torchy recalled the Xavier (LA) game day: "After our shoot-around, I asked Bo if *Sports Illustrated* had taken any pictures." Bo responded, "No, but I think Roger has a photographer with him today." The Knights coach was hoping *Sports Illustrated* would take a picture of the duo using either New Orleans' Bourbon Street or the famous St. Louis Cathedral as a backdrop; or possibly a picture of both before the Xavier game.

"Everybody was excited about having *Sports Illustrated* travel with the team. It's not like they travel with us every trip. We weren't the Boston Celtics," remembered Bo Clark. However, Torchy was nonetheless anxious about the picture.

Xavier is the alma mater of Donald "Slick" Watts, the first NBA player to lead the league in assists and steals in the same season (1976). Watts played most of his six-year career with the Seattle Supersonics. The bald, six-foot-one guard who wore a trademark headband, was an NBA fan favorite with his blazing quickness, defensive tenacity, and passing ability.

Another Xavier legend was Nat "Sweetwater" Clifton, one of the first African Americans to play in the NBA in 1950. Clifton later became more famous as a valuable superstar of the touring Harlem Globetrotters and the Harlem Magicians.

The on-campus gym at Xavier was nicknamed "The Barn" for its loud and crazy fans. "The Barn's" capacity was 1,300, but on many nights the Gold Rush squeezed in 1,500. The 75-year-old facility was one of the toughest small college gyms for opponents in the country. The Gold Rush had a 246–20 home court record at "The Barn." The tiny gym had its own spirit and was a boisterous "energy palace."

The clash at "The Barn" was wild. "The fans know we just beat Furman a week ago," said Torchy. "We had fans sitting a foot from our bench. Xavier was tough and came in the game with a 4–0 record. The floor was loaded with talent, and it was obvious from the opening tip, this would be a dogfight," observed the worried coach.

UCF took an early 10-point lead behind the dynamite play of Knights' Ruben Cotton, Gerald Jones, Dean Rossin, and Roland Ebron. The teams went back and forth with 1,500 fans going berserk after each Xavier basket. The Knights maintained their safe 10-point cushion going into the half. And yes, *Sports Illustrated* was in "The Barn" with a photographer to take a picture of the father-son duo against a team that loses at home once every five years.

"The second half starts and we haven't pressed yet, and that's our reputation," said Torchy. "Midway in the half, we are still in control by 10 points. With seven minutes left, our lead fluctuates between six and eight points. And with 1:45 remaining we are only up four. The place is bedlam! They're coming at us! I call a timeout," recalled the nervous, but in control Torchy. UCF led 79–75. "The Barn" was engulfed in flames of intensity as the Gold Rush were back!

Torchy remembered the emotional 1:45 timeout: "I'm thinking, should we press? Should we change tempo—or could we hang on to win? I haven't been mad that much the last two games: only once, briefly ripping Bo at Furman. I tried to calm down our guys saying, 'We have control of this game . . . keep it steady. No, we aren't going to press. We played this way and we'll finish this way.

"'Run triangles and be strong with the ball.' I'm still under semi-control, but I gotta rip somebody and I own him. So, I look at Bo and get right in his grill, yelling, 'Bo, what is wrong with you tonight?' Bo, with his innocuous look, now lashes out at me in a *rare* heat-of-the-moment exchange, 'What do you want, they have three guys all over me?'"

Torchy remembered, "I was hot as a firecracker pointing my finger at Bo's chest saying, 'You know what I want. I want,' etc. . . . ' *Sports Illustrated* took the darn picture at that precise moment during the timeout. *Sports Illustrated* is not the leading publication for nothing. And people wonder why I was worried about the timing of the picture."

The Knights hung on for their second "big" road win to beat Xavier 83–79. The Gold Rush found a way to shut down the nation's leading scorer, but was unable to stop UCF's six other stars. Bo Clark was held to only 12 points on 5 of 11 shooting from the field. An upbeat and relieved Torchy said, "I thought our kids played good, disciplined ball tonight. I was proud of our team in a tough environment; however, it did seem strange for me coaching *against* Xavier. It was a big win. A big win."

Cotton led all scorers with 24 points and was his phenomenal self in New Orleans. Also, Roland Ebron and Dean Rossin both had exceptional games. Ebron came off the bench to score 16 points. Rossin followed with a monster double-double with 13 points and 12 rebounds. Ray Ridenour added, "Rossin played a heck of a game tonight and was huge for us. This made all the recruiting trips to Lake City (FL) worth it. He was such a great teammate and a difference maker."

The Knights began the 1979–80 season "on fire," winning their first 15 games, earning a No. 1 NCAA Division II national ranking. For three straight weeks, Torchy's (15–0) Knights held the top spot in the nation before losing a heartbreaker to Hal Wissel's Florida Southern Mocs, 96–90. The game in Lakeland before a jam-packed crowd of 3,100 at Jenkins Field House was undoubtedly a classic. The Mocs were led by All-American forward John Ebeling and point guard Kurt Alston. But it was reserve forward Mark King's 23 points hitting jumper after jumper against the Knights' 2/3 zone that catapulted the Mocs to the win.

The UCF-Southern rivalry was a passionate, front-page rivalry, as were the UCF-Rollins matchups. Torchy always referred to those dogfights in his career as "white knucklers." The Knights finished the year with a fabulous 25–4 record. Three of the four UCF losses were at the hands of Florida Southern, who reached the 1980 NCAA II Final Four that year. One loss was in the NCAA South Region Championship in Lakeland.

Sports Illustrated (December 17, 1979) ran the feature story by Roger Jackson titled "A Tough Gun of a Son." The picture of Torchy tongue-lashing Bo was used in the magazine with a caption underneath,

"Being the coach's son and a 28 scorer doesn't mean Bo isn't a target for Lombardian taunts."

Torchy remembered seeing the picture for the first time, "The cords in my neck were bulging. I looked wild. How did Bo look? Like a cherub. We went to New Orleans to win a game, not to take a picture. *Sports Illustrated* is clever! You establish a reputation and you live with it. My reputation was one of fiery and intense. And that's the picture *Sports Illustrated* wanted. But sometimes in life things are like vapors: here and then gone. But the memories remain."

CHAPTER 29

Sawyer Brown Says Good-Bye

Written by
Mark Miller/Sawyer Brown (2018)

I have traveled the world with my band Sawyer Brown for 37 years now. No one was more proud of my success than Torchy. None of my awards and accomplishments compare to the honor of being asked to be a part of this book and sharing memories of my incredible coach, a man who was the ultimate example of faith, passion, and strength!

Growing up, my dream was to play college basketball. I was too often told that I didn't have the size for it and that it probably wouldn't be in my future. However, after hours and hours of practice, relentless hard work, and a decent high school basketball career, I found myself with several opportunities to realize my dream. The offers came from some small four-year colleges and several junior colleges. My sights, though, were set on playing for Torchy Clark, the coach who had an on-fire nationally ranked program at UCF, and who had the reputation for his unorthodox coaching style—as well as his larger-than-life personality.

Even from my first visit to UCF and meeting Torchy, he did not disappoint. Torchy was a rock star. He carried himself like a prize-fighter, confident with a quick and strong gait. He was fiery, with his strawberry-blond hair—and he looked like he could take me one-on-one. I was nervous and very intimidated when he started the interview, but his charisma and humor put me at ease—not to mention entertained me.

We were in his office with his assistant coach Ray Ridenour; and Ray was a perfect fit for Torchy. He was to Torchy what Ed McMahon was to Johnny Carson. Torchy would interact with Ray, and Ray would respond as if it were rehearsed. I started by telling them that I wasn't looking for a scholarship because my father had died as a result of the Korean War, and I was going to school on the G.I. Bill.

Coach Ridenour said, "Coach, I think he's just looking for an opportunity to make the team and to contribute."

Torchy just nodded his head at Ray for stating what must have seemed like the obvious. Torchy looked at me and said, "I actually saw you play a couple of times." He then turned to Ray and said, "Ray, I had no idea he was this short."

Ray instantly said, "Yeah, Coach, he is pretty short."

Torchy then said, "The games I saw, you only had 6 or 8 points." Then after an awkward pause, he broke out into a big smile and added, "I guess playing with those 6'7" Harris twins, you don't get much of a chance to shoot."

"No, sir," I said—and we all laughed.

"Well," Torchy said, "I don't care how tall you are. You can play. And you have the one thing it takes to play here: speed. Mark, you're quick as a cat and you'll fit in here."

I walked out of Torchy's office on cloud nine. I was on top of the world knowing my dream was going to come true. Torchy Clark had endorsed and validated me as a college basketball player. I had just had my first experience in being motivated by what the great coaches are able to do—make us think we are better than we really are. And Torchy Clark was a master at that.

My favorite part of practice was what I referred to as "the Monologue." We would warm up, and then Torchy would enter the gym. We'd all take a seat, and Torchy would take 15 minutes and talk to us about life, about God, and he'd challenge us to be better men and better students. He loved teaching moments like that in practice and in the classroom. I took every class he taught, and his classes were amazing—educational, insightful, and always entertaining. His antics at practice and on the court—especially during games—were legendary. There was the day we played football for an entire practice; or when Torchy would sit in the stands *during the game*; or the time he sent all 5'9" of me into the game to replace our 7-footer to play center. In the moment, I would at times scratch my head, but as I got older, I realized every single mildly bizarre or unorthodox event—and there were a lot—was a deep and incredible teaching moment. And Torchy found those moments everywhere.

To give more insight into Torchy the motivator, I have to give you some backstory. I'm told that Torchy's college basketball experience as a player at Marquette was not unlike my own experience at UCF. He didn't talk much about Marquette; and, though I never saw him play, I know I wouldn't have wanted him to guard me. Like Torchy, I prided myself on being a tough, hard-nosed defender.

We had a very successful season my sophomore year. The team had a highly talented group of players, and we were on a roll. I was working hard, yet due to the number of great players on the team, there was little playing time left for me—and rightfully so. One day, Torchy walked by me and said, "Mark, if you were at Valdosta State, you'd be a starter." Maybe, I thought—but Valdosta State doesn't have Torchy Clark.

Sensing some burnout midway through that season, Torchy pulled me aside to talk about the team, asking me about different players. He then looked me straight in the eye and said, "Why is Bo an All-American?"

Bo was our All-American shooting guard and led the nation in scoring. And he also happened to be Torchy's son. We were fortunate to have Bo—he wanted to play for his dad, otherwise he would have been playing in the ACC or SEC for sure. So the question "Why is Bo an All-American?" caught me off guard.

My answers seemed obvious. "Coach, Bo is the best shooter—he's averaging 32 points per game. And he's leading the nation in scoring. And Coach, you are pretty tough on him."

Torchy looked at me and said, "Bo is an All-American because he has to face you in practice every day. No one is going to guard him like you do, and that has prepared him to face any kind of pressure."

Now in reality, Bo was an All-American because of all the reasons I gave Torchy and because he worked his butt off and was the best shooter I've ever seen. But as only Torchy could do, he made me—the walk-on—feel like I was the reason for Bo's accolades and our team's success.

And it made me want to work twice as hard.

After making my decision to leave UCF and move to Nashville to pursue a music career, I met with Torchy to tell him I wouldn't be returning for my senior year. I was as nervous as the first day I'd walked into his office three years earlier. Singing and songwriting was a newfound talent for me, so even teammates and close friends weren't aware that I had any interest in music.

My announcement was intriguing to Torchy—and his reaction was unexpected. When I told him, he got that Torchy smirk on his face. It was a look I'd seen often—an expression that made you think he knew something you didn't. And he actually did.

Torchy looked at Ray and said, "Did you know about this?"

Ray quickly shook his head. "No, Coach. I had no idea."

Torchy looked back at me. "So, you can sing and write your own songs?" He paused for a second and then added, "I bet you're good. You have to be good or you wouldn't be doing this."

He spun and looked at Ray again. "Ray, I bet he's good."

Torchy then paused and closed his eyes for a moment. When he opened his eyes, he nodded his head and said to Ray, almost as if he'd had a premonition, "He's going to be famous."

Once again, I walked out of Torchy Clark's office like I had three years earlier—on top of the world, motivated, and ready to pursue another dream.

No one was happier for me or prouder of my success than Torchy. He followed my career right up to the end of his life. I loved stopping by his house over the years—unannounced. I loved sitting and visiting with him, ever the great conversationalist: thought-provoking, charismatic, downright clever, and funny. He was my coach. My teacher. My preacher. My friend. And in ways I see more and more as the years go on, I continue to learn from all that Torchy taught me. I probably always will.

I love you, Torchy.

CHAPTER 30

Tangerine Bowl

In December of 1980, Torchy began his scouting preparation for the prestigious, four-team Tangerine Bowl Basketball Tournament. The historic event at Enyart Alumni Fieldhouse in Winter Park, Florida, featured three Division I schools and one local Division II team, either Rollins or UCF. Stetson University, a Division I program, played annually in the popular tournament which was part of the festivities associated with the Tangerine Bowl Football Game. Glenn Wilkes was Stetson's coach for 36 years (1957–93) and compiled 552 career wins at the Deland, Florida, institution.

The tournament's opening game featured Stetson against Hofstra University. UCF was matched up with Central Michigan (MAC) in the nightcap.

Torchy recalled the dilemma he faced a week before playing Central Michigan: "I sat in my office weighing my options to scout them. We had a budget line for recruiting and scouting, but it was small. "Truthfully, we didn't have the money to scout Central Michigan. Their next game was against Big 10 power, Michigan State in East Lansing. The Spartans were hosting a classic with Central Michigan, Detroit, and Western Michigan. Detroit would play Western Michigan in the first game. Host Michigan State would play Central Michigan in the second game," continued Torchy.

The Knights' coach reminisced, "I went back and forth between going to East Lansing or buying the scouting report for $125.00. But I kept thinking I should see them live, so we wouldn't be embarrassed in the Tangerine Bowl. Central Michigan was 4–0 and receiving votes in the Top 25. Finally, I made the decision," as Torchy recalled, "I asked our athletic secretary to book a flight to Detroit and then a connecting flight to East Lansing."

"The next day as I flew to Michigan, I reviewed my scouting notes on the Chippewas. After landing in Detroit, I boarded a small commuter plane to East Lansing with eight passengers. When I arrived at the packed Jenison Fieldhouse for the first game, the ticket manager placed me in a seat down low—practically in the huddle of Western Michigan, who rallied to beat Detroit."

Torchy was uneasy about his seat location. "I was hoping that Central Michigan had the opposite bench for the second game. I didn't feel comfortable sitting inches (a row behind) from their players and coaches. Much to my dismay, Head Coach Dick Parfitt and the Chippewas had the bench where I was sitting. I was so close, it was embarrassing. I'm glad I wasn't recognized—it just bothered me."

The veteran coach with sound, moral integrity continued: "Did I listen? No, because I have my ethics which include not listening to my opponent's strategy. Before I knew it, 10,000 fans rose quickly in unison giving someone a standing ovation. It had to be Magic Johnson who was with the Los Angeles Lakers at the time. It was Magic, as he strolled into Jenison Arena in a leg cast, slowly hobbling to sit on the Spartan bench like George Gipp of Notre Dame legacy."

Torchy observed the incredible talent on the floor. "Michigan State versus Central Michigan. Both teams were excellent. Central Michigan was impressive. Every phase of their game was executed perfectly.

The Chippewas' best player was Melvin "Sugar" McLaughlin, a gifted player, shooter, and scorer. He could do it all!

"Who won? Central Michigan won. They pounded State 89–66 on the Spartans' home floor! Central Michigan was now 5–0 coming into the 1980 Tangerine Bowl. This was going to be tough!" added the worried, but always prepared Torchy.

Wilkes' Hatters defeated Hofstra 76–72 in the first game, as Stetson advanced to the championship behind the play of Wilbur Montgomery, Frank Burnell, and Brad Weston. McLaughlin is the all-time leading scorer at Central Michigan, scoring 2,071 points in his career. He averaged 20.8 points per game for the Chippewas in the 1980–81 season. In 1982, McLaughlin was named Player of the Year in the MAC.

The long-time UCF coach fondly remembered the Central Michigan game: "We started in a box-and-one defense. Roland Ebron and James Beacham, [a six-foot-two combo guard] alternated guarding McLaughlin. The other four defenders played zone, stopping any dribble penetration by shrinking the court. We took a lead midway in the first half and quickly went to the stall. Central Michigan was extremely talented, but the box-and-one confused them. Our strategy limited McLaughlin's scoring, keeping the ball out of his hands. Instead, we had the ball and held it most of the first half, much to the displeasure of many neutral fans."

Beacham, nicknamed "Spiderman" for his heroic efforts, had two superb years after transferring from Valencia Junior College. The clutch player had breakout games against Saint Leo and Rollins his prior year, scoring 19 and 14 points off the bench for the 25–4 Knights. "'Beach' was a tough player, and I enjoyed coaching him. He was super competitive and played the game the right way," said Torchy.

The smooth combo guard hit a jumper at the halftime buzzer against Central Michigan in Torchy's "triangles-delay" game, putting the Knights up 18–13. The former Xavier coach implemented his "Marty Crowe Marinette strategy (1964)," attempting to beat Central Michigan. The Chippewas were rattled both offensively and defensively by the unorthodox tempo of the game punctuated by Beacham's long-range bomb at the horn.

Torchy recalled an odd memory of the game: "Just before intermission, with us leading 16–13, a fan walked by our bench and said, 'This isn't basketball [the stall] . . . I'm leaving.' Russ (Salerno), my assistant, waved good-bye. I felt sorry for the guy. I was just trying to win the game."

Central Michigan was losing to a Division II team. This was the same team who a week prior pummeled Michigan State by 23 points in East Lansing. Now, they were losing 18–13 at halftime, wondering if their complimentary theme park passes for Sunday included not only Disney World but possibly Sea World too. Yes, the Chippewas were frustrated! The master of strategy had them just where he wanted.

"In the second half we played, delayed, pressed, delayed, and stalled. We won 70–65 and controlled the tempo of the game from start to finish. We gutted it out. I was so proud of my team," the humble Torchy added.

Two years prior, the Knights defeated Virginia Military Institute (VMI) 108–91 in the first round of the 1978 Tangerine Bowl. The next night, they would lose a heartbreaking 85–83 double-overtime championship game to American University, coached by a young Gary Williams. Losing to American was one of Torchy's most agonizing losses at UCF. He very much wanted to win the prestigious Tangerine Bowl in his now-hometown—and have the satisfaction of defeating two Division Is on back-to-back nights.

Ebron, a versatile two-way player, averaged 15.2 points per game as a senior. His ability to play multiple positions helped the Knights to a 23–5 record in 1980–81. In his prior year, he played a significant role in the Knights' 1979–80 successful season and a NCAA tournament berth. Torchy recalled the magnificent play of Ebron: "He had two outstanding years for us—and had a big-time senior year including his finest hour in the Tangerine Bowl. We were an excellent rebounding team with Ruben Cotton, Dean Rossin, and Roland Ebron."

Cotton was an elite rebounder who averaged 10 rebounds a game. In addition, he averaged 14.2 points per game in his two-year career. Every UCF fan that saw Cotton play knew what a special player he was. The Knights' mentor enjoyed coaching the "quiet leaper."

One of Torchy's favorite players, Rossin surprisingly did not play high school basketball. He was a physical player who had the body of an Atlanta Falcon defensive end. Rossin gave the strong-willed, energetic coach an unremitting effort each night. All four players, Rossin, Cotton, Ebron, and Beacham, led the Knights to 48 wins over a spectacular two-year period (1979–81).

The Stetson game gave Torchy one more chance to win a *sweet* Tangerine Bowl Championship. "Glenn Wilkes always had his teams ready to play and was a championship coach. Year in and year out, Stetson played a demanding schedule and were very good," recalled Torchy. Cotton and Ebron were all over the court in the championship game against the Hatters, racing for layups and rebounding like Division I players. Rossin was not only a skilled post presence, but guarded the lane and was a true rim protector.

Jimmie Ferrell, a five-foot-eleven, left-handed combo guard, was a key player for Torchy. Ferrell was a pure shooter who transferred from the Naval Academy. The former Orlando Boone High School star came home to finish his basketball career. He understood Torchy—one of the keys to playing for him. *If you did not "get it," your chance of success was quite limited.* Ferrell "got it." And his last-second pass to Rossin, who made a layup at the buzzer in double overtime, helped the underdog Knights upset the Hatters, 75–73.

It was a chaotic, but joyous ending at Enyart, as the Knights celebrated the Tangerine Bowl Championship. "Jimmie was gritty and ultra-competitive. He was a winner on and off the floor in his three years. His fiery and relentless passion was contagious," concluded the elated Torchy.

Ebron scored 28 points in the Stetson win and was named Most Valuable Player. Similar to UCF marvel Jerry Prather, Ebron was "sneaky good"—meaning he did a lot for the team that did not show up in the box score. It was a well-deserved award for one of the hardest workers in the Torchy era. Rossin and Cotton were also named to the All-Tournament team.

A quote close to Torchy's heart came from Saint Philip Neri: "We must always remember that God does everything well, although we may not see the reason of what he does."

Torchy recalled the excellence of the 1980–81 season: "Winning the Tangerine Bowl was one of my favorite coaching memories. Humbly, I still believe when you're outmatched, you have to protect your team and give them a chance to win! I'm glad I scouted Central Michigan in person and saw the greatness of 'Sugar' McLaughlin. All of our players, coaches, and managers received beautiful Tangerine Bowl Championship watches. Who said we didn't know what time it was? We had watches now! The stall lives another day! But sometimes in life things are like vapors: here and then gone. But the memories remain."

—Contributions from Bill Beekman, "Dribblings Including the Adventures of the Disco Winnebago & Blocked Punts: Fond and Foggy Memories from the Early Days of Knights' Athletics."

CHAPTER 31

Eight Zeros

In 1980, Ronald Reagan was elected to his first term as the 40th President of the United States. Ted Turner, the media mogul, that same year announced the creation of Cable News Network (CNN) in Atlanta, Georgia. Concurrently, in Orlando on the fabulous campus of UCF, diehard Knights basketball fans camped out overnight securing their place in line for a limited distribution of tickets for road games at Rollins and Florida Southern. The ticket lines for BIG home games are nostalgic memories of yesteryear.

This flashback is when the No. 2 nationally ranked Knights hosted the No. 1 Mocs of Florida Southern in 1980. UCF ticket lines opened promptly at 5:00 p.m. on game day for the 7:30 tip-off. The two lines south and north were organized at opposite entrances to UCF's Education Building as ardent Knights loyalists stood impatiently for a ticket. The line to the north extended through the building's lobby, across the terraced walkway, nearly to the parking lot. The line to the south extended for a half-mile through the wooded area outside the building leading to the main road and parking areas. The long lines yearning to watch a Gerald Jones pull-up jumper or a Ruben Cotton tomahawk dunk resembled the ticket line at the local cinema for the

Friday night premiere of *Jaws*. One ticket line sold out in 24 minutes and the other in 27.

Athletic Business Manager Bill Goldsby (a great guy) became the villain, making the harsh announcement to the remaining people in the lines that he was out of tickets. "The real villain," said an unsmiling Goldsby, "is the guy who designed this place [UCF Gym]." Torchy had created a monster just like he did at Xavier. The monster grew and grew each season.

Four hundred people were turned away. "We don't want anybody to be mad," explained Athletic Director Jack O'Leary afterward, trying to appease the crowd. "We want them to have a chance to see good basketball. That's why we worked out the closed-circuit videotaping for the media center and the village center cafeteria. We decided not to charge for that, either."

O'Leary continued, "It's just a darn shame that the Civic Center isn't completed. I believe we could have drawn 10,000. Wow, wouldn't that be a boom to our athletic program! That could be the answer to our prayers." In other big basketball games, tickets *were sold out a week in advance*.

As we fast-forward to the 1981–82 season, the Knights finished with an impressive overall record of 21–8, receiving an at-large bid to the NCAA South/Central Regional in Warrensburg, Missouri. UCF lost to Southeast Missouri State, 60–55 in the opening semifinal. The Knights were led by Alabama native and Southern Union Junior College transfer Willie Edison (1980-82). A six-foot-two "do everything" forward, Edison averaged 17.7 points per game. Edison's 29 points (with 13–15 of those points coming from the free throw line) helped the Knights defeat Rollins 79–72 at Enyart. After the emotional win, Torchy's top assistant Dave Shaw in his first year said, "NOW, I know what the Rollins rivalry is all about. The place was nuts! They knew what we were going to do and we knew what they were going to do. It's a great atmosphere." Shaw added, "Our kids played terrific. Edison was fantastic and so was Eddie Rhodes, Jimmie Ferrell, and Isaac McKinnon."

A Fond du Lac St. Mary's Springs legend, Shaw is the all-time leading scorer at Carroll College in Waukesha, Wisconsin. In 1977, he led the nation (NCAA III) in scoring, averaging 29.3 points per game for the Pioneers. The Wisconsin native pursued a career in coaching and joined Torchy's staff in 1981. He was a dynamic, relentless recruiter who signed several high-caliber athletes for the Knights. "Dave was an outstanding assistant and a great role model for our players. His basketball pedigree and work ethic were a huge part of our success, receiving an at-large bid to the NCAA Tournament. I was lucky to have him," said Torchy. Dave Shaw is Torchy Clark's nephew!

Marty Fisher of the *UCF Future* (1982) noted, "Willie Edison has a marvelous knack for being in the right place at the right time. Just look for the open man or loose ball underneath the basket and you'll find Willie Edison." Torchy reflected, "Willie was an excellent ball player and even a better person. What a great find for us! He was darn close to being as good as Jerry Prather. After his senior year, he became a student assistant and was an inspirational mentor."

Ronnie Thornton (1981–83), a six-foot-four forward and Orlando's (1981) Metro Conference Player of the Year from Winter Garden West Orange High School, was another Division I skilled player for the Knights. Thornton, recruited by assistant Russ Salerno, averaged 11.4 points and 8.0 rebounds per game, dazzling fans with his pure strength and tremendous athleticism. Thornton as a freshman corralled a record 23 rebounds in a game against Edward Waters College in 1981. "He was a mighty force on the boards. The thing about it . . . is I like Ronnie and he likes me. He seems to understand my personality," said Torchy.

After 14 years at UCF, Torchy won 274 games and lost 89. His teams were nationally ranked seven consecutive seasons. During that period from 1969–83, UCF won five of eight Sunshine State Conference Championships. The Sunshine State was considered the "toughest Division II basketball conference in the country."

Looking back at 1983, Torchy remarked, "I had a great run at UCF, but I decided to resign in July. I resigned under no pressure (yes, a few smiling faces). And, I received a one-year sabbatical from the university. This was the first full-paid sabbatical awarded in the school's history. Was it a sad time? Not really. Oh, you always reflect a little, *but my time had come and gone.*"

Why did Torchy resign from his coveted position at the young age of 54? Certainly, he still had plenty of prime coaching years ahead; however, the Continental Basketball Association's (CBA) Wisconsin Flyers, who played in Oshkosh, contacted him in early fall of 1983. The Flyers' owner approached him regarding the possibility of coaching and joining their franchise. Torchy was intrigued about the opportunity of coaching professional basketball. The return to Oshkosh, his hometown, played a small role in pursuing the new challenge.

From Torchy's perspective, the near future of UCF basketball looked *murky* from two fronts. First, the school decided to make the transition to NCAA Division I. The projected next six to eight years looked downright scary to the veteran coach. Torchy knew every facet of basketball, but also had a keen expertise of big-time athletic budgets, staffing, facilities, infrastructure, recruiting, academics, and most importantly, the much-needed financial commitment of the school to become successful.

In 1983, UCF did not fully understand the "Division I process" and the necessary steps involved in that serious and expensive commitment. Through no one's fault, it was a *new* venture into the unknown, but the timing was right for the growing university to make the move. Torchy knew that UCF in the distant future would reach Emerald City and see the Wizard. But for the beginning years, finding the yellow brick road would be a treacherous and difficult task. It would be *fool's gold* to think it would be an easy process.

Secondly, the NCAA in the mid-1980s placed Division II institutions who decided to make the jump to Division I on probation for five years as a provisionary member. During this phase of the process, the school was not eligible for any postseason play (Conference Tournament or NCAA postseason.) The provisionary status of five years was a "coaching purgatory," as recruiting becomes more difficult. Why? Every "potential" recruit wants the opportunity to play in the postseason. Winning becomes harder in purgatory. His sharp mind always stayed one step ahead.

Like many coaches, Torchy really enjoyed teaching. He knew if the Flyers job did not work out, he could come back and teach at the university. The Flyers opportunity/UCF sabbatical were the "perfect storm" for the former Marquette basketball player. When UCF guaranteed him a tenured faculty position on his return, the deal was sealed.

Several weeks after resigning, Torchy was hired as the head basketball coach of the CBA's Wisconsin Flyers. "It was an exciting time. I had already coached at the grade school, high school, and college level, and now I had my chance at the pro level," emphasized the Wisconsin and Florida Hall of Famer.

Torchy wanted Claire to join him in Oshkosh for the Flyers' year, but she knew it may only be a temporary situation. "She loved me, but wanted to stay in Winter Park and keep her job. Claire was well liked at St. Margaret Mary, but who wouldn't like Claire. Unfortunately for me, she decided to stay," said Torchy.

The Wisconsin Flyers played in Oshkosh from 1982–87. Torchy was hired for the 1983–84 season, becoming the third coach in the franchise's history. He signed a rare one-year contract. The plan was to only stay a year; however, Flyers owner Killian Spanbauer thought the lifetime coach would enjoy coaching at the pro level and not want to return to college.

The Flyers were affiliated with the Indiana Pacers and the Milwaukee Bucks of the NBA. The CBA team received the rights to any released players from either organization. At the time, most of the NBA teams worked with two CBA teams. The sole-hybrid partnership that flourishes today in the NBA with the G-League teams did not exist at this time.

"In September, I went to the Pacers' training camp at Hinkle Field House and spent three days with the team. I then visited Don Nelson's preseason camp in Milwaukee for two days," said the rookie CBA coach. Torchy, who had never coached at the professional level, became an astute student of the pro game in those five days and said, "The NBA game is much, much faster, more physical, and so, so competitive. These are the greatest players in the world."

The Pacers' assistant coach told Torchy, "You (Oshkosh) are going to get four *really* good guards from us. We have eight *really* good guards in camp who are all tough." Torchy's brief time in the CBA helped him understand the razor-edge difference between making the team or getting released. The first UCF basketball coach clarified his in-depth analysis of the last workout at Hinkle with a diagram. "These eight zeros below represent eight highly skilled players vying for Pacers' roster spots:

0 0 0 0 0 0 0 0

"Almost identical in ability, four would join the NBA and become Pacers, making huge salaries. The other four who were cut with similar talent would go to Oshkosh and play in the CBA." Torchy continued his thoughts on the intense competitiveness and fire of the NBA: "And you say it's close. Yes, you could hardly divide them;

and yet when they had to be divided, the financial differences, status, travel, and reputation were enormous. It was that close."

Torchy reminisced on his Pacers experience: "These are difficult decisions for NFL, MLB, NBA coaches, and general managers. And, coaches at all levels of sport. Sometimes a high school coach has 60 players at a tryout and has to make difficult decisions on cuts. I immediately thought of how that extra work and attention to detail may have paid off . . . all those little things."

Torchy explained in detail his scoring assessment in the chart below: "Each zero (a player) is intensely evaluated and graded on their talent and ability":

TORCHY'S EIGHT ZEROS

0	0	0	0	0	0	0	0
91	90	90	91	90	90	91	91

At the camp's conclusion, Torchy emphasized a major bullet point: "Wow, now the differences could be practice habits, heart, attitude, personality, handling pressure, or work ethic.

"Sometimes a coach or general manager will evaluate the player's mental toughness or 'general attitude' of being a sub. Is player 'B' a great teammate? Will he be a good bench guy? Many times it comes down to a fine line. Finally, we know if you are sent down, you can fight and claw your way back to the NBA. That is one of the great life lessons of sports."

Torchy recalled his short time with the Flyers: "We had a great guy named Jose Slaughter, and he played in the NBA, CBA, and the Philippines, all at high levels. Slaughter did it with class and dignity. He had all the necessary attributes needed for the NBA. Jose Slaughter, a six-foot-five guard, would have been a 91 on my chart." After a year highlighted by one season with the Pacers (1982–83), Slaughter played

10 years of professional basketball, having several stints with multiple CBA teams. The Compton, California, native was a "warrior" for the week of Flyers' training camp. Slaughter had a noteworthy career at the University of Portland and was drafted by Indiana in the second round of the 1983 NBA Draft.

Meanwhile, the Flyers' players had tremendous respect for the first-year pro coach. Torchy enjoyed the intensity level, work ethic, and emotion as the players fought doggedly for CBA roster spots. The intensity level of the pro game was a perfect match for the high-octane Torchy Clark.

However, he would not coach a game in the CBA. At the end of training camp, Torchy and Killian Spanbauer, the team's owner, disagreed on several issues: decisions on player cuts and allowing him to hire his *own* assistant coach. Their disagreements could not be resolved. Torchy resigned.

The coach returned to the Sunshine State, but learned a valuable life lesson from his short stay with the Flyers. He strongly advised players and coaches at all levels, "Try to give your best effort each day in these areas featured in this chapter, so when you're in the lineup, *you'll be ready.* You don't have to play in the NBA to be happy; the opportunity to play the game, work as a referee, or coach the game at any level is truly a *privilege.*"

Although brief, his CBA experience provided him with insight and knowledge of the professional game he often shared with his students: "Whether in middle school, high school, college, pros, coaching, teaching, the business world, or as a certified financial planner, remember the zeros. *If you have done your best, you have won.* But sometimes in life things are like vapors: here and then gone. But the memories remain."

CHAPTER 32

The Teacher

All coaches are teachers first—at least the good ones. Torchy was one of the best! Whether it was teaching Bill McGinnis the reverse dribble (1953) at St. Mary's, or teaching Jeff Bartosic the "Big Play" (1967) at Xavier, or teaching Ronnie Thornton the full-court press (1982) at UCF, or teaching Nick Pastis the "oranges" delay game (1988) at Trinity Prep, Torchy was a teacher.

After his Wisconsin Flyers experience, he returned to UCF as an assistant professor in the summer of 1984. Torchy taught six hours each semester and supervised physical education interns throughout the Orlando area. The engaging and dynamic teacher taught Coaching Theory, Team Sports, the Basketball and Football class, Bowling, and Actualization of Physical Potential. Other than his sabbatical year, he taught every year (1969–2004), many while serving as basketball coach.

His court now became the classroom. As a coach, he wanted to win every practice; as a teacher, he wanted to win every class. Torchy strived to meet his obligation as a classroom teacher by inspiring and motivating his students each day. He made the transition from coaching to full-time teaching rather seamlessly, always thinking of himself as a teacher first.

As an educator, Torchy was able to carry over his unremitting coaching zeal and fervor into vibrant teaching. This ability to bring students together and provide a forum to exchange ideas, philosophies, and strategies was one of his greatest strengths. The students devoured every word of his class, knowing they were hearing stories and examples from a person that "lived the life." His background and successful career created a spirited platform of credibility and knowledge he passed on to his students. Through his teaching, the students were more prepared for any coaching situations that would arise in their future "labor of love."

As he returned to the classroom full-time (1984), he shared an office with Martha Lue Stewart in the College of Education. She remembered students coming to his office in droves, not only to learn about coursework, but also to learn life lessons. Stewart recalled how devoted Torchy was to Claire and his children. "And we were his UCF family, and we loved him dearly."

Stewart continued, "When he coached, his persona was as much a part of the game, as the team that was on the floor," she relates. "He was able to transmit that same energy and enthusiasm in his classes. I had the pleasure of teaching next door to him in the Wayne Densch Center at UCF. Sometimes because of his enthusiasm, his voice would rise. I'd stop teaching so I could hear him, and my students would laugh along with his."

Torchy's classes were as popular as the Packers in Wisconsin. Each semester he signed numerous overrides from the UCF Registrar, allowing extra students into his courses. Many students picked his brain after class about job opportunities or engaging in sports talk. Each semester a student would ask the coaching lifer, "Are we going to cover any material from the textbook?" Torchy shot back decisively,

"My life is the textbook!!" Students from colleges within the university, like Joe DeSalvo, flocked to his classes, especially to hear the stories. De Salvo warmly reminisced, "He'd talk about his days coaching NFL great Rocky Bleier at Xavier."

The metamorphosis from coaching to full-time teaching was eased by the generous spirit of Frank Rohter. He was a steady influence on Torchy, especially through his sound teaching principles, insight, and knowledge he shared with the professor/coach he hired in 1969. Torchy remembered, "Dr. Rohter became my mentor and has been for all the years at UCF. He prepared me for college teaching."

The 38-year coaching veteran fondly looked back: "He taught me all the little things so well. For example, I always scrupulously labored over my grades. He never interfered, but one day he saw me struggling over grading. You know, grading can sometimes get sticky, like B+, A-, B-, and C+. He simply said to me calmly, 'Gene, I am not a grader; I'm a teacher.' I remind myself of that often. I have been a teacher since."

Rohter was a full professor (exercise physiologist) and a former DePaul University athlete who became a triathlete, participating in 350 triathlons, 11 marathons, and two Hawaiian Ironman Triathlons. Torchy recalled, "Frank is a gentle person who is so nice that his 10-year-old granddaughter called him 'Mr. Rogers.'

"The man is 67 years old [at the time] and is in the shape of an NCAA long jump champion. He is unbelievably healthy and has little stress. In my later years, we shared an office. One day, an insurance agent whom we both knew came to our office. The agent said, 'Torchy, it's time for you to convert your term insurance to whole life—your kids are now raised.' I responded, 'I've been thinking about that, too.'

"'And you, Dr. Rohter (who laid on the office couch with his head back), what about your life insurance?' said the curious agent.

"Dr. Rohter said simply, 'I'm not going to die!'

"'Oh?' the agent said, smirking, 'You're not going to die?'

"'That's right! I take care of myself. I eat right, sleep well, and train. I know exactly what my eight pints of blood are doing,' said Rohter.

"'Oh!' the agent repeated.

"'Let me explain,' continued Rohter, lying in absolutely perfect condition. 'Insurance is for people who don't take care of themselves or have a sickness. Or in need of that kind of protection. I'm doing something positive about my health!'"

Torchy continued, "The agent started to get really interested. He was learning. Dr. Rohter was teaching, and the pupil was listening. He continued in his humble, but firm way! The good doctor knows he's going to die someday. But, he's doing so much in nutrition, weightlifting, running, cycling, and swimming for himself to improve his health.

"The insurance agent was about 50 with his belly four inches over his pants, and his eyes slightly drooped. He smiled and said good-bye," continued Torchy. "Hopefully, the insurance agent went out and bought a good pair of walking shoes later that day. And he learned a strong and powerful lesson from the great *teacher*, Frank Rohter."

Russ Salerno fondly remarked, "Torchy has lots of knowledge. He tries to bring his faith, his feelings, his philosophies into coaching and in the classroom. Many instructors can pass out the paperwork, but they forget how to deal with kids. Torchy deals with the individual, and he can get more out of a kid than anyone else. He has lessons that can't come from a textbook."

Former point guard and one of the top three players in the Torchy era, Calvin Lingelbach (1973–77), described his coach as a "master teacher." Lingelbach added, "When it comes to physical education, he doesn't need a lesson plan or book. When I came to UCF, I thought I knew everything there was to know about basketball. I always had coaches that told me every little move to make and every detail of the game. Well, I looked at Torchy's practice as totally unorganized, and I thought all he was teaching were two plays. It wasn't until my junior year I realized that our 'organized confusion' practices taught me more than I had ever learned before, and there was a distinct method to the madness.

"One of my proudest moments came when we went to the Lawrence University Christmas Tournament in Wisconsin my senior year. My number was No. 14, and after the game a reporter from the *Appleton Post-Crescent* came up to Torchy and commented how well his son, No. 14, had played. Well, it was me and not his son Bo, and I was so proud. Torchy did communicate with me like I was his son," noted Lingelbach.

"At the end of the season, I played the last ten games with a blown-out knee. I was operated on after the season and was in the hospital for 17 days. Torchy came to see me at 6:00 a.m. every day, but didn't want anyone to know. That was the kind of person he is, his ego didn't need to be fed. I agree, Torchy Clark is different; he is a saint; he is gifted," proudly concluded Lingelbach, the former professional jai alai player, softball phenom, and the Knights' most fearless leader.

Torchy's youngest son Bob, an inspirational elementary physical educator and positive role model for 38 years in Orange County (Florida) reminisced, "We grew up in a gym and being around athletics. Sports was a huge part of our lives and brought us closer as a family. It was my dad's *humble* influence that helped me become the man I am today."

Brian Garvey, a truehearted ally of the Clark family over the years, served as Xavier's girls' basketball coach, accumulating an eight-year record of 135–57. Garvey remembers the special times he spent with Torchy on his visits to the Clark family in the Sunshine State: "I enjoyed his insight on other aspects of the game besides the

X's and O's. I can definitely say that I tried to incorporate many of his 'Torchy's Tips' into my own coaching philosophy. It was like being at a coaching clinic sitting with him in his living room, listening to him not only talk the game, but more importantly the life lessons he shared with his players."

Mike Cuff, a successful basketball and golf coach at Lake Brantley High School in Altamonte Springs, Florida, had Torchy for a class at UCF. Cuff played college basketball (1982–84) for Bo, at Flagler College. A lifetime friend of the Clark family, Cuff recalled, "Torchy was an inspiration for me personally in my coaching career. He motivated me tremendously, and his coaching stories will live forever."

Students in the 1960s will never forget his American History class at Xavier. "Torchy always found a way to bring sports into his lesson. All we had to do was mention Jim Bunning, and he would quickly stop discussing the Confederate surrender of the Army of Northern Virginia at the Appomattox Court House. He would then start talking about the Philadelphia Phillies, the 1962 National League pennant race, or Sandy Koufax, the Hall of Fame southpaw of the LA Dodgers," remembered Xavier's Kip Whitlinger, the basketball "franchise" who led Torchy to both a state football and basketball championship in the year of perfection (1962–63).

Another Torchy memory came from Lee Rabas, who coached the boys' basketball team at Xavier from 1997–2004 and was a key player in the Torchy Clark Gym Dedication, who reflected, "I had the good fortune of getting to know Coach Clark during my last two years at Xavier. We had a reunion for the 1963 state championship basketball team. The more information I gathered, the fonder I grew of him; not only as a teacher and coach, but as a person and man.

"It was a blessing to discover what Torchy meant to the players and students of Xavier. They spoke with great reverence about a man who taught them and motivated them to succeed. I'm so glad we renamed the gym in his honor."

Frankie McGinnis, former Hawk football player said, "Coach was one of the most important people I had the good fortune of knowing in my life. He was always an inspiration, not only to me, but to all he touched in his life. Torchy was a great man that made a significant difference in the lives of many students and athletes in his journey."

Many UCF students expressed that Torchy was the best professor they had in college. His unique, honest, colorful, and emotional style of teaching served as an engaging motivator for the soon-to-be coaches. And many said their lives are better because of Torchy Clark. His 33 years of teaching will never be forgotten.

UCF hasn't forgotten, either, and made sure his legacy was secure with the College of Education renaming its gymnasium the "Torchy Clark Gym" at a ceremony in 2005. At the present moment, Torchy's oldest son Mike is an adjunct instructor in the College of Education and Human Performance at UCF, teaching two classes every semester. Providentially, Mike's teaching classroom is the "Torchy Clark Gym."

The College of Education also created an endowment in his name to support scholarships for undergraduate students enrolled in physical education and graduate students in the Sports Leadership Program. The scholarship endowment recognized Torchy's many years as a gifted professor at the university. He retired from the Department of Teaching and Learning Principles in 2004. "Most people think of Torchy as a coach, but first and foremost he is a teacher," said Sandra Robinson, then-acting dean of the College of Education. "That's what made him so successful as a coach. He explained things in ways people can understand. Warm tributes from his students confirmed that many learned as much from his example as what he taught in class."

Ron Johnson, former UCF football player and physical education graduate, reminisced with deep gratitude about his days taking several courses with Torchy: "I wish every athlete in America could have Torchy for one season or even one class. We were extremely fortunate to have him as a mentor. Let's make sure we do the right thing and pass some 'Torchy' to our youth—he would want us to do that."

CHAPTER 33

Trinity Prep

In 1987, while teaching at UCF, Torchy had the opportunity to coach basketball at a local high school, Trinity Preparatory School (Trinity Prep) in Winter Park five miles from the university. The longtime coach was excited to return to the game he loved. He accepted the job but remained as a tenured assistant professor.

Jay St. John, the headmaster of Trinity Prep, thought by hiring Torchy Clark it would bring great prestige to the basketball program. He began at Trinity four years after stepping down at UCF. The decision for the school was a no-brainer: to hire a highly acclaimed Hall of Fame basketball coach that had won 550 games both at the high school and college levels.

Trinity Prep was a 1-A school and competed in the Florida High School Athletic Association District with Wymore Tech, Lake Highland Prep, Mount Dora Bible, Orangewood Christian, Montverde Academy, and Luther High School. The task of rebuilding the Trinity program was a Herculean challenge, as the district was loaded with talented players and outstanding coaches.

With a smile of contentment, Torchy recalled his Trinity days: "I had a fantastic administration and great kids to work with. The school had an *elite* academic reputation. I was happy to be back in coaching! And yes, we did full-court press, throw the long-court pass, run the three-man weave, and stall. We didn't have any Rocky Bleier-type pressers, but we had some good ones."

In his first two years (1987–89), he instantly changed the basketball culture as the Saints finished 20–5 each season. For Torchy, coaching was coaching, regardless of the level. The passionate coach had no ego and enjoyed teaching the game. He posted a spectacular six-year record of 98–45 which included three 20-game win seasons. "I always said your favorite team was either the one you play for or the one you coach. Trinity was my favorite team," emphasized the 58-year-old coach, often reminding his players of loyalty.

The former Xavier-UCF mentor enjoyed his player-coach relationships at Trinity. Some of Torchy's best players in his six-year run were three-point shooters. One of his mantras throughout his career was "you are only as good as your guards." And he didn't mind having four guards on the court at the same time—a visionary idea at the time that is now popular in the NBA. The comparisons of Torchy to his father are eerie, as Donald, also, frequently predicted radical changes in sports strategies as early as the 1940s.

Travis Van Dyke was a six-foot-two versatile player and natural leader who helped Torchy to his first 20–5 season. Other key players in his Trinity five-year run were Don Worden, a six-foot-two point guard who was a clutch performer in many big games; Todd Walker, a five-foot-eight combo guard and shooter; and Duke McLauchlin, a five-foot-ten playmaker Torchy trusted with the basketball (the same trust he had in Xavier's championship point guard Dick Weisner in 1963 and UCF's Calvin Lingelbach in 1976). Torchy's nickname for McLauchlin was "Mr. Trinity."

Gene Orr, a five-foot-eleven high-spirited floor general, ran his offense to perfection. Ron Veres, a six-foot-two power forward and an

All-State football player, was an undersized and relentless rebounder for the Saints. At Xavier in the 1960s, like Ron Veres, Torchy used many football-basketball combo athletes, such as Rocky Bleier, Kip Whitlinger, Dick Weisner, Brad Graff, and Mike Heideman.

Chris Guokas, a six-foot-two guard and son of then-Orlando Magic Head Coach Matt Guokas, played with great confidence and court savvy for Trinity. Another pure shooter was Andy Greenlee, a six-foot-two tough and hard-nosed competitor who had several impressive years under Torchy. A shooter's coach throughout his career, the 1951 Marquette graduate took full advantage of the three-point shot and his Saints' sharpshooters.

The *finest* player Torchy coached at Trinity was six-foot-five, 210-pound power forward, Nick Pastis. Pastis played at Trinity from 1985–89 (last two years for Torchy) and was an All-State and an All-County performer. The two had a tremendous player-coach relationship: Pastis thrived in his "Rat game." And thrived is truly an understatement to describe Nick Pastis' high school career.

In all four Trinity years, Pastis led the Saints in both scoring and rebounding. The power forward blossomed in Torchy's system, averaging 30.5 points per game and leading the Central Florida area in scoring. His Trinity career numbers of 25.1 points per game and 12.4 rebounds per game are Olympian statistics. "Nick Pastis was a Division I player and a joy to coach. He really improved in our system. His tireless, humble attitude was contagious for our entire team. As a coach, your team is *special* when your best player is your hardest worker," added the UCF Hall of Famer.

In Pastis' greatest moment, he helped Torchy's 1-A Trinity beat 6-A Orlando powerhouse Dr. Phillips High School in a shocking upset at the 1988 Dr. Phillips' Christmas Tournament. The Oshkosh-born coach was at his best that night, as Trinity hit three-pointer after three-pointer while using his stall at critical times in the colossal win.

It was a vintage David versus Goliath. In this upset Torchy Clark, like no other person, *understood* the pace, the beat, and the feel of the game. There were no game analytics, just "pure gut feelings" and coaching experience complete with an all-embracing understanding and *realistic* summation of his team's ability.

Pastis remembered his two unforgettable years with Torchy: "Any time we were preparing for an inferior opponent, those were the most demanding practices, when he tried to convince us we were about to lose. He focused on individual matchups and predicted that certain players on the other team were better than our key players. Then, in practices before playing better opponents, he filled us with confidence and laid out a specific strategy to keep us in the game. This strategy worked, because our teams never lost to inferior teams. Torchy understood 'the mental' game, and that's what I took away most from him."

Pastis' practice recollection in 1989 was similar to Kelly Kornely's practice flashback of 1962 as Torchy prepared his football team to play St. John's. Torchy ranted and raved about the incredible talent of the Dutchmen (St. Johns) who were the Hawks' next opponent. Quarterback Dick Weisner (Xavier's Bart Starr) rather innocently questioned his coach if he *really* thought St. John's could beat them. In an angry rage, Torchy dismissed the team from practice. For the 30-year-old football coach, preparation was the key; and yes, in his eyes, *defeat was right "smack" around the corner.*

The Trinity scoring sensation fondly recalled, "Torchy was so far ahead of his time that other coaches couldn't compete against him. He went against everything the others expected to defend. It's amazing how he went back and forth between lightning fast and a snail's pace. I think I'm subjective in saying this because I loved the post in the 1980s and 1990s, but Torchy was prophetic in predicting its near disappearance."

After graduating from Trinity in 1989, Pastis, nicknamed "The Chief," played college basketball at prestigious NCAA Division III Emory University. Today, Pastis is a pulmonary and critical care physician in Charleston, South Carolina.

One of Torchy's most satisfying games as a coach had an unusual ending in 1991 at Trinity. He recalled the sequence of events in a late February game: "I had one of the craziest games in my career, but also one of my greatest. And no one knew it was my greatest, but me. That's what I like about getting to the 'soul' of the game. The crowd was real. Claire wasn't there, no family. Just a few parents; a small attendance of 93 people.

"We were playing a basketball dynasty and district opponent, Wymore Tech (Eatonville, Florida). Wymore in the past had beaten Trinity like a drum. I had never beaten Wymore. I was 0–6 against them. Earlier in the year, they nipped us by 58 points. Yes, we lost by 58. Baskets for us were like touchdowns. We barely got the ball across the half-court line. But now it's the second game.

"The calm side of my demeanor was evident in this game. We 'flat-out' slowed it down and used our stall. This second game against Wymore had a completely different rhythm. It was boring! Both teams looked lethargic: sluggish and apathetic. But this is what I wanted. It was our small window of opportunity to win the game.

"We stalled the whole first half and were only down four points at the break—maybe a possible miracle in Winter Park after the 58-point debacle. I told our team, I want to keep stalling in the second half. This gives us the greatest opportunity to win."

Torchy continued, "Wymore had possession of the ball to start the half, but did not score. We went to the stall to run time off the clock—thinking in Wymore's mind . . . why would anybody in their right mind stall when losing by four points? Wrong! That's the time to stall if you are completely overmatched. Nick Pastis had graduated and was playing at Emory in 1991. My theory was: Try to keep the score as close as possible against a superior opponent; and then strike at the end. You might win! Hey, we lost by 58 in the first game! My mind flashed back *again* to Marty Crowe.

"We kept stalling and stalling. Wymore became impatient and frustrated with our strategy. They backed off from their intense ball pressure and slid into a soft zone. The Wymore players started talking to each other haphazardly while on defense and began doing calisthenics to stay loose. I loved it! We stalled the ENTIRE third quarter and it's still a four-point ballgame," continued the flabbergasted coach.

The fourth quarter began as Torchy recalled, "Wymore got the ball to open the fourth. I assumed they would score, press us, and then press us again. I was worried now the fourth quarter would be a replay of the first game. But that didn't happen. Wymore, to my surprise, began to run their own version of a stall. They showed us: We can play your game too. Great!! All my kids had to do was stunt and fake defensive effort. I was hoping we could get it down to the last minute or two. That is exactly what happened! With 48 seconds left in the game, we were only down four. It was time to play up-tempo and try to win this thing (strike at the end). If we scored five points we could win!"

Torchy concluded with an enormous feeling of accomplishment and pride, "My plan didn't work, and we lost. But it gave our guys a *chance* to win. It was one of my top seven games as a coach, and we lost! But sometimes in life things are like vapors: here and then gone. But the memories remain."

CHAPTER 34

Darling, You'll Be Fine

In their retired life, Torchy and Claire were active parishioners at St. Charles Borromeo Catholic Church, a mile from their home. Both served the church at the 9:00 a.m. Mass; Claire as a Eucharistic Minister and Torchy as an usher. The "passing on of the faith" to the next generation was important to the grandparents of 17. In difficult times, Torchy often quoted Bishop Fulton Sheen who said, "Unless there is a Good Friday in your life, there can be no Easter Sunday."

A few times each basketball season, the couple drove to St. Augustine to watch Bo coach at Flagler. After every game, home or away, Bo had a ritual of calling his dad. On game nights, Torchy and Claire waited anxiously for the 10:00 p.m. call.

Bo fondly remembered, "Torchy was a pro at knowing what to say and how to say it. He had tremendous empathy and was always honest, yet encouraging. Many times watching a Flagler game in person, Torchy would get fidgety and leave at halftime." For many parents, it can be nerve-wracking watching the game from the stands, especially being a former coach. It's much easier to coach the game and "be in the fray" than being a parent-spectator.

"When my dad left early, I understood. Talking to him put things in perspective. I coached for eight years after he died. I thought about calling him after every game," said Bo.

One day in early fall 2004, Torchy complained to Claire about one of his teeth and how the pain would not go away. The lifetime coach thought he may need a wisdom tooth pulled or, possibly, a dreaded root canal.

The dentist immediately examined his sore tooth after X-rays, but it was quickly clear his problem wasn't going to be solved by a dentist. "I knew I was in trouble when the hygienist started calling me 'darling.' They weren't telling me what I had, but I knew I was in trouble," said the worried Torchy. "You don't just pass around words like 'darling' and 'honey' and 'Oh my God, baby.' I thought something is really wrong. And it was," he added.

An oral surgeon in Orlando found a malignant cancerous tumor in his right jawbone. Torchy was diagnosed with cancer—squamous cell carcinoma, Stage IV of the jawbone. The news jolted him. The same-type jolt that shocked through his body with the deaths of his two brothers at such young ages. But with faith as his solid foundation, he knew God was in control. All along, he had been thinking the pain was a wisdom tooth; cancer had never crossed his mind.

Now, the Clarks teamed together to research as much information about jawbone cancer as possible. They found he would need extensive surgery, follow-up chemotherapy, and radiation treatments. At this stage in the process, the two options were: (1) Have surgery to remove the cancer from the jaw bone and reconstruct the area, or (2) Opt to not have the surgery and live a year or two as the cancer metastasized. The former St. Mary's Menasha (1945–47) boxer was indeed a *fighter*. The 75-year-old Torchy frequently said he lived a "charmed life" and was truly blessed. But this by far would be his most difficult challenge.

The three potential sites for the surgery were the M.D. Anderson Cancer Clinic (Houston, Texas), UF Health Shands Hospital (Gainesville, Florida), or Memorial Sloan Kettering Cancer Center (New York City). Sloan Kettering was strongly recommended by trusted friend and diehard UCF fan, Mike Daspin.

The family advised Torchy to begin with Sloan Kettering to get a strong opinion and some direction. He was accompanied by Claire, Bob, and Bo as the foursome flew to New York. At the hospital, he was then introduced to one of the top ENT-otolaryngologists in the country, who thoroughly examined the affected area while looking at various scans. In the small, crowded patient room, the surgeon was positive and sincere with Torchy and his nervous family.

The surgeon explained in detail the possible 12-hour surgical procedure which would remove the tumor, bone, and soft tissue in the first phase; the second phase included the reconstruction of his jaw using part of his leg or hip bone. The surgeon was a straight-shooter and understanding, but told the family . . . this was a difficult surgery. The lengthy procedure would be followed up by weeks of chemotherapy and radiation. He would lose taste buds, lose some ability to produce saliva, his speech would be affected, and he would lose teeth during radiation. In addition, he would be forced to live on a soft diet the rest of his life.

Torchy liked the straight-forwardness and bluntness of the surgeon. He developed an immediate trust in him. As he left the doctor's office, he knew the surgery would be a *grinder*, but remained positive, knowing he had immeasurable support from family and friends. "Sloan Kettering had such a renowned reputation in its treatment of cancer. This type of cancer was definitely unique. We wanted only the best for Dad," said daughter Patty. He decided to have the surgery in New York. It would not be easy.

Claire handled the cancer news bravely with deep faith, praying frequently while attending daily Mass with Torchy. But she, too, was worried about the length of the surgery and its grueling intensity. Although her mobility was quite limited, her support and love for her husband never wavered. She was in the fight. "We were all nervous for Torchy and knew it would be a rough road ahead," said the devoted Claire.

Friends of the Clarks poured in with prayers and uplifting support. During this time, Torchy heard from a multitude of friends, former players, coaches, managers, and students he had coached or taught in 50-plus years. With deep gratitude, he said, "It was encouraging to get all the phone calls, letters, and home visits. One Xavier player who constantly called was Greg Steinhorst, my former quarterback who threw the long pass to receiver Jeff Bartosic in 'The Big Play' in our huge win at Premontre in 1967 (Chapter 14). Greg was so supportive when I was sick."

In Jim Nantz's *Always by My Side: A Father's Grace and a Sports Journey Unlike Any Other*, President H.W. Bush in his Foreword emphasized, "Few of us will walk this earth and not be touched in some way by tragedy, but there's an old saying that adversity has a way of introducing you to yourself."

The family huddled, once again, to discuss the logistics of having surgery in New York—the flights, the hotels, the dates—and who would accompany Claire and Torchy during the two-week hospital stay. The city is expensive, especially in December; however, the Clarks had two living angels who came to their rescue.

The first was Russ Salerno, who along with his youngest son, Tony, brainstormed for ideas on how to assist the Clarks financially in New York. The Salernos embarked on an ardent Torchy Clark Cancer Fund, a fundraising campaign to help raise money to offset the costs of medical bills, hotels, flights, cabs, and other expenses during the ordeal.

The former assistant was not done helping his mentor. At Errol Estates Country Club in Apopka, Florida, he organized the Torchy

Clark Golf Classic in 2006, with all proceeds going directly toward his cancer-related expenses. Salerno's "labor of love," along with 80 enthusiastic "Torchy" golfers who played in the tournament, was a spectacular event. The stylish Torchy Golf Classic brochures were designed and printed by Yvette Salerno, Bubba Salerno's wife. "Russ did a fabulous job organizing the tournament. It was a picture-perfect day and a powerful testament to Torchy's legacy!" reminisced Mike. Patty added, "There was a lot of *love* on the golf course that day. It meant so much to our dad and family."

Another angel was Mike Daspin, not only for his strong recommendation of Sloan Kettering, but his timely arrangement in securing the Roger Smith Hotel in Manhattan for the Clarks' two-week stay. Daspin's daughter lived in New York, and he and his wife Sara had been frequent visitors to the city. He had a business relationship with the owner of the Roger Smith, who assisted the family with their lengthy accommodation.

The surgery was on December 17, 2004. The nurses at Sloan Kettering politely told the Clarks after Torchy's pre-surgery check-in at 6:00 a.m. to leave the hospital and return at dinner. "We prayed a lot that day. It was tough emotionally knowing your dad is going through a 12-hour surgery," said Bob. "The hospital staff discouraged us from sitting in the waiting area all day. They told us we could call and get updates. And we did, several times," he added of the stressful day.

At 7:00 p.m., the 12-hour procedure was completed. Claire remembered that December night: "The surgeon told us the operation was successful and they had removed all the cancer. He then explained that his team did not use bone to restore the jaw, but instead opted to create a "skin flap" using skin from his thigh." Claire continued, "The kind-hearted doctor stressed that Torchy would be heavily sedated for two to three days because of the delicate nature of facial reconstruction and the intensity of the procedure."

Relief and reality both set in quickly for Claire, Bob, and Bo, who had been in non-stop contact during the day with family and friends in Florida, Wisconsin, and Kentucky. The surgery was over, but the battle was just beginning. Torchy loved the powerful quote from St. Rose of Lima who said, "Apart from the cross, there is no other ladder by which we may get to heaven." (Catholic Company, 2019)

On the fourth day at Sloan Kettering after surgery, Torchy finally regained consciousness, but it took several *long* days to orient himself to his surroundings and understand the severity of the procedure. "The waiting was emotionally draining. Seeing Dad suffer was difficult and we felt helpless. We wanted to be there for both of them," recalled Bob, of the exhausting recovery.

Before the surgery, the Clark family discussed in detail "the changing of the guard." This included the coordination of four-to-five-day New York shifts for the Clarks flying in from Florida. The siblings spent many hours at the hospital and assisted Claire, who was in the city for the duration. Patty, who was incredibly compassionate and nurturing with Torchy, came to New York on the fourth day, relieving Bob. Mike came the fifth day, relieving Bo.

The Clarks worked like an efficient team in Torchy's recuperation. Spending hours and hours at Sloan Kettering, Mike, Bob, and Patty constantly lifted his spirit, as their presence and support were vital in his recovery. The stressful post-surgery weeks were overwhelming and an *emotional* roller-coaster for the Clark family.

Torchy and Claire returned to Orlando 17 days later, a day after his 76th birthday on New Year's Day. He recalled the welcome relief of returning back to Florida: "I was so glad to be home. *It was the toughest thing I've ever been through in my life.* My kids and Claire were unbelievable and so supportive. We're a tight family!"

The Sloan Kettering doctors allowed Torchy to have his post-surgery treatments at UF Health Shands Hospital in Gainesville. Eight weeks after the surgery, the married couple of over five decades who fell in love at Marquette drove the two hours to Gainesville to begin the intense regimen. He received radiation five days a week Monday through Friday and chemotherapy once a week.

During this time, the couple would leave Monday morning from Orlando, receive treatment and then spend four nights in a Gainesville hotel. While most people find the post-surgical procedures to be a torturous part of the cancer treatment, Torchy said he wasn't in any pain, despite massive swelling around his right jaw. One of his favorite inspirational quotes is from St. Josemaria Escriva who said, "Suffering overwhelms you because you take it like a coward. Meet it bravely, with a Christian spirit: And you will regard it as a treasure." (Catholic Company, 2018)

After the treatments were completed, he was declared cancer free!! At this time, the skin flap on Torchy's jaw was quite large and noticeable; however, he handled his physical appearance like a true champ. The surgeon had reminded him that after a year, he could have liposuction surgery to remove the excess skin buildup. And he did, at Sloan Kettering, which made his jaw look much better.

As part of his mandatory soft diet, Torchy experimented, eating foods such as pudding, eggs, ice cream, yogurt, soft vegetables, smoothies, and applesauce. The nutritional experiment was unsuccessful and eating remained a continual struggle. The family desperately tried to persuade him to eat soft foods, but he liked the smoothness and ease of swallowing homemade blended shakes. Torchy's daily caloric intake consisted of three chocolate shakes made from Boost chocolate drink, a banana, protein powder, and yogurt.

The shakes were his nutrition the rest of his life. Claire was already an expert at making shakes. Sixty years earlier, she had made hundreds of chocolate malts at her father's Covington, Kentucky, drugstore in the summers. Now, in 2005, Claire was blending three liquid meals a day for her husband's survival. Torchy handled his plight like a trooper and enjoyed a semi-active life with his children, grandchildren, and friends. He often attended local high school football and basketball games and missed being in the "fray" of coaching. The former coach enjoyed his close relationships with the fine people of the St. Charles community.

Jim Flanagan faithfully supplied his former UCF coach with a large canister of protein powder every other month. In a thank-you letter to Jim for a lifetime of kindness, Torchy thanked his "friend" for his tremendous loyalty and countless visits to his home. Both Flanagan and Russ Salerno had dug deep "in the trenches" to help their revered mentor at a *critical* time in his life. With great appreciation, Torchy concluded, "That's the beauty of coaching—the lifetime relationships and the unbreakable player-coach bond that lives forever. But sometimes in life things are like vapors: here and then gone. But the memories remain."

—Contributions from Stuart Korfhage/
St. Augustine Record/*March 1, 2005*

CHAPTER 35

Good-Bye Lovely Lady

Claire Theis was born in Cold Spring, Kentucky, to Dorothy and William Theis. The second oldest of four daughters, Joan, Mary, and Lois, Claire grew up in Southgate. She went to an all-girls school, Notre Dame Academy in Park Hills. After graduating from Notre Dame, Claire attended Marquette University in Milwaukee, Wisconsin, where she met her future husband.

On the kindness and gentleness of his mother-in-law Dorothy Theis, during the celebration of her 102nd birthday, Torchy said, "Today, we honor Dorothy on this amazing day. But more important we honor a very special, special lady. Nobody was a better mother, and everyone here was touched and loved by her."

He continued his adulation of Claire's family: "Bill [father] was the protector, the breadwinner, and Dorothy was the *heart!* She was the ideal mother and had four beautiful girls that called her the 'perfect mother.' Joan, Claire, Mary, and Lois are just like her—smart, humble, thoughtful, radiant, the best morals, and with no arrogance whatsoever. They are all class and loved to laugh. Dorothy and Bill were great parents in a pure, tender-hearted home. She raised her girls like herself." Torchy fondly closed by adding, "*They say you can't raise canaries in a crow's nest.* The Theises had four beautiful canaries, and I was incredibly blessed to have been married to one."

Teaching physical education at St. Margaret Mary for over 25 years, Claire also coached girls' volleyball, track, and softball. She was a vibrant role model for her students and became a huge part of the St. Margaret Mary community.

A loyal and supportive coach's wife, Claire attended most home football and basketball games in his 38 years of coaching. Many times at UCF, she helped to entertain recruits at the Clarks' home on official visits. Her dynamic and charismatic personality assisted her husband-coach on many occasions, helping the recruit feel comfortable and welcome.

Claire was truly a giver. She was a guiding force in Torchy's cancer recovery, encouraging him in his fight through surgery, radiation, and chemotherapy. She was there every second, every minute while she, herself, battled her own health problems. Claire admired the eloquent quote of St. Gianna Molla, who said, "Love is the most beautiful sentiment the Lord has put into the soul of men and women."

The year 2004 was both an eventful year, yet a stressful year for Torchy and Claire. The present-day Xavier Athletic Director Kathy Bates, who was remarkably a student at the school during the Torchy years, was influential in the renaming of the gym. Bates remembered the special night: "In February of 2004, the gym was named the Gene 'Torchy' Clark Gym, and the now-Orlando resident was able to come home for the dedication ceremony, which was fittingly held the night of a boys' basketball game. A plaque engraved with Torchy's picture hangs in the 'Torchy' lobby, sporting the phrase, 'The Torch Will Never Go Out.' The evening was a memorable event to honor a coaching legend, and we were thrilled that he was able to attend. His Xavier legacy still lives on today. He will never be *forgotten*." A special thank you goes to the members of the Gene "Torchy" Clark Gym Planning

Committee: Kathy Bates '71, Kelly Kornely '63, Kip Whitlinger '63, Rocky Bleier '64, Brad Garvey, Chris Richter, Rick Vander Wyst, Becky Weiske, Jim Weiland, Lee Rabas, Matt Reynebeau, Sena Gray, Sister Patrice Hughes, and Tom Simon.

Kristin Lease, the 2004 *Xavier High Prospector Alumni News* editor, wrote of Torchy's special honor that night:

> When Xavier opened its doors in 1959, Mr. Gene "Torchy" Clark said "he looked at the trophy case and it was empty." Because the school was built to offer a strong Catholic education above everything else, Mr. Clark said to himself, "I don't see how we're ever going to win."
>
> That didn't stop Mr. Clark from coaching his team to 15 conference championship titles and maintaining a 62-game winning streak. The Hawks under Mr. Clark's direction never had a losing season. The spirit with which Mr. Clark coached the team will never die. From February on, students who play at Xavier will play in the gym that bears his name.
>
> The gym was dedicated to Mr. Clark on February 21 before the varsity boys' game in front of 2,000 fans. The sold-out gym that housed Mr. Clark's past players, members of Mr. Clark's family, alumni, students, and faculty greeted both Mr. Clark and his former player, Mr. Rocky Bleier, with a standing ovation.
>
> The Super Bowl champion and decorated Vietnam War veteran opened the evening with fond words and memories of Mr. Clark: "The greatest gift he brought to Xavier was his will to win. He wanted you to succeed. You either loved Torchy or you didn't… He's not okay: he's opinionated. He's not nice; he's passionate." Bleier added, "It's not about Torchy," noting that with Mr. Clark, it has always been about faith, teaching, and

the players. "If faith is number one, then his wife is number 'IA,' because she has to be a saint." When future students ask about the man for which the gym is named, Mr. Bleier responded by saying, "He is a selfless man who gave his all and started a tradition... a simple man who was the greatest coach anyone could ever have, who taught us to believe."

The boys' basketball coach [2004] Lee Rabas presented Mr. Clark with a plaque commemorating the dedication. Mr. Clark accepted the plaque and addressed the crowd. He had a unique system for writing out his speech. A file folder decorated in colorful word clusters contained the notes for the oration that captivated the crowd. Every line drew laughter, cheers, or applause.

Throughout his speech, he commended both his players and Xavier, shared memories, and rattled off a litany of "thank yous." "There are very few legends and he [Rocky Bleier] is the greatest thing that ever happened to Appleton," Mr. Clark said. "I could tell Bleier stories all night long." The NFL star was not the only player Mr. Clark wanted to address. He added, "To my players—you guys were talented, you were humble, no one bragged... you were great students... you were winners."

His thoughtfully crafted speech did not lack humor. "Since this is about the basketball gym, I want to tell some football stories," he said. Mr. Clark's genuine adoration of Xavier showed throughout his speech. "I love the crucifix on the wall... this school is extremely blessed. *This school is a slice of Heaven.*"

The audience, which included many young people who had never met Mr. Clark, responded warmly to him. "This is very, very touching tonight, and a lot of you don't even know me," he said.

The 75-year-old coach wanted to keep the focus of the night on the current varsity boys. "The game is the thing," he affirmed countless times. Indeed, he managed to watch the game despite all of the attention. In an interview after his speech, he said he did not think about how people would remember him: "I want the Lord to say, 'he worked hard.' I'm not concerned with what people think," he said, "I just want to be a good father and grandfather." (By Kristin Lease, *XHS Prospector*, Alumni News, Xavier High School–Spring 2004)

Eight months after the gym dedication came the unexpected, fearful jawbone cancer diagnosis, followed by the 12-hour surgery in December. As a nurturer, Claire was the best. Torchy's primary health issues post-surgery were general weakness and dehydration.

In August 2007, on a trip to a local department store, Torchy and Claire parked their car and proceeded into the store about 100 feet away. As Claire walked, she tripped, lost her balance and fell hard to the pavement. From the fall, she immediately lost consciousness as Torchy hurried to her aid. The local EMTs were called, rushing her to the hospital. When Claire arrived, she still was unconscious; the trauma from the fall caused internal bleeding as many of her vital organs began to shut down. The Clark family raced to the hospital as their mom fought for her life.

After two days of great uncertainty, Claire regained her consciousness, but her organs had suffered severe damage as she tried to gain strength. She was hospitalized for several months. Now, it was Torchy's turn to be the loving nurturer and support system. The Clark family helped by taking shifts staying with both of them. Claire was in and out of consciousness as her health slowly declined.

On November 4, 2007, with the family at her side, Claire passed away. The day she died, November 4th, coincidentally was the Feast Day of St. Charles Borromeo, the patron saint of their home parish. One of Claire's favorite quotes from the great saint was, "Be sure that you first preach by the way you live. If you do not, people will notice that you say one thing, but live otherwise, and your word will bring only cynical laughter and a derisive shake of the head." Claire lived her life by that precious quote. She preached by the meek and humble way she lived.

Claire was 77 when she died. Torchy lost his best friend. "When Mom died, a huge part of Dad's heart died too. Nobody was a better person than our mom. They were attached to each other and kept each other going," said Bob, in a warm tribute. The eldest son, Mike, wondered how Torchy would survive without his golden gem: "When Mom died, we were all concerned how Dad would handle the loneliness and the day-to-day functioning. It was difficult, and we knew he needed us."

Several months after Claire's death (2007), Torchy wrote a five-paragraph letter to the editor of the *Marquette Alumni Newsletter/Magazine* entitled "Like We Were Still at Marquette."

"Like We Were Still at Marquette"

"Claire Theis and I, Gene 'Torchy' Clark, fell in love at Marquette University in 1950. Claire was a sophomore and I was a junior. I wrote my dad and said, 'I'm going to marry a girl from Kentucky who is going to Marquette. I've never been happier.' My father took my letter to our parish priest in my hometown of Oshkosh, Wisconsin. The priest said to my dad, 'You're lucky you got the letter.'

"In 1950 we got married, and for 57 years we loved each other as much as we did when we fell in love at Marquette. I wanted to coach, which we did, coaching and teaching for 51 years until I retired. We had four boys and one daughter, all of whom attended UCF in Orlando, Florida.

"On August 13, 2007, beautiful Claire fell down, and all her organs shut down. Six doctors said we should let Claire go. I said no—I wanted Jesus to have his time. Three weeks later everything came back perfect. The next ten days were like we were still at Marquette. Claire was so popular and beautiful. We were ready to put her in rehab when a terrible sepsis infection hit Claire, and on November 4th, 2007, Claire died.

"On our very last day, in a dark hospital room in which the love of my life hadn't spoken for several days, I kissed Claire and said, 'I love you, Claire.' It came from my soul and 57 years of joy. I was shocked to hear her say clearly 'and I love you!!'

"Those were our last words, said like we were still at Marquette; Claire, the beautiful co-ed in Liberal Arts, and me, the Liberal Arts Education major. Our Marquette days were perfect and it continued for the next 57 years, which I thank God for." (*Marquette, 2007*)

■　■　■

Torchy's daughter Patty and her husband Bernie Budnik stepped in wholeheartedly, as did all the Clarks after Claire's death. But, Patty's tenderness and compassion simulating Claire's kindness helped Torchy considerably in his time of grief and transition.

Claire lived the self-sacrificing life, and her family meant everything to her. Torchy was the head of the family, but Claire was the *heart* and *soul*. The mother of five loved the powerful words of Pope Benedict XVI:

"The family is the privileged setting where every person learns to give and receive love. The family is an intermediate institution between individuals and society and nothing can take its place. The family is a necessary good for peoples, an indispensable foundation for society and a great and lifelong treasure for couples. It is a unique good for children, who are meant to be the fruit of love, of the total and generous self-giving of their parents. The family is also a school that enables men and women to grow to the full measure of their humanity." (Pope Benedict XVI, the *Magnificat*, 2017)

The day after Claire's death there was a perfect tribute to her in the *Orlando Sentinel* with the headline "Good-Bye Lovely Lady" written by columnist and Clark family friend, Jerry Greene. The 78-year-old Torchy was so proud of the deeply, moving farewell to his lovely lady of 57 years.

"If you didn't know Claire Clark, wonderful wife of former UCF basketball coach Torchy Clark, you missed a constant ray of sunshine in your life. Claire, who left us this week, brightened the day of anyone she met. If you did know her, you don't need me to know how much she will be missed. Godspeed Claire."

CHAPTER 36

Our Role is to Return to God

The most important virtue in Torchy's life was his faith. He read the Bible every day, attended daily Mass, and had a strong devotion to the *Novena of the Twelve Year Prayers of St. Bridget of Sweden on the Passion of Jesus,* which he fervently prayed, seldom missing a day.

In fall 2008 in an interview with Jerry Greene of the *Orlando Sentinel,* Torchy was asked by his close friend and reporter if he ever embraced the idea of death and did he fear it? The legendary Xavier/UCF coach replied, "I'm Catholic. I still have my family, including 17 grandchildren, which is motivation to hang around. But I'm not afraid of death because my faith gives me strength." Greene then quickly asked, "And, what about Claire?" Torchy confidently said, "I expect to see her again. We'll have a lot of time. My only worry is that I'll get to Heaven and find out she's married to *John the Baptist*." The outstanding *Sentinel* columnist continued by asking the two-time cancer survivor (prostate and jaw bone) how his present health was. The quick-witted king of the one-liner said, "I've had everything except leprosy. I'm good." Greene inquired if it was tough on the former Marquette basketball player not having a hard meal in almost four years. Torchy shot back with his Wisconsin humor, "I don't miss eating much, although every once in a while, I'd love a Grand Slam at Denny's."

It was a collective Clark team effort after Claire died as Torchy fought a broken heart. To ease his pain, however, he did stay at daughter Patty's house off John's Lake in Oakland (outside of Orlando, 30 minutes from his house) several times a week. The lake has tremendous fishing, and the Florida Sports Hall of Famer loved to fish with his son-in-law Bernie and his grandchildren.

Unlike most men, Torchy actually liked to shop, looking for bargains (usually clothes). He enjoyed the busyness and energy of a mall. "Torchy loved shopping. He was so sweet and fun to be around. But he missed Claire so much. I tried to help him as often as I could because I knew how lonely he was," said Patty.

Another one of his hobbies was watching old movies with Bernie for endless hours. Many days during the week, his sons would stop by his house to spend time with him watching an MLB, NFL, or NBA game or in conversation about family. Torchy cherished the company of family and friends during countless home visits, usually engaging them with coaching story after story.

Patty, in her devotion to Torchy as unofficial nurse and totally official best friend, went above and beyond her "labor of love" after Claire's death. With humor that never deserted him, Torchy said, "I give Patty a quarter an hour." In sincere gratitude, he wrote a beautiful letter that was left among his many notes and writings thanking Patty for her gentle, Claire-like kindness. Torchy wrote, "Mom would be proud! Patty picks up and orders my prescriptions, makes all necessary phone calls, cleans everything, and kept my dog (Jessie) when I was not feeling well. Patty has asked for nothing and has done so much. She always begs me to stay at her house. We get along perfect."

Son Mike remembered, "Torchy enjoyed going to high school football games at Bishop Moore. Walking the sidelines following the ball, he loved being close to the action. I think he missed the X's and O's of coaching football." Son Bob recounted Torchy's last year: "We all knew he was lonely without Claire. We helped as much as possible with doctor appointments, errands, and stayed at his house a night or two trying to fill the Claire-void. But Patty did an unbelievable job of nurturing him, which he needed at that time. She was great and Bernie was terrific with Torchy too."

Throughout his life, the longtime coach was caring and compassionate, often visiting the sick or dying in hospitals or homes. He always had kind words for the brokenhearted and suffering. Pope Francis encourages us that "time spent with the sick is holy time. It is a way of praising God who conforms us to the image of his son." Saint John Paul II said, "It is in care for the sick more than in any other way that love is made concrete and a witness of hope in the Resurrection is offered." John Paul II added, "Christ did not come to remove our afflictions, but to share in them, and, in taking them on, to confer on them a salvific value." (*Magnificat*, February 2018)

Torchy, reflecting back on his "charmed life" having grown up in Oshkosh, playing at Marquette, meeting the love of his life, teaching and coaching over 50 years, believed that God in his infinite wisdom places individuals or role models in our lives to guide us. These influential "helpers" may be teachers, coaches, friends, bosses, or peers who help us carry out God's will as we strive each day to be Christ-like. For Torchy, six "helpers" influenced him eminently in his earthly journey from Oshkosh, Wisconsin (1929) to Orlando, Florida (2009): his father Donald, Bob Kolf Sr. of Oshkosh State, Monsignor Adam Grill of St. Mary's, Brother Peter of Xavier, Frank Rohter of UCF, and close friend Bob Willis of the Orlando Twins/Appleton Foxes. All played meaningful roles in Torchy's cornerstone of values, beliefs, and philosophy in his 80 years.

In April of 2009, Torchy's health slowly began to deteriorate, as general weakness and dizziness forced a worried Patty to take him to the doctor. The doctor diagnosed dehydration and instructed him to drink more fluids and increase his daily caloric intake. After the doctor's visit, Patty lovingly ordered her dad to stay with their family a few nights as he recovered. Bernie and Torchy that night enjoyed a movie at the house.

The next morning around 6:00 a.m., Bernie left for work, and Patty before leaving made a shake for Torchy. She set him up comfortably on the couch in their family room (downstairs) to watch TV and drink his breakfast. She then headed on her commute. Thirty minutes later, Patty's daughter Kaley came into the family room and asked, "Grandpa, are you okay?"

"Yeah, I'm fine, Kaley," said Torchy.

"I'm going to take a shower and get ready for school," added Kaley.

"Okay," Torchy replied.

And then he returned to watching ESPN's MLB highlights of last night's games. Torchy loved baseball! When Kaley came back into the family room at 6:45 a.m., *Torchy had died.* The date was April 22, 2009. He was 80 and died of congestive heart failure. But Torchy did not die alone in his house—he was in his daughter's home—a home full of love and warmth.

The funeral was two days later at an overflowing St. Charles Borromeo, a parish close to Claire and Torchy's heart. The beautiful Mass was attended by many of his former players, coaches, managers, students, fellow professors, and friends. The hymn "Ave Maria," the same at Claire's funeral 17 months prior, was sung devoutly by a parishioner.

The night Torchy died, Patty, still overwhelmed with grief, went to gather his valuables and keepsakes at his house. Upon entering Torchy and Claire's bedroom, the first thing she noticed immediately was a paper note on his bedroom dresser. It was a plain, white index card with a handwritten sentence in Torchy-print (big letters). Once a teacher, always a teacher, the *coach* left a strong, faith-inspired message of spiritual guidance before he left this earth. The note read:

OUR ROLE IS TO RETURN TO GOD*

Torchy had written the note the same day (prior day before he died) he left his house with strict orders from Patty. With faith as his cornerstone, he believed that after death, he would *return to God* and be in the presence of his Maker, the Almighty God. And see his beloved Claire once again. The reunion of the Hilltoppers in Heaven would be one of everlasting and immeasurable joy ("Back at Marquette"). Torchy, too, would reunite with his father (Donald), mother (Florence), and two brothers (Dutch and Jim), who he had profoundly missed throughout his life.

John Wooden in *The Greatest Coach Ever* said, "Winning seems so important, but it actually is irrelevant. Having attempted to give our all is what matters—and we are the only ones who really know the truth about our capabilities and performance. Did we do our best at this point in our life? Did we leave all we had to give on the field, in the classroom, at the office or in the trenches? If we did, then we are a success—at that stage in our life."

Torchy's gauge of earthly happiness was simple and humble, like many things in his life. "To me, coaching is the second best thing a person can do in sports. The No. 1 thing is to PLAY! There is nothing better than playing. Most coaches loved playing so much they just hung around longer and coached. Third, would be broadcasting sports, working as a team manager, officiating, or sports writing. I've done them all and it was a privilege.

"What a beautiful vocation—to go to school every day of your life. My father once asked me, 'Do you like teaching and coaching?' I said, 'I love it.' Playing sports and the early coaching roots (Bob Kolf Sr.) have been a part of my life since I was seven years old growing up in Oshkosh," recollected Torchy of his passion for teaching.

Sports was a huge part of Torchy and Claire's family. "My wife and five children have positively been affected from my work. Remember the classic 1989 movie, *Field of Dreams* with Kevin Costner and the cornfield? Someone asked me, 'Torchy, did you see *Field of Dreams?*' I replied, 'I not only saw it, but I lived it.' In our family, I played catch with my boys many days in our Appleton backyard. We were constantly talking ball—Xavier sports, pennant races, college football, college basketball, and Super Bowls. All of us followed Jim Bunning's (Uncle Jim's) career closely. We always knew how the Phillies were doing in the National League, and we followed Jim's individual pitching record."

Torchy recalled how fortunate he was to teach and coach at St. Mary's and Xavier: "Appleton was a great place to raise our family. I believe we had one of the nicest outdoor basketball courts in the city. Several of my friends and coaches helped pour the cement and install the state-of-the-art metal fan-shaped backboard. My kids loved it!" added the proud father.

Torchy's "fiery" reputation will always be a part of any discussion about the legend's career. Jim Rather, a player on the 1962–63 State Basketball Champion Hawks, recalled a different side to his personality that delighted him: "Torchy had a human side. My fondest memory of him occurred during my junior year in 1963. We basketball players would like to try trick shots before and after practices. It was the 'kid in us' having fun. The trick shots varied from half-court, three-quarter, stage, doorway, behind the basket and bleachers. We never knew Torchy silently took note of our efforts.

"One day late in 1963 as the players were getting ready for practice, Torchy came racing into the locker room and proudly announced that he had made a most improbable shot, one that we players had been trying all year without success. The shooter would stand in the doorway leading to the gym and attempt to carom the ball into the basket off the supporting structure of the backboard. The team was *stunned* because: (1) None of us had ever made that shot, (2) Torchy was doing this 'trick shot stuff,' and (3) Torchy would admit to it. In that moment, I realized all the hard work and sacrifices were truly worth the effort. Torchy showed us his human side, for he had a 'little kid' in him just like us."

Rocky Bleier, a member of the Pittsburgh Steelers Hall of Honor (2018 inductee), reminisced with deep emotion about his esteemed coach: "To some degree he's in a better place. It's easier to say that to make you feel better, but in this case it's true. And he is. It's always a sad and tragic moment as time passes and that era passes and people who were a part of your life, a big part of your life have passed on." (Woods, 2009)

On the life-after, Torchy blissfully explained his grandiose vision of heaven: "I thought I'd coach again in the next world. We do go around twice. In heaven, besides praising and honoring God, I plan, along with my coaching job, to direct a dance band! A big band with a great brass section, singles, a choral group, maybe twin pianos and even a comedian, a juggler and a tap dancer just like in the old Riverside Theater in Milwaukee. A band with a girl vocalist like Peggy Lee or Ella Fitzgerald; a male singer like Frank Sinatra; the whole ensemble: trumpet section, clarinet, trombone, saxophone, drums . . . the works. A lot of the band includes musicians like: Al McGuire, Hank Raymonds,

Ray Meyer, Jim Valvano, Cesar Odio, Ed Jucker, Clarence 'Big House' Gaines, and Phog Allen. What a band! What a group! And the best part, it will play forever!!

"So, you think it's childish—I hope it is because I've got to believe like a child to get into heaven. It will be like high school. First, the big game will take place, and then following the game, the big dance. Everybody will win—because being with God is the *ultimate* win."

Torchy continued the next duty of directing his all-star band: "Okay coaches, let's strike up the band! A-one, a-two, a-three." We all know what the first, angelic song Torchy's band played on April 22, 2009. It was "Sweet Georgia Brown."

CHAPTER 37

Legacy 37

Torchy Clark will be remembered as one of the greatest high school coaches this state has seen and be remembered for so much more to all the lives he touched. Torchy was a master teacher in the athletic arena as well as the classroom. Gene "Torchy" Clark's life story is a long list of stories told by others. Torchy was a once-in-a-lifetime kind of man. Colorful, passionate, polite, religious and rambunctious. He was 30 when he came to Xavier High School in 1959, the year the school opened. He started the programs from scratch and built them immediately into state powers. (Mike Woods, *Appleton Post-Crescent*, 2007)

Torchy articulated often there is more to the heart, the soul of coaching than just the wins and losses. He recalled one of his Xavier stories close to his heart: "Mike Gregorius played football for me. Mike was six-foot-one, 185-pounds: a tall pulling guard, a class kid, a worker, and the ultimate team player. Gregorius just did everything he was supposed to do. After graduating from Xavier in 1965, he was sent to Vietnam.

"Mike was wounded there and wrote me a letter of appreciation from the hospital. Gregorius thanked me for so many things—I actually felt unworthy. He praised me for everything I had done for him. Shortly thereafter, I wrote Gregorius a letter. I told him it was my pleasure, that he did it all and it was an honor to have coached him.

"The reason I tell you this story is because to certain athletes, you give all your thoughts and energies. You praise them, you correct them, you laugh with them and cry with them. You feel tremendously close to and needed by them. But surprisingly, Mike Gregorius wasn't like that—he just did his job perfectly, asked for nothing and was an excellent teammate. In 1969, three weeks after I wrote the letter to Mike, the hospital he was recuperating in was bombed. Mike was killed."

Jerry Prather, who led Torchy to the Final Four in 1978, wrote this about his beloved coach: "I often wonder what people will think of me when I am gone. Was he a good man, was he a hard worker, was he a good family man, was he a God-loving man, and was he good to others? *All these define Torchy Clark.* From the time I took my first drive up State Road 436 from Orlando International Airport with Torchy on a recruiting trip, I knew I was home. He was so engaging, and for a quiet boy from Mississippi, that was comforting. Even when I got homesick midway through my freshman year, he sat me down and talked about what I wanted to do with my life. That talk made me stay, and I will forever love him for that. I even love him for the many times he told me to go back to Mississippi after messing up on a play. I knew he was joking. Later, he would give you a hug. I want to thank Torchy for leaving unforgettable memories and for creating a legacy not only in basketball (and football), but in the FTU/UCF community."

Torchy's lifetime hero was Dr. Frank Rohter. After hiring the young coach from Xavier in 1969 and listening to the Appleton anonymous burger flipper who said, "Torchy Clark is the best coach in the state of Wisconsin," Rohter changed the lives of the Clark family forever. Without the wisdom of the former athletic director and friend in his life, Torchy's legacy would not be complete. Rohter proudly recalled the decision to hire the Wisconsin legend: "One of my most significant contributions was to recommend Torchy Clark as the university's first basketball coach, because he was indeed a 'winner.' He was a 'winner' on the court, in the classroom, and in the community."

Russ Salerno, Torchy's former player and assistant coach, grew up without a father and said, "Torchy Clark was one of the three most influential men in my life," and credits him for much of the success he has achieved. "He found me at an intramural game and changed my life." Salerno continued on his mentor's lasting impact, "He was one of a kind. He taught you how to win and he taught you how to gracefully accept a loss. Torchy wasn't into losing, but when you did, you became better for it and learned something. He taught you how to reach deeper than you could reach."

Jim Flanagan, one of the early Knights, remembered his mentor's lasting impact: "Torchy was one of God's special creations. He may not have been a very big man in stature, but he had the *heart* of a lion." Flanagan added, "I spoke and represented the Nautilus Corporation for 20-plus years, meeting a lot of big-time Division I basketball coaches during the process in my travels. Orlando had no idea of the treasure we had in Torchy Clark. He was way ahead of his time. I feel fortunate to have played for him."

Another life Torchy touched was Brad Garvey, a childhood friend of the Clarks who lived five houses away from their Appleton home in the 1960s. Garvey grew up with the Clarks, riding along with Torchy and his sons, Bob and Bo, to many Xavier football and basketball practices. His future dream was to coach his own team someday.

After high school Garvey left Wisconsin and attended UCF in 1977, following the Clarks to Orlando. He seldom missed a Torchy-coached UCF game. As a keen observer, Garvey watched the Knights win 24 consecutive games (1977-78) and several Sunshine State

Championships—similar to Torchy's success he had witnessed at Xavier. After his 1982 graduation, he returned to Appleton to assist his mom, Marge, in the family Hertz Business. A year later, he was named Xavier girls' basketball coach, guiding the Hawks' program for five years, amassing a Torchy Clark-type record of 110–18.

"I lost my father when I was in eighth grade. Torchy became my father figure and mentor," said Garvey. "They say everything is begged, borrowed, or stolen in coaching; and I'll tell you, I pilfered from Torch as much as I could, no doubt. I used his offense, defense, full-court press, and out-of-bounds plays. The one other thing I got from Torchy was his old blue sport coat, but it didn't fit me," continued Garvey.

During four of the five Brad Garvey years (1983–88), he and younger brother Brian, who served as Hawks' assistant, led Xavier to the WCIAA State Catholic Girls' Basketball Championship Game. Ironically, the Hawks faced the same Wisconsin girls' juggernaut, Milwaukee Pius XI High School, all four times in the title game. Losing three times, his greatest opportunity to beat the Lady Popes (Pius) was in 1988. Earlier that season, his No. 1-ranked Hawks had defeated Pius 61–49 to snap the Lady Popes' mind-blowing 70-game winning streak in a Thanksgiving Tournament. They would face a second time at the Milwaukee Arena in March for the 1988 State Championship. In this riveting matchup, his (25–0) Hawks led 66–64 with three seconds left in the game and had possession of the ball. Pius was forced to foul Xavier, sending the Hawks to the free throw line for a bonus situation. Garvey's Hawk player missed the front end of the one-and-one; Pius rebounded the free throw, threw the outlet pass to half court, and a Lady Pope guard heaved a 40-foot Hail Mary making the shot (three-point shot) at the buzzer. Milwaukee Pius won miraculously, 67–66 to win yet another WCIAA State Catholic Girls' Basketball Championship.

After talking to his inconsolable and sobbing Hawks after the painful loss, Garvey's *first* phone call was to Torchy. Garvey remembered the 1988 call: "Torchy was understanding, compassionate, and wise. He helped me see life's big picture in a crushing, emotional loss. The Torch does live forever, and his legacy is not just about the wins, trophies, and championships, but his legacy is much deeper. It's more about his simplicity, humility, and the many lives he impacted, one being mine."

Kelly Kornely, a steadfast, true-blue leader during Xavier's phenomenal run in the early 1960s, warmly reminisced, "Torchy was an important influence in my life. He taught me how to win, be a great teammate and prepare to win!" Kornely added on his coach's legacy, "Torchy had the characteristics and coaching abilities of: Vince Lombardi in his preparedness, Al McGuire in his showmanship, Bobby Knight in his intensity, and John Wooden in his teaching."

Don Jonas was the first football coach at UCF. He coached the Knights for the program's first three seasons (1979-81), compiling a 14–12–1 record. Jonas, an excellent coach, was a former Penn State football player. The quarterback also played pro football in the NFL, Canadian Football League, and Continental Football League. He was a close comrade of Torchy's, and the two loved talking sports, especially football.

In 1979, Torchy and Jonas were sitting a few rows behind the scorer's table, waiting for a junior college basketball game to start in UCF's Education/Gym Complex (now appropriately called the Gene "Torchy" Clark Gym). Torchy recalled the series of events: "With a minute left on the pregame clock, one of the game's referees suddenly collapsed to the floor. Don Jonas, sitting next to me yelled, 'Heart attack!' Jonas rushed to the stricken official as I ran down the hallway to get Dr. Ed Stoner." After quickly moving the referee from courtside to the UCF training room a few minutes later, the referee was lying, still unconscious, on one of the treatment tables.

Stoner said, "This has happened to him before!" Looking in his wallet, the doctor discovered the referee was a dentist from West Palm Beach. A few minutes later the referee was conscious and alert; and told the doctor that he had been under a lot of stress and had not been sleeping well. As a precautionary measure, Stoner told him that he would have to stay overnight and could go home in the morning. Torchy, without hesitation, said, "I'll come back tomorrow and drive him to West Palm."

The next morning, Stoner called the Knights' coach to tell him that he had checked the referee's condition and he was fine, ready to go home. Stoner offered to drive his own car and follow behind the referee's car to drive Torchy back to Orlando. The coach told the kind doctor it was not necessary for him to go. Stoner fired back, "It's 180 miles to West Palm Beach! How will you get back?" With every fiber of his Oshkosh-bred toughness Torchy said, "I'll hitchhike."

"The dentist/referee and I had a great conversation as I drove his Oldsmobile. We arrived at his home near the freeway as his wife came out to thank me. She kissed her husband after a scary 12–15 hours while their three-year-old boy rushed from the house to hug his daddy. I felt good and after a few minutes, we all said good-bye," remembered Torchy.

As the coach "without a ride" walked to the freeway, his plan was to hitchhike back to Orlando. Claire would not have been happy with that decision. Now, guess how many rides it took him to get back to Orlando? *One!* The cool and calm Torchy recalled, "After about 15 minutes of hitchhiking, a shiny, new van came to a quick stop ahead of me on the freeway entrance ramp.

"Astoundingly, the driver of the van said, 'Torchy, what the heck are you hitchhiking in West Palm Beach?' It was a friend returning to Orlando. Do I believe in angels? Certainly, I shake hands with my Guardian Angel at least once a week. I live day by day inspired by St. John Vianney's quote, 'Our Guardian Angels are our most faithful friends because they are with us day and night, always and everywhere.'" (Perna, 2018)

Ray Ridenour, Torchy's trusted assistant (1974–80), remembered, "Dr. Rohter was a smart man to hire Coach Clark. Torchy is a catalyst. He teaches students to think, to evaluate and to evaluate what is right or wrong. The highlight of my career was working with Torchy.

"When people ask me if he got mad or was tough, I always answer 'Yes,' but he was funny and good. There was always humor in everything he did."

Former UCF team manager Tim Grayson (1977–81), now a Campus-wide Executive Chef at the College of William and Mary, reminisced, "Torchy would always inspire everyone around him to do better and better. I was a 'dorky' high school kid that went to interview him my senior year (1976) for a school paper. Knowing very little, I asked stupid questions and got ripped. He told me after that, 'I like you because you came back.' I ended up being the team manager for Torchy my four years at UCF. I was proud to be his friend through the rest of his life."

Yvan Kelly, the Knights' loyal student assistant, recalled hearing Torchy say, "I'm not running Father Flanagan's Boys Town here! I'm trying to win basketball games." Kelly continued, "As typical with our team, when Torchy started yelling, the gym got very quiet. I don't recall what led to Torchy making that comment, but with his outburst I quickly caught the eye of a player, Mark Miller, and fellow manager Tim Grayson. Mark and I lost our fathers at a young age. All I knew was that all of us looked up to Torchy as a father figure. I'm sure there were others who did so as well, we just never talked about it.

"At the time, some of us felt guilty that Torchy would be distracted from coaching in order to spend time with us when he should have been focusing on what the team needed to be successful. What were we as players and team members asking from our coach? Was it fair to be needing his time and attention? I carried that moment with me for years.

"Around 25 years later, I brought that comment back up with Torchy. I asked him if he remembered saying it. I told him that after a long contemplation, that I had determined that yes, indeed, he was running a type of Boys Town for guys like Mark and I. Torchy laughed and said he did remember saying it. And that he knew when he said it that it was exactly what he was doing.

"He told me, 'You have to really care when you say something like that.' Torchy had time for his guys. Not just a few minutes, all the time you needed. When I was off and on my own, I'd call him every now and then. We would always be at least an hour on the phone. Cancer robbed us of this later in his life; speaking clearly became so difficult and frustrating for him. When he was gone, we all knew he cared for us. Especially those who were from Boys Town."

With a deep reverence, Torchy regarded his teaching and coaching as a true vocation, a duty deemed particularly worthy and requiring great dedication. He was inspired by the quote from Blessed John Henry Newman, who said, "Realize it, my brethren—every one who breathes, high and low, educated and ignorant, young and old, man and woman, has a mission, has a work. We are not sent into this world for nothing; we are not born at random . . . God sees every one of us; He creates every soul, He lodges it in the body, one by one, for a purpose. (The Catholic Company, 2019)

Vince Cotroneo, presently the play-by-play radio announcer for the Oakland Athletics and formerly with the Houston Astros and Texas Rangers, remembered his days at UCF fondly: "As an aspiring play-by-play announcer as a Communications Major at UCF (1983 graduate), I was fortunate to learn a lot about basketball and life sitting just 10 feet away from Torchy Clark. My colleagues and I treated every broadcast with professionalism, and I believe Torchy saw that and respected our efforts. Crouching down at the scorer's table within earshot of every Torchy emotion, we were regaled with coaching acumen and life lessons at the same time.

"He understood in the early days of the program, his teams were undersized, played in a small gymnasium, and the budget extended his recruiting challenges. And yet season after season, Torchy assembled a team with fire, and he constantly found ways to wring every drop of talent his roster had to offer on a nightly basis to build a powerhouse.

"No, it wasn't Duke or North Carolina or UCLA, but Torchy's teams in the Sunshine State Conference brought enormous prestige to his program. It gave kids like me a chance to experience what it means to give the most and get the most of what you have, even if the odds weren't in your favor. He helped lay the foundation for the kind of moments every announcer dreams of, even if it wasn't on the biggest stage. It was his stage, and he was kind enough to bring myself and fellow co-workers along for the greatest ride in my days at UCF and share that platform.

"My broadcasting career has continued, and I've enjoyed many moments working in Major League Baseball. Part of achieving that success was built with every fast break and score by a Knights' team up and down the floor with Torchy. I am forever thankful for his looks our way. His kindness, encouragement, and respect for our group trying to keep up with him stays with me to this day. Torchy, thanks for including me on the path."

Calvin Lingelbach aka "Calvin Cool" who willed the Knights back against Rollins in 1976 during the greatest comeback of Torchy's career, said, "After I graduated from UCF, I became a high school basketball coach. I frequently drew upon strategies I learned from him, used 'Torchyisms' to communicate with my players, and found myself wandering down memory lane when faced with 'déjà vu' game situations. More importantly, Torchy remained a close friend and confidant. I can truly say I was blessed to know him."

Tom Klusman, the Rollins College basketball coaching legend and one of the game's finest, remembers, "Torchy was a brilliant, unique coach who thought out of the box. When I began my coaching career, he was an important mentor, and I was honored that as the years went by, we became friends. He would visit me at my office to drop off notes about my team or to offer words of encouragement. I would even pop over to his house, at any hour, to talk about my recent game or to discuss the fundamentals of coaching. Our chats would sometimes last for hours. An added bonus to knowing Torchy was that I became friends with players he had coached, with many of them being players I played against during my college career. I always enjoyed hearing stories about Torchy, as there were many."

Klusman continued, "Torchy was unique in that he had me look at coaching and even life in a different way, making me a better coach and a better person. Torchy had knowledge and courage to do what he believed in and stood behind it. I try to follow him in that regard, and it is harder to do than many may think. As Torchy taught me, coaching involves players, fans, media, school administrators, and families. Torchy was a winner at all of it. His record speaks for itself."

"Icon. Legend. Hero. Husband. Father. Coach. Teacher. Friend. Eugene 'Torchy' Clark was all of these and more. The UCF family lost a part of its heart when Clark passed away in 2009, *but his legacy lives on.* Talk to anyone who knew the legendary founder of the university's basketball program, the man who became the favorite teacher of many a student, and faces light up as the stories flow." (Judy Creel, 2005) His

274 wins came with great passion and an unsurpassed competitive spirit. Yes, the eternal flame of Torchy stills burns bright.

Mike Woods of the *Appleton Post-Crescent* (2004) wrote a humorous, yet sad article about a letter he received from Torchy. The following is an excerpt from that piece: "The first thing I noticed about the letter was the return address. In the upper corner was 'Torchy.' That was it.

"That immediately brought a smile, because I figured that if the letter were somehow lost, the U.S. Postal Service would have little difficulty returning it to its rightful owner.

"For anyone who has been lucky enough to meet Torchy Clark, he's one in 293,027, 571, which just happens to be the United States' estimated population (2004).

"When I opened the correspondence, the smile disappeared. In it was a story from the *Orlando Sentinel.* 'Ex-UCF coach has cancer' barked the headline. That was it. No other form of communication.

"So, I called the man who helped make Appleton and Xavier High School famous to see what was up. All I really knew was that this 75-year-old who made a name for himself coaching basketball was now caught in a double-team. Father Time had him on one side, cancer on the other. 'I sent you the article,' said Torchy, showing he was still one step ahead of the competition, answering my question before I could even ask it, 'because if someone in Appleton would ask you, What's up with Torchy, I didn't want you not to know anything about it.' Proof again he's one in 293,027, 571."

Joe DeSalvo, a native New Yorker and a 1975 FTU/UCF graduate, was a close friend of Torchy's. DeSalvo went on to become a sports journalist and spent two years as the executive director of the Florida Sports Hall of Fame, where Torchy is one of three inductees (with Michele Akers and Winston DuBose) from UCF. A key player in his induction in 1993, DeSalvo affectionately recalled, "He touched the lives of many UCF students—so much that almost 45 years later, we still hold him in high regard," DeSalvo says with a catch in his voice. "With all due respect to the talents of those who came after him, there's only one *Torchy*. Alabama had Bear Bryant; Ohio State had Woody Hayes; the Packers had Vince Lombardi; and we had Torchy Clark."

Jerry Greene, former *Orlando Sentinel* columnist, said, "Torchy was a man I truly admired because he liked people, had a great sense of humor, and made you feel great." Greene continued on Torchy's lasting legacy, "I don't know how many wonderful men or women people get to meet in their lives, but Torchy was one of the truly wonderful people I met."

Torchy's 50 Tips

O ver the years I have attended and spoke at numerous coaching clinics and camps. I have collected several pet philosophies and coaching tips from these experiences I would like to share. I realize that you are not going to agree with everything. I sincerely respect that. Many are basketball specific, but several are applicable to coaches of any sport:

1. Coach, get yourself a confidant, a person who understands you and doesn't depress you in any way. Keep good people around you.
2. Officials: I like them. They don't beat you any more than they help you win. It's all evened out for me.
3. Go to your strength, to your reservoir, what you do best. I yell and scream, but my players understand me. They are motivated and don't get tight running freely as themselves.
4. On rules, I don't have a lot. I've tried to stay up with the times. The rules I have: I want hard practices and great effort. I want my players to be good people on and off the court.

5. I don't believe in useless running. We don't do any line running or suicides. We work off *specificity* by using our press and game situations which results in intense, game-like running.

6. When giving a banquet speech: Talk about the school to whom you are addressing your speech. Ask the managers in all the sports to stand up and be recognized. They are often overlooked.

7. In high school, I always tried to keep two or three sophomores on my varsity basketball team. I did this to get them ready for the varsity pressure of a packed gym at 7:30 p.m.

8. You can't fool kids. Don't try—they are too sharp. Be yourself. Don't con them. They will see your strengths and weaknesses. If you are insecure, remember there is a strength that goes with insecurity.

9. Each team establishes a personality of its own.

10. Off-season players make you a better coach.

11. Coaching is all repetition. If they don't get it the first fifty times they have heard it, they will after that. Besides the actual sport, I try to give my players something spiritual or humorous and then try to develop it through our entire team.

12. Every *coach* should be an *official* and every *official* should be a *coach*.

13. There are arrogant *coaches*. There are arrogant *officials*.

14. Be a leader! The players are looking for your leadership. There are times in history when a dictator is needed; however, don't be afraid to listen to your players. It doesn't hurt for you, the coach, to show some *transparent realism*.

15. Remember DISCIPLINE can be a form of LOVE. I don't believe in an excessive amount of awards or punishments, just fairness, a pat on the back.

16. If you have done your best, you have won.

17. On yelling and not controlling your tongue—you will have REMORSE. In real estate they call it "Buyer's Remorse." Two days after the purchase of the house, the buyer regrets the purchase. The remorse also holds true with controlling your emotions. The technical foul, ejection, poor body language, or the bad scene is hard to explain the next few days.

18. What you do (style of play) in your early preseason practices is exactly what you will see during your season.

19. The difference between winning and losing is often ENERGY.

20. Some games I've worked so hard and was so mean that I won, but lost. Other games, I've lost, but won because I had the feeling my team did everything possible to win the game. You establish a *reputation* and then you live with it. At one point in my career, I only had four technical fouls in 18 years, but I was still regarded as fiery and volatile.

21. Now, for my worse coaching *mistake*: I share this with you because if I started coaching again at the age of 22, I would eliminate all swearing for two reasons: (1) It's God's name, (2) You are an example to youth. I believed it was necessary for motivation, *I was WRONG.*

22. Keep your opponents out of the BONUS SITUATION. Too often coaches overlook the BONUS.

23. The success of our team is dependent upon our conversions, converting from offense to defense and from defense to offense. The conversions are predicated on our quickness and speed: It's the way we practice, the key to our success.

24. The cornerstone of character is HUMILITY.

25. Work hard and think, but don't OVERCOACH. These kids are young and learning every day, so on any level don't OVERCOACH.

26. Try to get your players to hate losing as much as you do. When you do lose, show some class. Shake your opponent's hand. Remember—adversity is the great teacher.

27. Try to eliminate your players' fears. Example: Facing a tough opponent that full-court presses and blitzes the ball with hard, aggressive traps . . . use *six* players on the second team to press your first team at practice.

28. Stay with *simplicity*. As Coach Vince Lombardi said, "Block, Tackle, and Execute." Too many coaches complicate the game with too much strategy. Keep It Simple.

29. If you are going to stay in coaching, you better have a sense of *humor*. Every coach needs a happy ball club.

30. I give my team everything I've got for the two-hour practice. And it's usually two hours of solid teaching. Always give 100 percent, you can't give more than that.

31. During timeouts, we stress *two* major points that need direction and correction, not five or six.

32. We try to get seven or eight players ready to play (more if possible), then build a family around them, including our substitutes. I spend a lot time talking with our subs on the bench at practice and games.

33. Teach your system so well that your players know it, can teach it, and then can freely operate in it.

34. Get the ball back to the hot shooter, if possible. We aren't taking turns shooting, we are trying to WIN a game. That is my obligation to my team.

35. We always play the same. HARD in practices. HARD in games, even HARDER against poor opponents. This keeps us ready for our best opponents.

36. Don't run up scores. Remember the opposing coaches and players have to get on the bus, go home, and report to their AD or principal. Don't make it harder on them.

37. Have a system in which your team can score *easy baskets*. *Easy baskets* win games.

38. It takes 10 years to be a good coach.

39. Remember it is a *privilege* to coach and be a part of this great game. Find a profession in your life you truly enjoy.

40. I believe that overlooked areas in basketball are proper cutting, pivoting, and footwork.

41. Our practices are short, always crisp, hard, and to-the-point. Remember your players' attention span is between five-to-seven minutes, and that's on a good day.

42. Sports should help make you a better person. If they don't, then find the road that takes you home to God.

43. As a basketball coach, my best friend was always the janitor (custodian).

44. On pressure shooting: We will often stop practice and have a player take a jumper while everyone is watching. We also do this by having a player shoot a free throw . . . then convert immediately into our "live" full-court press.

45. In college coaching, the three most important areas are: scheduling, recruiting, and coaching (in that order). Very few coaches can win by being over-scheduled.

46. During the first part of our practice, I like music pumped into the gym while our players are shooting. It breaks the monotony and adds motivation.

47. The relationship with the press, TV, and radio must be excellent. Most of the time, the press is fair, but occasionally you'll get burned. Always protect your team when dealing with the media.

48. Coaches, get some exercise. Work daily on your cardio, strength training, and healthy eating. You owe it to your family. Find 30–45 minutes each day.
49. Get along with administrators. They are here to stay. You'll get a lot of attention in coaching, but remain *humble* in your profession. There are probably 200 people waiting to apply for your job.
50. As teachers and coaches, we have an *obligation* to visit the sick and bury the dead. Oftentimes, we are the primary source of support for our players and families in difficult periods.

Acknowledgments

This book would not have come to fruition without major contributions from my dad's unpublished manuscript, *I Live by the Scoreboard* (1988). A significant amount of the stories, recollections, and quotes came directly from the original chapters. During the project I was blessed to have an understanding wife who was supportive during the writing process. Nancy, thank you for your patience (of Job) on this project, an undertaking close and dear to my heart. You are my everything. You are my hero.

I would like to thank my two editors (coaches), Tim Pollock and John Meyer, who encouraged and advised me every step of the way. Your positive feedback and input motivated me to finish the race.

A big thank you to my family, Mike, Tom, Bob, and Patty for your tremendous support, love, and encouragement. A project like this doesn't become a reality unless you surround yourself with good people. Mike's photographic memory and countless recollections of not only Xavier, but also UCF were uncanny. Mike, Tom, and I were all blessed to have played for our dad in our careers. Playing for your dad is not always easy, but Torchy's personality, success, drive, and

HUMOR made the dynamic work. The father-son stories have the potential to be a colorful and entertaining book in itself; however, in this manuscript I concentrated *solely* on my dad's humble life and the mighty handprint he left. My three advance scouts: Mike Clark, Bob Clark, and Brad Garvey were terrific!

I am grateful to my dad's former players, assistants, managers, students, and friends who contributed in a myriad of interviews, phone calls, and e-mails during the 16-month writing experience. Thanks to Rocky Bleier for his powerful, inspirational Foreword to open the book. My sincere appreciation to Peter and Mike Bates from Appleton, Wisconsin, for their elaborate and informative Xavier Athletics website. The "Torchy Legacy" was truly an integral and valuable resource in this project. The contributions from UCF's Mark Miller, Bill Beekman, and Yvan Kelly were not only uplifting, but indeed sensational. A special thank you also to Menasha, Wisconsin's, gifted author Adrian Martin for his advice and recollections. My heartfelt gratitude to Dick Bennett, Lee Corso, Tim Povtak, and Hal Wissel for their insightful Torchy testimonials.

The intricate research throughout the book emanated from the gifted and brilliant sportswriters that covered Torchy's football and basketball teams in the many stories and newspaper articles from: *the Orlando Sentinel, Appleton Post-Crescent, UCF Future, UCF Pegasus, Memphis Press-Scimitar, Memphis Commercial-Appeal, Springfield (MO) Daily News, Chattanooga News Free-Press, Fond du Lac (Wisconsin) Commonwealth Reporter, Milwaukee Journal, Milwaukee Sentinel, Lakeland Ledger, Sports Illustrated, Miami Herald,* and the *St. Augustine Record.*

Gene "Torchy" Clark was an incredible dad, grandfather, person, teacher, coach, and role model. I referred to my dad as "Torchy" throughout the chapters, not due to lack of respect, but to tell the story and make it easier for the reader. Lastly, but most importantly, my sole purpose of writing this tribute was for the honor and glory of God. *And we know that God causes all things to work together for good to those who love God, to those who are called according to His purpose.*" Romans 8:28.

—*Bo Clark*

References

Chapter 1   I'm from Oshkosh

Clark, T. (1988). "I Live by the Scoreboard." Unpublished manuscript.

Kolf Center, University of Wisconsin-Oshkosh Athletics Website. Retrieved October 17, 2017, from www.http://uwoshkoshtitans. com

Goldstein, R. (2009, December 1). "Tommy Henrich, Yankee clutch hitter, dies at 96." *New York Times.*

Lefty Edwards. Retrieved October 8, 2017, from www.bigbluehistory.net

Oshkosh All-Stars. Retrieved December 2, 2017, from nbahoopsonline.com

Clark, M. (2017, October 15). Phone interview.

Clark, B. (2017, October 17). Phone interview.

Steinberg, M. (2018, March 1). "Herd to honor Oshkosh All-Stars on March 3." Retrieved from wisconsin.gleague.nba.com

Chapter 2   Let 'em Play

Clark, T. (1988). "I Live by the Scoreboard." Unpublished manuscript.

Malatesta, M. (2018, April 17). Phone interview.

McClernon, J. (2007). *Sermon in a sentence: A treasury of quotations of the life of St. Thomas Aquinas.* San Francisco, CA: Ignatius Press.

Bishop Moore Catholic High School Athletics. Retrieved October 15, 2017, from https://bishopmoorecatholicathletics.com

Chapter 3   Sister Joseph Mary
Clark, T. (1988). "I Live by the Scoreboard." Unpublished manuscript.
Feeney, M. (2010, December 16). "Bob Feller, 92, Hall of famer had blazing fastball." *Boston Globe.*

Chapter 4   Road to Marquette
Clark, T. (1988). "I Live by the Scoreboard." Unpublished manuscript.
St. Mary's Catholic High School Athletics Website, Menasha, Wisconsin. Retrieved December 8, 2017, from http://smcatholicschools.org/st-mary-catholic-high-school/
Detloff, W. (2015). *Ezzard Charles: A Boxing Life.* New York, NY: McFarland.
Marquette University Athletic Website. Retrieved December 17, 2017, from www.gomarquette.com/athletic-dept/marq-athletic-dept.html

Chapter 5   Claire
Clark, T. (1988). "I Live by the Scoreboard." Unpublished manuscript.
Clark, M. (2017, October 15). Personal interview.
Clark, B. (2017, November 10). Personal interview.
The Catholic Company, Charlotte, N.C. Retrieved September 9, 2018 from https://www.catholiccompany.com

Chapter 6   Appleton
Clark, T. (1988). "I Live by the Scoreboard." Unpublished manuscript.
McGinnis, B. (2018, January 19). Personal interview.
Garvey, Brad. (2018, January 20). Personal interview.
Garvey, Brian. (2018, January 21). Personal interview.
Lindsay, J. (2017). "All About Appleton." Retrieved March 6, 2018, from www.jefflindsay.com

REFERENCES

Chapter 7 Soul of Xavier

Clark, T. (1988). "I Live by the Scoreboard." Unpublished manuscript.

Roman Catholic Diocese of Green Bay. Retrieved November 30, 2017, from https://www.gbdioc.org

Bates, P. & Bates, M. Xavier High School Athletics Website. Appleton, Wisconsin. Retrieved October 17, 2017, from https://xaviercatholicschools.org

Bleier, R. & O'Neil, T. (1998). *Fighting Back*. Pittsburgh, PA: Rocky Bleier Inc.

Chapter 8 Perfection–1962–63

Clark, T. (1988). "I Live by the Scoreboard." Unpublished manuscript.

Moore, M. & Mihalik, L. (2013, November 23). "President Kennedy is dead: Readers remember a terrible day." *Los Angeles Times*. Retrieved from http://www.latimes.com

Bates, P. & Bates, M. Xavier High School Athletics Website. Appleton, Wisconsin. Retrieved December 17, 2017, from https://xaviercatholicschools.org

McGinnis, B. (2017, December 10). Phone interview.

Clark, M. (2017, September 5). Phone interview.

Whitlinger, K. & Kornely, K. (2018, January 23). Personal interview.

Garvey, Brad. (2018, November 5). Phone interview.

Bleier, R. (2017, December 1). Phone interview.

34th Annual WCIAA State Basketball Tournament Program, Milwaukee, Wisconsin (March 1963).

Paustian, J. (1963, March 4). "Hawks down Marquette, win State Catholic title: Finish fast to score 71–66 win before 7,095 fans in Milwaukee." *Appleton Post-Crescent*.

Lassanske, J. (1963, March 4). "Xavier State Catholic: Pins 71–66 loss on Marquette." *Milwaukee Sentinel*.

Bleier, R. & O'Neil, T. (1998). *Fighting Back.* Pittsburgh, PA: Rocky Bleier Inc.

Torchy Clark Gym Tribute, Xavier High School, (2004). Appleton, Wisconsin.

Bledsoe, T. (1963, March 4). "Appleton wins Catholic title." *Milwaukee Journal.*

Chapter 9   Rocky

Woods, M. (October, 2007). "Being true to his school: Bleier doesn't stray from roots." *Appleton Post-Crescent.*

Woods, M. (2007, May 17). "Rocky has always embraced his past." *Appleton Post-Crescent.*

Bleier, R. & O'Neil, T. (1998). *Fighting Back.* Pittsburgh, PA: Rocky Bleier Inc.

Clark, T. (1988). "I Live by the Scoreboard." Unpublished manuscript.

Bleier, R. (2017, December 1). Phone interview.

Kornely, K. & Whitlinger, K. (2018, January 22). Personal interview.

Xavier High School Athletics. "Rocky Bleier Field Dedication," October 2007.

Bates, P. & Bates, M. Xavier High School Athletics Website. Appleton, Wisconsin. Retrieved on January 10, 2018, from https://xaviercatholicschools.org

Chapter 10   Knee and the Ankle

Bates, P. & Bates, M. Xavier High School Athletics. "Rocky Bleier Field Dedication," October, 2007.

Clark, T. (1988). "I Live by the Scoreboard." Unpublished manuscript.

Whitlinger, K. (2018, February 5). Phone interview.

Bleier, R. (2018, January 5). Phone interview.

Oskola, J. (2018, February 16). "Plamann sets Xavier career scoring record, passing Kip Whitlinger as Hawks roll to win." *Appleton Post-Crescent.*

Whitlinger, W. (2012). *Timeless Tips.* Charleston, SC: Wendy Whitlinger.

Martin, A. (2010). *Marty: The Man Who Refused to Punt. The Life and Times of Legendary Marty Crowe.* Neenah, WI: Adrian Martin Inc.

Martin, A. (2018, July 20). Phone interview.

Chapter 11   Ouch! Who's Al McGuire?

Gross, M. (2017). From 2009: "Jim Bunning remembers his perfect game." *Lancaster Online.* Retrieved April 17, 2018, from www.lancasteronline.com

Clark, T. (1988). "I Live by the Scoreboard." Unpublished manuscript.

Lawther, J. (1951). *Psychology of Coaching.* Upper Saddle, NJ: Prentice-Hall.

Whitlinger, W. (2012). *Timeless Tips.* Charleston, SC: Wendy Whitlinger.

Bates, P. & Bates, M. Xavier High School Athletics Website. Appleton, Wisconsin. Retrieved January 10, 2018, from https://xaviercatholicschools.org

Martin, A. (2010). *Marty: The Man Who Refused to Punt. The Life and Times of Legendary Coach Marty Crowe.* Neenah, WI: Adrian Martin Inc.

Martin, A. (2018, May 11). Phone interview.

Chapter 12   Frankie McGinnis and Torchy's Tales

Clark, M. (2017, December 17). Phone interview.

Garvey, Brad. (2017, November 10). Phone interview.

Clark, T. (1988). "I Live by the Scoreboard." Unpublished manuscript.

Kornely, K. & Whitlinger, K. (2018, January 23). Personal interview.

Chapter 13   Obligation—Preparation

Clark, T. (1988). "I Live by the Scoreboard." Unpublished manuscript.

Kornely, K. & Whitlinger, K. (2018, January 23). Personal interview.

Clark, M. (2017, December 20). Phone interview.

UCF Basketball 1982–83 Yearbook, Orlando, FL.

Chapter 14   The Big Play

Clark, T. (1988). "I Live by the Scoreboard." Unpublished manuscript.

Chapter 15   Torch Will Never Go Out

Clark, T. (1988). "I Live by the Scoreboard." Unpublished manuscript.

Kohl, T. (1966, February 5). "Ledgers snap Xavier's 53-game win streak: 4th quarter rally brings 60–57 triumph for Saints." *Fond du Lac (Wisconsin) Commonwealth Reporter.*

Clark, M. (2017, December 18). Personal Interview.

Tom Rankin Torchy Clark Gym Dedication Tribute, Xavier High School, 2004.

Bates, P. & Bates, M. Xavier High School Athletics Website. Appleton, Wisconsin. Retrieved December 10, 2017, from https://xaviercatholicschools.org

University of Wisconsin-Green Bay Athletics Website. Retrieved February 8, 2018, from https://www.greenbayphoenix.com

Clark, B. (2017, November 25). Phone interview.

Clark, P. (2017, October 20). Phone interview.

Xavier University Athletics Website. Retrieved from https://www.GoXavier.com

Bob Fullarton. "Real GM." Retrieved on March 1, 2018, from https://www.basketball.realgm.com

REFERENCES

Bob Fullarton. "Euro Basketball." Retrieved from https://www. basketball.eurobasket.com

Kersten, J. (2018, January 27). Personal interview.

Garvey, Brian (2018, January 27). Personal interview.

Shaw, K. (2018, September 28). Phone interview.

Martin, A. (2010). *Marty: The Man Who Refused to Punt. The Life and Times of Legendary Marty Crowe*. Neenah, WI: Adrian Martin Inc.

Chapter 16   Meeting Lombardi

Green Bay Packers Website. Retrieved November 7, 2017, from https://m.packers.com

Clark, T. (1988). "I Live by the Scoreboard." Unpublished manuscript.

Cheyney State Athletics Website. Retrieved January 9, 2018, from https://www.cheyneywolves.com

University of Wisconsin-Green Bay Athletics Website. Retrieved February 9, 2018, from https://www.greenbayphoenix.com

Chapter 17   Humble Beginning

Wallin, S. (2005, May). "Honoring a legend: Coach Torchy Clark: An inspiration, both on and off the court and in the classroom." *UCF Pegasus*.

Creel, J. (2009, July). "Eternal flame. The Torchy Clark legacy burns bright." *UCF Pegasus*.

Rohter, F. (2017, November 1). Phone interview.

Salerno, R. (2017, November 15). Personal interview.

Flanagan, J. (2017, November 15). Personal interview.

Clark, M. (2017, November 15). Personal interview.

Clark, T. (1988). "I Live by the Scoreboard." Unpublished manuscript.

Beekman, B. (2000). "Dribblings including the adventures of the disco winnebago & blocked punts: Fond and foggy memories

331

from the early days of Knights' athletics." Orlando, FL: Bill Beekman.

Chapter 18   New York City

Salerno, R. (2017, December 10). Phone interview.

Flanagan, J. (2017, December 10). Phone interview.

UCF Basketball Media Guide, 2017–18. Orlando, FL.

Clark, T. (1988). "I Live by the Scoreboard." Unpublished manuscript.

Chapter 19   Common Denominator

Clark, T. (1988). "I Live by the Scoreboard." Unpublished manuscript.

Clark, M. (2018, January 10). Phone interview.

Chapter 20   The Dragon Slayer

Guest, L. (1976, February 4). "Rollins-FTU tickets: Hold on to your scalp." *Orlando Sentinel.*

University of Cincinnati Athletic Website. Retrieved December 17, 2017, from https://gobearcats.com

Beekman, B. (2000). "Dribblings including the adventures of the disco winnebago & blocked punts: Fond and foggy memories from the early days of Knights' athletics." Orlando, FL: Bill Beekman.

McCarthy, M. (1976, February 8). "Jucker in racy post-mortem after FTU speed stops Tars." *Orlando Sentinel.*

Archer, D. (1976, February 8). "FTU, Tars renew Sunshine rivalry." *Orlando Sentinel.*

Guest, L. (1976, February 8). "FTU formula: Speed and heart." *Orlando Sentinel.*

Archer, D. (1976, February 8). "Bo Clark: 'Wanted this for my dad.'" *Orlando Sentinel.*

"UCF 2015–16 Basketball Media Guide." Retrieved January 11, 2018, from https://www.UCFKnights.com

Clark, T. (1988). "I Live by the Scoreboard." Unpublished manuscript.

Lingelbach, C. (2018, January 17). Personal interview.

Prather, J. (2017, November 5). Phone interview.

Chapter 21   Rollins—Down 22

Clark, T. (1988). "I Live by the Scoreboard." Unpublished manuscript.

Lingelbach, C. (2018, January 17). Personal interview.

Prather, J. (2017, November 15). Phone interview.

Archer, D. (1976, February 25). "Down by 22. FTU rallies in OT, 95–78." *Orlando Sentinel.*

Guest, L. (1976, February 25). "A new course at FTU: Hollywood endings 101." *Orlando Sentinel.*

Archer, D. (1976, November 30). "Prather: Star in his own right." *Orlando Sentinel.*

Beekman, B. (2000). "Dribblings including the adventures of the disco winnebago & blocked punts: Fond and foggy memories from the early days of Knights' athletics." Orlando, FL: Bill Beekman.

Coble, D. (1976, February 25). "Incredible comeback!!! OT surge too much for Tars, Knights clinch conference title." *Orlando Sentinel.*

Buchalter, B. (1976, February 25). "FTU unbelievable comeback not for faint of heart." *Orlando Sentinel.*

Archer, D. (1976, February 25). "Knights comeback. Lingelbach leads FTU comeback past Rollins into NCAA South Regionals." *Orlando Sentinel.*

Chapter 22   Family

Clark, T. (1988). "I Live by the Scoreboard." Unpublished manuscript.

Budnik, P. (2017, December 1). Phone interview.

Clark, B. (2017, December 8). Phone interview.

Clark, T. (2018, July 8). Phone interview.

Clark, M. (2017, October 20). Phone interview.

McCarthy, L. (1988, January 10). "The storied career of Bob Willis has touched all the bases." *Orlando Sentinel.*

Chapter 23   Real Pressure

Green, L. (1977, March 4). "Torchy Clark: Not just another basketball coach." *Chattanooga News Free-Press.*

Chapter 24   Memphis—Lonely Bench

Clark, T. (1988). "I Live by the Scoreboard." Unpublished manuscript.

Sandburg, Carl (1916). "The Fog." Retrieved March 20, 2018 from https://www.poets.org/poetsorg/poem/fog

Lingelbach, C. (2018, February 10). Personal interview.

Prather, J. (2018, March 17). Phone interview.

Hall, B. (1976, November 28). "Tigers show little concern with second-half show." *The Commercial-Appeal.*

Cobb, R. (1976, November 27). "Short on vets, Tigers open season." *Memphis Press-Scimitar.*

Team rosters cited in *The Commercial-Appeal*, November 27, 1976.

Helwig, B. (2012, February 28). "The upstart vs. the elite." Retrieved from UCFsports.comPublisher, http://ucfrivals.com/content.asp?CID-1336799.

Chapter 25   Final Four

Prather, J. (2018, May 5). Phone Interview.

Archer, D. (1977, December 1). "Bo to watch rest of FTU season." *Orlando Sentinel.*

Archer, D. (1976, December 1). "Prather: Star in his own right." *Orlando Sentinel.*

Bilas, J. (2013). *Toughness: Developing True Strength On and Off the Court*. New York, NY: Penguin Group.

Beekman, B. (2000). "Dribblings including the adventures of the disco winnebago & blocked punts: Fond and foggy memories from the early days of Knights' athletics." Orlando, FL: Bill Beekman.

Buchalter, B. (1978, February 1). "FTU gives Division II a chemistry lesson." *Orlando Sentinel*.

Cobbs, C. (1978, April 6). "A smaller Knights unhorsed in national tournament." *FTU Future*.

Cobbs, C. (1976, February 8). "FTU even in defeat did 'absolute best.'" *Orlando Sentinel*.

Cobbs, C. (1978, March 18). "Ice-cold Knights chilled by Cheyney." *Orlando Sentinel*.

Greene, L. (1978, February 26). "Knights earn a day of rest." *Orlando Sentinel*.

Greene, L. (1976, December 1). "Prather paces Bo-less FTU." *Orlando Sentinel*.

Jaffe, R. (1978, January 6). "Team play a must for Knights." *Orlando Sentinel*.

Jaffe, R. (1978, March 20). "The year." *UCF Future*.

"Lamar Cardinals, Coach Billy Tubbs." Retrieved January 11, 2018, from www.lamarcardinals.com

NCAA Basketball Quarterfinal Game Program, Orlando, Florida, Florida Tech University vs. University of San Diego, March 11, 1978.

NCAA South Region Tournament, Orlando Florida (UCF), Game program, March 5, 1978.

Welch, A. (1978, March 17). "Final Four to decide Division II crown: Florida Tech vs. Cheyney State." *Springfield (MO) Daily News*.

Chapter 26 Tap Your Emotions and Intensity

Clark, T. (1988). "I Live by the Scoreboard." Unpublished manuscript.

Kelly, Y. Retrieved transcript from e-mail on May 13, 2018.

Kelly, Y. (2018, May 10). Personal interview.

Buchalter, B. (1980, January). "UCF's Torchy burns with intensity." *Orlando Sentinel*.

Beekman, B. (2000). "Dribblings including the adventures of the disco winnebago & blocked punts: Fond and foggy memories from the early days of Knights' athletics." Orlando, FL: Bill Beekman.

Criswell, H. (1975). "Basketball strictly a family affair: Father and son team." *FTU Future*.

Valerino, J. (1979, November). Torchy's 'scoring machine' will be tough to beat in SSC. *Lakeland Ledger*.

Chapter 27 Champion of the Underdog

Wood, M. (2018, March 12). Personal interview.

Shaw, D. (2018, January 25). Personal interview.

Hayes, E. (July, 1976). "A moment that's lasted six years." *Orlando Sentinel*.

Bennet, B. (1997, February 7). "Coach still ignites students' spirits." *Knight Times*.

The Catholic Company, Charlotte, NC. Retrieved March 1, 2018, from http://www.catholiccompany.com

Chapter 28 Establish a Reputation

Jackson, R. (1979, December 17). "A tough gun of a son." *Sports Illustrated*.

Clark, T. (1988). "I Live by the Scoreboard." Unpublished manuscript.

Schmitz, B. (1979, December 2). "UCF registers greatest win 84–77." *Orlando Sentinel*.

Chapter 29   Sawyer Brown Says Good-Bye
Written by Mark Miller (October, 2018).

Chapter 30   Tangerine Bowl

Clark, T. (1988). "I Live by the Scoreboard." Unpublished manuscript.

Beekman, B. (2000). "Dribblings including the adventures of the disco winnebago & blocked punts: Fond and foggy memories from the early days of Knights' athletics." Orlando, FL: Bill Beekman.

Beekman, B. (2018, March 30). Phone interview.

Central Michigan Athletic Website. Retrieved January 11, 2018, from http://www.cmuchippewas.com/sportsm -basketball

The Catholic Company, Charlotte, NC. Retrieved December 10, 2017, from http://www.catholiccompany.com

Jaffe, R. (1977, February 9). "UCF's Clark bowing out, 'Beach' rolling in." *Orlando Sentinel.*

Sugar McLaughlin. "Beer City Hoops." Retrieved from http://www.beercityhoops.com

Chapter 31   Eight Zeros

Clark, T. (1988). "I Live by the Scoreboard." Unpublished manuscript.

Fisher, M. (1982, January 22). "Knights edge Rollins." *UCF Future.*

Fisher, M. (1982, January 29). "UCF romps St. Leo in conference game. Edison scores a career high 31 points." *UCF Future.*

Buchalter, B. (1980, February 10). "UCF-Florida Southern game SRO in half-an-hour." *Orlando Sentinel.*

Dillon, B. (1980, February 15). "Tickets as rare as oil and in as much demand." *UCF Future.*

Chapter 32   The Teacher

Lingelbach, C. (2018, March 20). Personal interview.

Clark, M. (2017, December 7). Personal interview.

Cuff, M. (2018, April 24). Phone interview.

Kreel, J. (2009, July). "Eternal flame: The Torchy Clark legacy." *UCF Pegasus.*

Wallin, S. (2005, May). "Honoring a legend Coach Torchy Clark: An inspiration, both on the court and in the classroom." *UCF Pegasus.*

Whitlinger, K. (2018, January 20). Personal interview.

Clark, B. (2018, March 1). Phone interview.

"Torchy Clark Tributes." (2004). Xavier High School Gym Dedication. Appleton, Wisconsin. Information from Peter Bates.

Johnson, R. Torchy Clark Funeral Tribute (2009, April).

Chapter 33   Trinity Prep

Clark, T. (1988). "I Live by the Scoreboard." Unpublished manuscript.

Pastis, N. (2018, February 5). Phone interview.

Pastis, N. Retrieved transcript from e-mail on October 30, 2018.

Clark, M. (2018, January 10). Phone interview.

Chapter 34   Darling, You'll Be Fine

Korfhage, S. (2005, March 6). "Winning percentage: Torchy and Bo Clark have won a combined 624 games. But the biggest battle now for the father-son duo is finding a way to beat cancer." *St. Augustine Record.*

Budnik, P. (2018, February 26). Phone interview.

Clark, B. (2017, December 5). Phone interview.

Clark, M. (2017, October 15). Phone interview.

Salerno, R. (2018, January 5). Phone interview.

Fulton Sheen Quotes, Goodreads. Retrieved December 10, 2018 from https://www.goodreads.com/author/quotes/2412.Fulton_J_Sheen

Salerno, Y. "First Annual Torchy Clark Golf Classic Brochure." (2006), Orlando, Florida.

Flanagan, J., Written transcript to Torchy Clark. (March, 2018). Orlando, Florida.

The Catholic Company, Charlotte, NC. Retrieved March 26, 2019 from http://www.catholiccompany.com

Chapter 35 Good-Bye Lovely Lady

Clark, T. (1988). "I Live by the Scoreboard." Unpublished manuscript.

Xavier High School Website. Retrieved January 20, 2018, from http://xaviercatholicschools.com

Clark, T. (2007). "Like we were still at Marquette." *Marquette Alumni Newsletter.*

Lease, K. (2004, spring). "Clark returns to a touch of heaven." *Xavier High School Prospector Alumni News.*

Greene, J. (2007, November 7). "Good-Bye lovely lady." *Orlando Sentinel.*

Quote from Pope Benedict XVI. (2017, December). *Magnificat.* Yonkers, NY:Magnificat.

The Catholic Company, Charlotte, NC. (St. Charles Borromeo). Retrieved January 9, 2018, from http://www.catholiccompany.com

Bates, K. Retrieved transcript from e-mail on April 25, 2018.

Chapter 36 Our Role is to Return to God

Novena of the Twelve Year Prayers of St. Bridget of Sweden on the Passion of Jesus, DuPage Marion Center, Westmont, IL. Retrieved from https://www.catholicshoppeusa.com/collections/medjugorie-magazine-official-marian-devotional-website

Budnik, P. (2018, March 18). Personal interview.

Budnik, B. (2018, March 18). Personal interview.

Garvey, Brian. (2018, March 18). Personal interview.

Clark, M. (2018, March 18). Personal interview.

Fellowship of Christian Athletes. (2016). *Greatest Coach Ever: Timeless Wisdom and Insights of John Wooden.* Ventura, CA: Regal.

Rather, J. (2003). "Xavier Gym Dedication Tributes." Xavier High School, Appleton, WI.

Greene, J. (2009, February 15). "Torchy still a coach at heart." *Orlando Sentinel.*

Chapter 37   Legacy 37

Beekman, B. (2000). "Dribblings including the adventures of the disco winnebago & blocked punts: Fond and foggy memories from the early days of Knights' athletics." Orlando, FL: Bill Beekman.

Kornely, K. (2018, January 22). Personal interview.

Garvey, Brad. (2018, January 18). Personal interview.

Garvey, Brian. (2018, January 21). Personal interview.

Flanagan, J. (2017, November 8). Personal interview.

Salerno, R. (2018, March 3). Phone interview.

Creel, J. (2009, July). "Eternal flame. The Torchy Clark legacy burns bright." *UCF Pegasus.*

Wallin, S. (2005, May). "Honoring a legend Coach Torchy Clark: an inspiration both on the court and in the classroom." *UCF Pegasus.*

Kelly, Y. Retrieved transcript from e-mail on May 15, 2018.

Perna, T., (2015). 7 quotes from St. John Vianney on the Feast of the Guardian Angels. Retrieved from tomperna.org on December 10, 2018.

Grayson, T. Retrieved transcript from e-mail on May 15, 2018.

Prather, J. Retrieved transcript from e-mail on December 12, 2018.

Miller, M. Retrieved transcript from e-mail on July 12, 2018.

Woods, M. (2009). "Torchy burns bright." *Appleton Post-Crescent.*

Woods, M. (2004). "With fighting spirit, Clark faces one of his biggest challenges.' *Appleton Post-Crescent.*

Rohter, F. (2017, October). Phone interview.

Clark, T. (1988). "I Live by the Scoreboard." Unpublished manuscript.

Lingelbach, C. (2018, March 20). Personal Interview.

Klusman, T. (2018, September 5). Phone interview.

Klusman, T. Retrieved transcript from e-mail on October 8, 2018.

Cotroneo, V. Retrieved transcript from e-mail on October 29, 2018.

The Catholic Company, Charlotte, NC. Blessed John Henry Newman quote. Retrieved March 10, 2018 from http://www.catholiccompany.com

About the Author

Bo Clark was the head basketball coach at NCAA Division II Flagler College in St. Augustine, Florida, for 31 years. Torchy and Claire Clark's third son was a UCF basketball All-American and a 1980 graduate. He also earned master's degrees from both UCF and the United States Sports Academy. Clark currently directs summer youth basketball camps in Florida and resides in St. Augustine with his wife Nancy. They are the proud parents of three sons, JP, David (Charlsea), and Matt (Alexandra).

The Clarks (left to right), Matt, David, Bo, Nancy, and JP.

Made in the USA
Columbia, SC
15 May 2020